Treasury Dep[artment]
6 January 1792

There are various arrangements
between the Government and
[Uni]ted States, which will better
[per]sonal conference than
request therefore that such
[ap]pear proper to the director,

The Founding Fathers

The Founding Fathers

ALEXANDER HAMILTON

A Biography in His Own Words

VOLUME 2

Edited by
MARY–JO KLINE

JOAN PATERSON KERR
Picture Editor

NEWSWEEK
New York

ISBN: Clothbound Edition 0-88225-045-0; ISBN: Deluxe Edition 0-88225-046-9
Library of Congress Catalog Card Number 72-92140
Copyright © 1973 by Newsweek, Inc.
All rights reserved. Printed and bound in the United States of America
Endpapers: Hamilton to the President and Directors of the Bank of the United States,
January 18, 1792; HISTORICAL SOCIETY OF PENNSYLVANIA

To the President, Directors & Com=
pany of the Bank of New York.

Pay to Samuel Meredith Treasurer of
the United States, or Order, the Sum of
Twenty thousand Dollars being the A=
=mount of a Loan agreed to be made by the said
Bank to the Secretary at War, in pursuance of
an Appropriation made by an Act of Congress
of the twentieth day of August 1789: for
which this shall be your Warrant.

No. 1.

Dollars 20,000.

Entered in the Register
Office this 13 day of
September 1789.
Joseph Nourse Reg.r

Given under my Hand and
the Seal of the Treasury on the
thirteenth day of September 1789

Alexander Hamilton
Secretary of the Treasury

Countersigned by

N.s Eveleigh Compt.r

An order of payment drawn on the Bank of New York, signed and sealed by Hamilton

Chapter **8**

Mr. Secretary

Alexander Hamilton spent only a little more than three decades of his short life as an American. In the first half of this period he had accomplished more than he could have dreamed of when he sailed from St. Croix late in 1772. By the summer of 1788, Hamilton had a devoted wife and a lively family of three sons and a daughter. His personal friends and political allies were among the most powerful men in the country. He had helped win ratification of the Constitution, which established a government that could give America national security and prestige and that would provide him with a stage for his own talents. But Hamilton knew that it was not enough to have established this form of government on paper. In the last sixteen years of his life he fought to see that his own vision of America's "respectability" was insured, by seeking to place the right men in office and by persuading these men to enact legislative and administrative programs that conformed to his ideals. Two weeks after New York had ratified the Constitution, Hamilton undertook the task of insuring that the Presidency would be held by the only man who could unite the nation. In mid-August, he wrote to George Washington.

> [New York, August 13, 1788]
> I take it for granted, Sir, you have concluded to comply with what will no doubt be the general call of your country in relation to the new government. You will permit me to say that it is indispensable you should lend yourself to its first operations—It is to little purpose to have *introduced* a system, if the weightiest influence is not given to its firm *establishment,* in the outset.

In reply, Washington wrote that he could not commit himself on an event that "may never happen." In any case, he confided, it

209

was his "greatest and sole desire to live and die, in peace and retirement" at Mount Vernon. Alarmed, Hamilton wrote again.

New York September 1788

I should be deeply pained my Dear Sir if your scruples in regard to a certain station should be matured into a resolution to decline it; though I am neither surprised at their existence nor can I but agree in opinion that the caution you observe in deferring an ultimate determination is prudent. I have however reflected maturely on the subject and have come to a conclusion... that every public and personal consideration will demand from you an acquiescence in what will *certainly* be the unanimous wish of your country. The absolute retreat which you meditated at the close of the late war was natural and proper. Had the government produced by the revolution gone on in a *tolerable* train, it would have been most adviseable to have persisted in that retreat. But I am clearly of opinion that the crisis which brought you again into public view left you no alternative but to comply—and I am equally clear in the opinion that you are by that act *pledged* to take a part in the execution of the government. I am not less convinced that the impression of this necessity of your filling the station in question is so universal that you run no risk of any uncandid imputation, by submitting to it. But even if this were not the case, a regard to your own reputation as well as to the public good, calls upon you in the strongest manner to run that risk.

It cannot be considered as a compliment to say that on your acceptance of the office of President the success of the new government in its commencement may materially depend. Your agency and influence will be not less important in preserving it from the future attacks of its enemies than they have been in recommending it in the first instance to the adoption of the people. Independent of all considerations drawn from this source the point of light in which you stand at home and abroad will make an infinite difference in the respectability with which the government will begin its operations in the alternative of your being or not being at the head of it....

[Hamilton omitted any considerations with "a more personal application," but drew these "inferences" from the factors he had already listed.]

This Gilbert Stuart portrait of George Washington was owned by Hamilton.

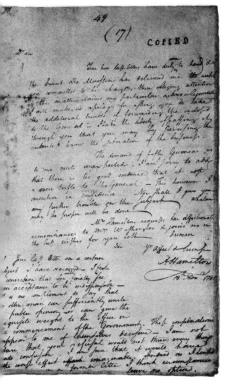

In the postcript of this letter of 1788, Hamilton again tried to persuade Washington to accept the Presidency.

First— In a matter so essential to the well being of society as the prosperity of a newly instituted government a citizen of so much consequence as yourself to its success has no option but to lend his services if called for.... it would be inglorious in such a situation not to hazard the glory however great, which he might have previously acquired.

Secondly. Your signature to the proposed system pledges your judgment for its being such an one as upon the whole was worthy of the public approbation. If it should miscarry ... the blame will in all probability be laid on the system itself. And the framers of it will have to encounter the disrepute of having brought about a revolution in government, without substituting any thing that was worthy of the effort. They pulled down one Utopia, it will be said, to build up another. This view of the subject ... will suggest to your mind greater hazard to that fame, which must be and ought to be dear to you, in refusing your future aid to the system than in affording it. I will only add that in my estimate of the matter that aid is indispensable.

...I doubt not the considerations mentioned have fully occurred to you, and I trust they will finally produce in your mind the same result, which exists in mine. I flatter myself the frankness with which I have delivered myself will not be displeasing to you. It has been prompted by motives which you would not disapprove.

Although he still did not know whether Washington would serve as President, Hamilton began to weigh the virtues of the candidates for Vice President. Theodore Sedgwick, a political leader in Massachusetts, asked Hamilton for his opinion of John Adams, who was then representing the United States in Great Britain. Hamilton sent his reaction.

[New York, October 9, 1788]

On the subject of Vice President, my ideas have concurred with yours, and I believe Mr. Adams will have the votes of this state....

The only hesitation in my mind with regard to Mr. Adams has arisen within a day or two; from a suggestion by a particular Gentleman that he is unfriendly in his sentiments to General Washington. Richard H Lee who will probably, as rumour now runs, come from Virginia is also in this state. The Lees and Adams' have been in

211

the habit of uniting; and hence may spring up a Cabal very embarrassing to the Executive and of course to the administration of the Government. Consider this. Sound the reality of it and let me hear from you.

What think You of Lincoln or Knox? This is a flying thought.

Sedgwick answered that Adams, "formerly infinitely more democratical than at present," could now be trusted. Massachusetts, he reported, was divided between the supporters of Adams and those of John Hancock for Vice President. Hamilton replied early in November.

[New York, November 9, 1788]
On the question between Mr. H— and Mr. A— Mr. [Rufus] King will probably have informed you that I have upon the whole concluded that the latter ought to be supported. My measures will be taken accordingly. I had but one scruple; but after mature consideration I have relinquished it. Mr. A to a sound understanding has *always* appeared to me to add an ardent love for the public good; and as his further knowlege of the world seems to have corrected those jealousies which he is represented to have once been influenced by I trust nothing of the kind suggested in my former letter will disturb the harmony of the administration.

Two weeks later, Hamilton wrote to James Madison to announce his endorsement of Adams as Vice President.

[New York, November 23, 1788]
My principal reasons are these—First He is a declared partisan of referring to future experience the expediency of amendments in the system...[and this sentiment] is much nearer my own than certain other doctrines. Secondly a character of importance in the Eastern states, if he is not Vice President, one of two worse things will be likely to happen—Either he must be nominated to some important office for which he is less proper, or will become a malcontent and possibly espouse and give additional weight to the opposition to the Government.

As the day approached when the presidential electors would cast their ballots, Hamilton faced another problem: the Constitution made it impossible for electors to indicate which of their votes were for President and which were for Vice President. The situation was further complicated by scattered support in South Carolina for John Rutledge and in Virginia for George Clinton. In January, little more than a week before the Electoral College was to convene, Hamilton advised James Wilson of Pennsylvania of the strategy to be followed if the Rutledge and Clinton electors decided to throw their votes to Adams.

New York, January 25, 1789

As the accounts of the appointments of electors will satisfy the partisans of those Gentlemen in each of those States that they will have no coadjustors elsewhere, it seems not improbable that they will relinquish the attempt in favour of their intended candidates. Here then is a *chance* of unanimity in Adams. Nothing is so apt to beget it as the opinion that the current sets irresistibly towards him. Men are fond of going with the stream. Suppose personal caprice or hostility to the new system should occasion half a dozen votes only to be witheld from Washington—what may not happen? Grant there is little danger. If any, ought it to be run?

. . . the chance is that there will be Eight votes to spare from Adams leaving him still a majority. Take the probability of unanimity in the North in Adams & of division in the South . . . and the chances are almost infinite in his favour. Hence I conclude it will be prudent to throw away a few votes say 7 or 8; giving these to persons not otherwise thought of. Under this impression I have proposed to friends in Connecticut to throw away two to others in Jersey to throw away an equal number & I submit it to you whether it will not be well to lose three or four in Pensylvania. . . . for God's sake let not our zeal for a secondary object defeat or endanger a first. I admit that in several important views and particularly to avoid disgust to a man who would be a formidable head to Antifoederalists—it is much to be desired that Adams may have the plurality of suffrages for Vice President; but if risk is to be run on one side or on the other can we hesitate where it ought to be preferred?

John Adams as Vice President, painted by Charles Willson Peale

After the presidential electors met on February 4, 1789, and chose Washington as President and Adams as Vice President, Hamilton turned his attention to the New York campaigns. On February 11, he presided at a meeting in Manhattan, which nominated Antifederalist

Robert Yates for governor. As chairman of "a committee to correspond with the other counties" Hamilton wrote to the supervisors of Albany urging them to support Yates.

[New York, February 18, 1789]

...it is highly necessary that the Chief Magistrate of the State should be free from all temptation wantonly to perplex or embarrass the national Government, whether that temptation should arise from a preference of partial confederacies, from a spirit of competition with the national rulers for personal pre-eminence, from an impatience of the restraints of national authority, from the fear of a diminution of power and emoluments, from resentment or mortification, proceeding from disappointment, or from any other cause whatsoever....

In the consideration of the character most proper to be held up at the ensuing election, some difficulties occurred. Our fellow citizens in some parts of the state had proposed Judge Yates, others had been advocates for the Lieutenant Governor [Pierre Van Cortlandt], and others for Chief Justice [Richard] Morris. It is well known that the inhabitants of this city are...strongly attached to the new constitution, and...that Lieutenant Governor Cortlandt and Chief Justice Morris...were zealous advocates for the same cause. Had it been agreed to support either of them for the office of governor, there would have been reason to fear, that the measure would have been imputed to party, and not to a desire of relieving our country from the evils they experience from the heats of party. It appeared therefore most advisable to select some man of the opposite party, in whose integrity, patriotism and temper, confidence might justly be placed; however little his political opinions on the question lately agitated, might be approved by those who were assembled upon the occasion.

Among the persons of this description, there were circumstances which led to a decision in favor of Judge Yates....It is certain, that as a man and a judge, he is generally esteemed. And though his opposition to the new constitution was such as its friends cannot but disapprove; yet since...its adoption, his conduct has been tempered with a degree of moderation and regard to peace and decorum which entitle him to credit; and seem to point him out as a man likely to compose the differences of the state, and to unite its citizens in the

BOTH: ALBANY INSTITUTE OF HISTORY AND ART

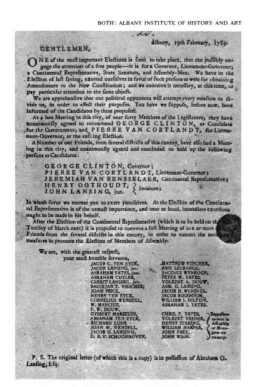

An Antifederalist, pro-Clinton broadside of the heated 1789 elections in New York State

harmonious pursuit of their common and genuine interest.

Of this at least we feel confident, that he has no personal revenge to gratify...nor any promises for personal purposes to be performed at the public expence. On the contrary we trust he will be found to be a man, who looks with an equal eye on his fellow citizens, and who will be more ambitious of leaving a good name, than a good estate, to his posterity.

Hamilton and the Federalists were determined not to repeat their mistakes of 1788, when their opponents had won control of the Poughkeepsie Convention by concentrating on local organization. Hamilton supervised every detail of an all-out statewide campaign against Clinton. Discarding the lofty style of Publius, he used the pen name "H.G." while producing a series of letters that examined Clinton's personal character and public record. In the first of these letters, H.G. reflected on Clinton's early life.

New York, February 20, 1789.

The present Governor was bred to the law, under William Smith, Esquire, formerly of this city. Some time before the late revolution, he resided in Ulster county, and there followed his profession with reputation, though not with distinction. He was not supposed to possess considerable talents; but upon the whole, stood fair on the score of probity. It must however be confessed, that he early got the character with many of being a very *artful* man; and it is not to be wondered at, if that impression, on the minds in which it prevailed, deducted something from the opinion of his integrity. But it would be refining too much to admit such a consequence to be a just one. There certainly are characters (tho' they may be rare) which unite a great degree of address, and even a large portion of what is best expressed by the word CUNNING, with a pretty exact adherence, in the main, to the principles of integrity.

A Federalist broadside published during the 1789 election campaign for the New York governorship

In the dozen years that Clinton had led New York, many of his exploits had been embroidered by popular legend. In his second letter, H.G. sought to puncture the Clinton myth.

New-York, February 21, 1789.

There is...no part of his character, which has been more misrepresented than the military part of it. His

Hamilton's friend John Laurance ran for Congress in the 1789 election.

panegyrists describe him to us as the "war worn veteran"—the complete soldier—the consummate general. One would imagine from their stories of him, that he...was the first of American generals; a Marius in courage, a Caesar in skill, inferior in nothing to a Turerne or a Monteculli, an Eugene or a Marlborough. But trust me, my dear Sir, this is mere rant and romance. That Mr. Clinton is a man of courage, there is no reason to doubt. That he was upon most occasions active and vigorous cannot be justly disputed. In his capacity of governor he was ever ready to promote the common cause—prompt in affording the aid of the militia, when requisite, and scrupling not, when he thought his presence might be of use, to put himself at the head of them. But here his praise as a soldier ends. Beyond this he has no pretension to the wreath of military renown. No man can tell when or where he gave proofs of generalship, either in council or in the field. After diligent enquiry, I have not been able to learn that he was ever more than once in actual combat. This was at Fort Montgomery [in October, 1777], where he commanded in person; and which, after a feeble and unskilful defence, was carried by storm... One particular in this affair deserves to be noticed. It is certain that the governor made a well-timed retreat, (I mean personally, for the greatest part of the garrison were captured), a thing which must have occasioned no small conflict in the breast of a commander nice in military punctilio. But squeamishness on this head, had been ill placed. It was undoubtedly the duty of the BRIGADIER to provide in season for the safety of the GOVERNOR.

The New York polls opened on April 28, and on that day Hamilton issued a last-minute election bulletin to Manhattan voters.
[New York, April 28, 1789]
Hitherto Fellow Citizens you have left no opportunity of manifesting your zeal for the firm establishment of the Constitution of the United States....Your work is now to be completed. We will ask you a few questions, and leave the answers to your own minds. Is there a man in America, who has more early, more decidedly, or more pertenaciously, opposed that constitution than the present governor? Is there a man in America from whose

future opposition to it, so much would be to be feared, as from that of the present governor, if suffered to continue *at the head of this State?* Is it *wise* to continue him in a situation, which will leave it so greatly in his power to counteract what you deem the true interest of your country? Is it *safe,* after all you have seen and known, to put the least confidence in the assurances you receive from those, who advise you to re-elect him...? Are there not appearances which *authorise* you to suppose, that the views of the present governor, in some important respects, have not coincided with the wishes or interests of the city?...These, Fellow Citizens, are serious question. Ponder them well, and act accordingly. Let every man, who believes a change necessary, step forward with the INDEPENDENCE of a FREEMAN and lend his aid!

While Hamilton waited for the verdict of New York's voters (a decision narrowly in favor of George Clinton), Washington was inaugurated on April 30. Five days later, in response to the President's request, Hamilton offered his ideas on the proper etiquette for the Republic's new Chief Executive.

[New York, May 5, 1789]

The public good requires as a primary object that the dignity of the office should be supported. Whatever is essential to this ought to be pursued though at the risk of partial or momentary dissatisfaction. But care will be necessary to avoid extensive disgust or discontent. Men's minds are prepared for a pretty high tone in the demeanour of the Executive; but I doubt whether for so high a tone as in the abstract might be desireable. The notions of equality are yet in my opinion too general and too strong to admit of such a distance being placed between the President and other branches of the government as might even be consistent with a due proportion. The following plan will I think steer clear of extremes and involve no very material inconveniences.

I   The President to have a levee day once a week for receiving visits. An hour to be fixed at which it shall be understood that he will appear and consequently that the visitors are previously to be assembled. The President to remain half an hour, in which time he may converse cursorily on indifferent subjects with such persons as shall strike his attention, and at the end of that half hour

Washington's inauguration

Pages from Hamilton's draft of his suggestions regarding the etiquette to be followed by the President

disappear.... No visits to be returned.

II The President to accept no invitations: and to give formal entertainments only twice or four times a year on the anniversaries of important events in the revolution.... The members of the two houses of the legislature Principal officers of the Government Foreign ministers and other distinguished strangers only to be invited. The numbers form in my mind an objection — But there may be separate tables in separate rooms. This is practiced in some European Courts....

III The President on the levée days...to give informal invitations to family dinners on the days of invitation. Not more than six or eight to be invited at a time & the matter to be confined essentially to members of the legislature and other official characters. The President never to remain long at table.

I think it probable that the last article will not correspond with the ideas of most of those with whom Your Excellency may converse but on pretty mature reflection I believe it will be necessary to remove the idea of too immense an inequality....

It is an important point to consider what persons may have access to Your Excellency on business. The heads of departments will of course have this privilege. Foreign Ministers of some descriptions will also be intitled to it. In Europe I am informed ambassadors only have direct access to the Chief Magistrate. Something very *near* what prevails there would in my opinion be right.... I have thought that the members of the Senate should also have a right of *individual* access on matters relative to the *public administration*. In England & France Peers of the realm have this right. We have none such in this Country, but I believe that it will be satisfactory to the people to know that there is some body of men in the state who have a right of continual communication with the President. It will be considered as a safeguard against secret combinations to deceive him.

I have asked myself — will not the representatives expect the same privilege and be offended if they are not allowed to participate with the Senate? There is sufficient danger of this, to merit consideration. But there is a reason for the distinction in the constitution. The Senate are coupled with the President in certain executive functions; treaties and appointments. This makes them in a degree his constitutional counsellors and gives them a *peculiar* claim to the right of access. On the whole, I think the discrimination will be proper....

I have chosen this method of communication, because I understood...that it would be most convenient to you. The unstudied and unceremonious manner of it will I hope not render it the less acceptable. And if in the execution of your commands at any time I consult frankness and simplicity more than ceremony or profession, I flatter myself you will not on that account distrust the sincerity of the assurance I now give of my cordial wishes for your personal happiness and the success of your administration.

Hamilton, meantime, was awaiting with special interest the outcome of congressional debate over the functions of Cabinet officers. Special heat was generated in discussions of the office of Secretary of the Treasury, a post for which Hamilton was being considered. The arguments dragged on through the summer of 1789, and not until September 11 was Hamilton's appointment approved. He himself had no doubt as to what must be his first priority. Import duties were the primary source of revenue for the Federal Government, and Hamilton knew that their efficient collection was essential. A practical man, he realized that only reliable statistics would enable him to review the system and make recommendations for reform when Congress reconvened. At the beginning of October he dispatched a circular letter to the collectors of customs.

Treasury Department
New York October 2d. 1789.

As in the first establishment of Revenue systems, imperfections and inconveniencies will naturally present themselves in practice, which could not have been foreseen in their formation; it is of the greatest moment, that the best information should be collected for the use of the Government as to the operation of those, which may have been adopted.

To the obtaining this information, as it respects the plan for the imposition and collection of the duties, the situation of the collectors and naval Officers of the several Ports is in a peculiar manner favourable, and... it is equally their duty and their interest to make the best use of their opportunities for that purpose.

Not doubting that their inclination will coincide with both; I am to request that they will carefully note and

219

Washington's nomination of Hamilton to be Secretary of the Treasury

from time to time communicate to me whatever may serve to discover the merits or defects of that plan, and to point out the means of improving it.

Though the complaints of the Merchants will not always be infallible indications of defects, yet they will always merit attention, and when they occur, I shall be glad to be particularly informed of them.

. . . it was in the contemplation of Congress to employ Boats for the security of the Revenue against contraband. I shall be glad to have your Ideas, as to the expediency of employing them in your quarter, and . . . of the number and kind you deem requisite; their equipments, and the probable expence. . . .

It has been very much apprehended that the number of Ports in several of the States would conduce to great evasions of the duties. It is my wish to be informed how far experience has justified this apprehension, and what can be done to correct the Mischeifs, which may have ensued. . . .

In hinting these particulars it is not my aim to confine your attention to them only; It will give me pleasure to find that your observation has been as diffusive as the object is extensive.

The revenue officers were valuable agents for the new Secretary. When Hamilton decided to allow customs duties to be paid in the notes issued by the Massachusetts Bank in Boston, he offered this suggestion to Benjamin Lincoln, the collector of customs at that port.

Treasury Department November 20th. 1789
It is my wish to have an *eye* on the spot to attend to the operations of the Bank, in order that the measure now adopted may be continued or discontinued, as considerations of safety shall dictate. My own situation with regard to Philadelphia and New York answers this end; but I am too far distant from Boston to have it in my power to pay the same attention there. This hint you will of course perceive to be confidential and designed only for yourself.

Should you therefore at any time perceive it to be unsafe to continue the receipt of the Notes of the Bank of Massachusets or to make that Bank the depository of the public Monies received in your State, I authorize you not only to discontinue the receipt yourself but *as from me* to countermand that receipt at, and . . . the proposed remittance...from the other ports.

This discretion I confide in you from the intire confidence I have in your prudence and judgement.

Private citizens could serve the Department of the Treasury as well, a fact Hamilton made clear in a letter to William Bingham, a wealthy Philadelphia merchant and director of the Bank of North America. Bingham's knowledge of American and British business made him an excellent source of information.

Private New York October 10th, 1789
There is a species of information highly requisite to the Government in adjusting the policy of its Treaties and Laws respecting Navigation for obtaining which with proper accuracy and detail no regular plan has ever yet been persued in this Country. It relates to the comparative advantages with which the Navigation of the United States and that of other Nations with whom they trade is or can be carried on. The utility of the Knowledge of the facts on which this comparison will depend need not I am sure be explained to you.

Knowing as I do your Zeal for whatever concerns the public good and relying upon your care and intelligence I take the Liberty to request your aid in making the enquiries requisite to the attainment of the Knowledge I have mentioned....

May I also take the Liberty to request of you that you will from time to time favor me with communications with regard to the operation of the Revenue and Navigation Laws which have been adopted the defects and inconveniences which have been experienced and the proper remedies. And with any thoughts that may occur to you concerning the Finances and Debts of the United States.

Washington's signature and the presidential seal adorn Hamilton's commission as Treasury Secretary.

Hamilton was aware that the Treasury Department might have problems when Congress reconvened in January, 1790. Indeed, he had already had a taste of James Madison's pronounced anti-British bias in the recent House session, as George Beckwith, Britain's unofficial minister to the United States, reported after a conversation with Hamilton.

[New York, October, 1789]
[Hamilton]...I confess I was likewise rather surprised at it, as well as that the only opposition to General Washing-

ton was from thence. The truth is, that although this gentleman [Madison] is a clever man, he is very little Acquainted with the world. That he is Uncorrupted And incorruptible I have not a doubt; he has the same End in view that I have, And so have those gentlemen, who Act with him, but their mode of attaining it is very different.

If Hamilton considered Madison "little Acquainted with the world," he knew the Virginia congressman was well acquainted with American public opinion. During the congressional recess, while he was preparing for the House a plan for payment of the public debts, Hamilton asked Madison for his thoughts on the subject.

[New York, October 12, 1789]

I dont know how it was but I took it for granted that you had left town much earlier than you did; else I should have found an opportunity after your adjournment to converse with you on the subjects committed to me by the house of Representatives. It is certainly important, that a plan as complete and as unexceptionable as possible should be matured by the next meeting of Congress; and for this purpose it could not but be useful that there should be a comparison and concentration of ideas of those whose duty leads them to a contemplation of the subject.

As I lost the opportunity of a personal communication May I ask of your friendship to put to paper and send me your thoughts on such objects as may have occurred to you for an addition to our revenue; and also as to any modifications of the public debt which could be made consistent with good faith the interest of the Public and of its Creditors?

In my opinion, in considering plans for the increase of our revenues, the difficulty lies, not so much in the want of objects as in the prejudices which may be feared with regard to almost every object. The Question is very much What further taxes will be *least* unpopular?

LIBRARY OF CONGRESS

The chambers in New York City's Federal Hall, where the House of Representatives first met in 1789

Provision for the public debt required careful attention to international opinion as well. France, beset by political unrest and economic problems, was an increasingly impatient creditor. With this in mind, Hamilton wrote to his friend the Marquis de Lafayette of his plans for the Treasury Department.

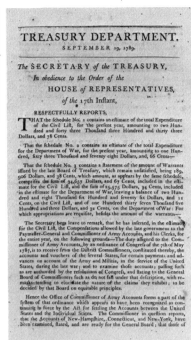

One of Hamilton's first reports to Congress as Treasury Secretary: an account of Government expenditures

New York October 6th, 1789

The debt due to France will be among the first objects of my attention. Hitherto it has been from necessity neglected. The Session of Congress is now over. It has been exhausted in the organization of the Government, and in a few laws of immediate urgency respecting navigation and commercial Imposts. The subject of the debt foreign and domestic has been referred to the next session which will commence the first Monday in January with an instruction to me to prepare and report a Plan comprehending an adequate Provision for the support of the Public Credit....

From this sketch you will perceive that I am not in a situation to address any thing officially to your administration; but I venture to say to you, as my friend, that if the installments of the Principal of the debt could be suspended for a few years, it would be a valuable accommodation to the United States. In this suggestion I contemplate a speedy payment of the *arrears* of *interest* now due, and effectual Prov[is]ion for the punctual payment of future interest as it arises. Could an arrangement of this sort meet the approbation of your Government, it would be best on every account that the offer should come unsolicited as a fresh mark of good will.

During the three months of the congressional recess, while Hamilton was preparing his report on public credit, the Secretary also began publicizing his new administration and its new standards. In mid-December, he issued a circular letter to customs officials concerning the bonds given by shipowners as security for their payment of import duties.

Treasury Department 18 Decr. 1789

As one of the periods for the payment of Bonds taken for Duties is arrived, it is proper that the respective Collectors should be apprised of my expectation with regard to the conduct to be observed by them. It is, that if the Bonds are not paid, *as they fall due* they be immediately put in Suit. On this point, the *most exact punctuality* will be considered as *indispensable*.... I am not unaware that the relaxations in this respect, which obtained in many instances under the State Laws, may give an Air of rigor to this Instruction; but I consider its *strict observance* as *essential,* not only to the order of the finances, but even to the propriety of the indulgence, which the Law allows of procrastinated terms of payment of the Duties, and hence I regard this Strictness, as eventually most convenient to Individuals, as well as necessary to the Public.

The Secretary of the Treasury was equally firm concerning his own standards, as when he replied to Henry Lee of Virginia, who had asked for advance information on the provisions for the payment of the public debt.

[New York, December 1, 1789]
I am sure you are sincere when you say, you would not subject me to an impropriety. Nor do I know that there would be any in my answering your queries. But you remember the saying with regard to Caesar's Wife. I think the spirit of it applicable to every man concerned in the administration of the finances of a Country. With respect to the Conduct of such men—*Suspicion* is ever eagle eyed, And the most innocent things are apt to be misinterpreted.

Public interest in Hamilton's plans for the public credit ran high, but, as he explained to a friend in Philadelphia, he was reluctant to invite discussion in advance.

[New York] November 27, 1789.
With regard to feeling the public pulse about the debt I have several times had an inclination to the measure; but this inclination has given place to the reflection, that bringing on a discussion might be as likely to fix prejudices as to produce good, and that it may be safest to trust to the effect of the Legislative sanction to good measures, and to the reasons that will accompany them at the time.

Early in January, 1790, Hamilton's *Report Relative to a Provision for the Support of Public Credit* was ready for submission to the legislature. In accordance with a rule established by Congress—that officers of the executive departments could not appear personally to present their programs—Hamilton laid his plans before the legislature in a series of massive written reports like this one. The Secretary of the Treasury opened the first of his reports—a major document in the evolution of American government—with a lecture on the benefits of "funding" the national debt: that is, of establishing permanent funds for paying that debt and for converting the various forms of the debt (loan office certificates, certificates issued by the Army, and so forth) into interest-bearing government bonds. Then he dealt with the claims of the various classes of public creditors.

Treasury Department, January 9, 1790.

It is agreed on all hands, that that part of the debt which has been contracted abroad, and is denominated the foreign debt, ought to be provided for, according to the precise terms of the contracts relating to it. The discussions, which can arise, therefore, will have reference essentially to the domestic part of it, or to that which has been contracted at home. It is to be regretted, that there is not the same unanimity of sentiment on this part, as on the other.

The Secretary has too much deference for the opinions of every part of the community, not to have observed one, which has, more than once, made its appearance in the public prints.... It involves this question, whether a discrimination ought not to be made between original holders of the public securities, and present possessors, by purchase. Those who advocate a discrimination are for making a full provision for the securities of the former, at their nominal value; but contend, that the latter ought to receive no more than the cost to them, and the interest: And the idea is sometimes suggested of making good the difference to the primitive possessor....

The Secretary, after the most mature reflection on the force of this argument, is induced to reject the doctrine it contains, as equally unjust and impolitic, as highly injurious, even to the original holders of public securities; as ruinous to public credit.

It is inconsistent with justice, because in the first place, it is a breach of contract; in violation of the rights of a fair purchaser....

The difficulties too of regulating the details of a plan for that purpose, which would have even the semblance of equity, would be found immense. It may well be doubted whether they would not be insurmountable, and replete with absurd, as well as inequitable consequences, as to disgust even the proposers of the measure....

[Hamilton knew that his proposal that all public creditors be treated equally would be fiercely debated. His next point, however, was also to raise a great deal of controversy.]

The Critical Period, FISKE

One-penny notes issued by the Bank of North America in August, 1789

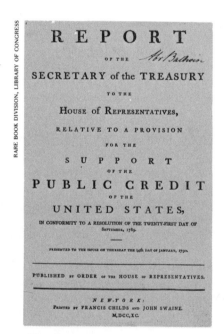

The House of Representatives had Hamilton's first report on the public credit printed in 1790.

The Secretary, after mature reflection on this point, entertains a full conviction, that an assumption of the debts of the particular states by the union, and a like provision for them, as for those of the union, will be a measure of sound policy and substantial justice.

It would, in the opinion of the Secretary, contribute, in an eminent degree, to an orderly, stable and satisfactory arrangement of the national finances.

Admitting, as ought to be the case, that a provision must be made in some way or other, for the entire debt; it will follow, that no greater revenues will be required, whether that provision be made wholly by the United States, or partly by them, and partly by the states separately.

The principal question then must be, whether such a provision cannot be more conveniently and effectually made, by one general plan issuing from one authority, than by different plans originating in different authorities.…

If all the public creditors receive their dues from one source, distributed with an equal hand, their interest will be the same. And having the same interests, they will unite in the support of the fiscal arrangements of the government.… These circumstances combined will insure to the revenue laws a more ready and more satisfactory execution.

If on the contrary there are distinct provisions, there will be distinct interests, drawing different ways. That union and concert of views, among the creditors, which in every government is of great importance to their security, and to that of public credit, will not only not exist, but will be likely to give place to mutual jealousy and opposition. And from this cause, the operation of the systems which may be adopted, both by the particular states, and by the union…will be in danger of being counteracted.…

[The report next explained how these debts were to be funded into a new issue of government securities. The old domestic debt was to be viewed as a form of annuity. Creditors were entitled to prompt payment of annual interest, but the Government was not required to redeem the principal of the debts at any set time. Hamilton then outlined a complicated system by which public creditors could accept various forms of bonds, public lands, or annuities for their old certificates. He estimated that government expenses and interest on the debt would require an annual income of $2,839,163.09.]

This sum may, in the opinion of the Secretary, be obtained from the present duties on imports and tonnage, with the additions, which... may be made on wines, spirits, including those distilled within the United States, teas and coffee.

The Secretary conceives, that it will be sound policy, to carry the duties upon articles of this kind, as high as will be consistent with the practicability of a safe collection. This will lessen the necessity, both of having recourse to direct taxation, and of accumulating duties where they would be more inconvenient to trade, and upon objects, which are more to be regarded as necessaries of life.

That the articles which have been enumerated, will, better than most others, bear high duties, can hardly be a question. They are all of them, in reality — luxuries — the greatest part of them foreign luxuries; some of them, in the excess in which they are used, pernicious luxuries. And there is, perhaps, none of them, which is not consumed in so great abundance, as may, justly, denominate it, a source of national extravagance and impoverishment. The consumption of ardent spirits particularly, no doubt very much on account of their cheapness, is carried to an extreme, which is truly to be regretted, as well in regard to the health and the morals, as to the œconomy of the community....

The Secretary computes the nett product of the duties proposed in this report at about one million seven hundred and three thousand four hundred dollars ... which... will, together with the probable product of the duties on imports and tonnage, complete the sum required....

[Having listed his proposed import duties and taxes, Hamilton promised the House yet another plan.]

...the Secretary... ardently wishes to see it incorporated, as a fundamental maxim, in the system of public credit of the United States, that the creation of debt should always be accompanied with the means of extinguishment....

Under this impression, the Secretary proposes, that the nett product of the post-office, to a sum not exceeding one million of dollars, be vested in commissioners, to consist of the Vice-President of the United States..., the Speaker of the House..., the Chief Justice, Secretary of the Treasury and Attorney-General of the United States, for the time being, in trust, to be applied, by them, or any three of them, to the discharge of the existing public debt, either by purchases of stock in the market, or by payments on account of the principal, as shall appear to them most adviseable...; to continue so vested, until the whole of the debt shall be discharged....

The Secretary contemplates the application of this money, through the medium of a national bank, for which, with the permission of the House, he will submit a plan in the course of the session.

The violent opposition that greeted Hamilton's report on the public debt made it impolitic for him to present a report on the bank at that time. Worst of all, Hamilton found that chief among the opponents of his program was his old friend James Madison. Two years later, Hamilton recalled his pain and surprise at Madison's behavior in early 1790.

Philadelphia May 26th, 1792
When I accepted the Office, I now hold, it was under a full persuasion, that from similarity of thinking, conspiring with personal goodwill, I should have the firm support of Mr. Madison, in the *general course* of my administration. Aware of the intrinsic difficulties of the situation and of the powers of Mr. Madison, I do not believe I should have accepted under a different supposition.

I have mentioned the similarity of thinking between that Gentleman and myself. This was relative not merely to the general principles of National Policy and Government but to the leading points which were likely to constitute questions in the administration of the finances. I mean 1 the expediency of *funding* the debt 2 the inexpediency of *discrimination* between original and present holders 3 The expediency of *assuming* the state Debts....

Hamilton's military hat and saber and a copy of his report on funding adorn this engraved portrait.

Under these circumstances, you will naturally imagine that it must have been matter of surprize to me, when I was apprised, that it was Mr. Madison's intention to oppose my plan on both the last mentioned points.

Before the debate commenced, I had a conversation with him on my report, in the course of which I alluded to the calculation I had made of his sentiments and the grounds of that calculation. He did not deny them, but alledged in his justification that the very considerable alienation of the debt, subsequent to the periods at which he had opposed a discrimination, had essentially changed the state of the question—and that as to the assumption, he had contemplated it to take place *as matters stood at the peace.*

While the change of opinion avowed on the point of discrimination diminished my respect for the force of Mr. Madison's mind and the soundness of his judgment...Yet my previous impressions of the fairness of Mr. Madison's character and my reliance on his good will towards me disposed me to believe that his suggestions were sincere; and even, on the point of an assumption of the debts of the States as they stood at the peace, to lean towards a cooperation in his view; 'till on feeling the ground I found the thing impracticable, and on further reflection I thought it liable to immense difficulties.

Madison quickly lost his fight to institute a policy of monetary "discrimination" between the Government's original creditors and the men who had later purchased their certificates. The battle over Federal assumption of state debts, however, was longer and more difficult. Alexander White, a Virginian opposed to this provision, argued that debate on the matter was pointless until the House had some information on how the United States might pay the state debts. On March 3, hoping to delay debate, White moved that the Secretary of the Treasury report on funds to be used for the payment of interest on state debts. This delaying action failed and the very next day Hamilton submitted lists of revenues such as those that follow.

[Treasury Department, March 4, 1790]
An increase of the general product of the duties on goods imported, by abolishing the discount of ten per Cent allowed...in respect to goods imported in American bottoms, and adding ten per Cent to the rates specified, in respect to goods imported in foreign bottoms....

This change, without impairing the commercial policy of the regulation, or making an inconvenient addition to the general rates of the duties, will occasion an augmentation of the revenue little short of two hundred thousand dollars.

An additional duty on imported Sugars. Sugars are an object of general consumption, and yet constitute a small proportion of the expense of families. A moderate addition to the present rates would not be felt.

House debates on the assumption of state debts raised the old question of state rights and the new question of "constitutionality." Personal attacks were as bitter as they had ever been in the old Continental Congress. When Hamilton learned that Ædanus Burke of South Carolina had denounced him for his supposed insults to southern militiamen, he replied promptly and indignantly.

[New York, April 1, 1790]

I have been informed that in the house of Representatives yesterday, you made use of some very harsh expressions in relation to me.

As I cannot but ascribe so unprovoked an attack to misapprehension or misrepresentation I have concluded to send you an extract from the Eulogium pronounced by me on General Greene, of the part to which alone your animadversions do relate. It is in these words—

"From the heights of Monmouth I might lead you to the *plains of Springfield*, there to behold the Veteran Knyphaussen, at the head of a veteran army, baffled and almost beaten by a General without an army—aided, or rather embarrassed by small fugitive bodies of volunteer militia, *the mimicry of soldiership.*"

From this, you will perceive that the epithets, to which you have taken exception, are neither applicable to the Militia *of South Carolina* in particular, nor to *Militia* in general, but merely to "*small fugitive* bodies of *volunteer* militia."

Having thus Sir stated the matter in its true light it remains for you to judge what conduct, in consequence of the explanation will be proper on your part.

The first sessions of the Senate were held in this chamber in New York City's Federal Hall.

On April 12, the House rejected assumption as part of the funding program. The Senate had yet to act. But, if Congress was slow to adopt Hamilton's financial policies, speculators abroad were eager to invest in the nation's future. Indeed, the Dutch banking house of Willink, Van Staphorst, and Hubbard was too eager, having opened a loan for the United States without any authority from the Federal Government. In May, Hamilton wrote to the bankers in Amsterdam.

The President and his Cabinet, in an engraving by Currier and Ives: from left, Washington, Knox, Hamilton, Jefferson, and Randolph.

Treasury Department May 7th. 1790. The distinguished zeal you have in so many instances shewn for the interests of this country, intitles you upon all occasions to a favourable interpretation of the motives by which you are actuated....Nor should I be apprehensive, that a sanction to the step you have taken, would form an inconvenient precedent for the future.

But the delays naturally incident to deliberations on a matter of the first consequence, the road to which had not been made easy by the antecedent state of things, having hitherto suspended any definitive resolutions concerning the public debt, I am not now in a situation to speak explicitly in regard to the measure you have undertaken. I can only say that the United States will stand in need of the aid of Loans abroad, and that I expect the requisite provision for making them upon solid, and consequently advantageous terms, will shortly be concluded upon; in which case you will immediately hear from me.

One Virginian, James Madison, had done his best to defeat Hamilton's program in the House; another native of that state soon came to Hamilton's aid. Thomas Jefferson, recently returned from his diplomatic post in Paris, took his oath as Secretary of State on March 22. He and Hamilton discovered several points of mutual interest, such as Jefferson's cherished plan to give America a decimal coinage and standardized system of weights and measures. Hamilton responded enthusiastically.

[New York, June 16, 1790] Mr. Hamilton presents his Compliments to Mr. Jefferson. He has perused with much satisfaction the draft of his report on the subject of weights and measures. There is no view which Mr. H has yet taken of the matter which stands opposed to the alteration of the money-unit as at present contemplated by the regulations of Congress either in the way suggested in the report or in that mentioned in the note of yesterday. And there are certainly strong reasons to render a correspondency desireable. The idea of a general standard among nations...seems full of convenience & order.

Together, Jefferson and Hamilton solved the problem of Federal assumption of state debts by tying the issue to the debate over the future location of the Federal capital. Many southern Congressmen, opponents of assumption, were anxious to see the capital moved to the Potomac River, whereas many northerners were in favor of assumption but were reluctant to see the capital in the South. The new Secretary of State took credit for persuading Madison to cooperate in a "bargain" by which the South accepted assumption in return for northern votes on the site of the capital city. On July 21, the Senate restored assumption to the House bill on funding; three days later the House agreed to let the amendment stand. Hamilton's program had survived. As he later recalled, he could even forgive James Madison his obstinacy.

> Philadelphia May 26th, 1792
>
> At this time and afterwards repeated intimations were given to me that Mr. Madison, from a spirit of rivalship or some other cause had become personally unfriendly to me; and one Gentleman in particular, whose honor I have no reason to doubt, assured me, that Mr. Madison in a conversation with him had made a pretty direct attempt to insinuate unfavourable impressions of me.
>
> Still I suspended my opinion on the subject. I knew the malevolent officiousness of mankind too well to yield a very ready acquiescience to the suggestions which were made, and resolved to wait 'till time and more experience should afford a solution.

Hamilton could afford to be generous to his critics at the end of July, 1790. His political balance sheet for the last two years had been decidedly in his own favor. Although he had failed to defeat George Clinton in New York, that loss seemed trivial compared to his victory in helping to persuade George Washington to serve as President. With so many of the "right men" in national government, state politics seemed relatively unimportant.

As Congress prepared to adjourn that summer, Hamilton could look forward to working with old friends like John Jay, first Chief Justice of the Supreme Court, and Henry Knox, Secretary of War, and with a new ally, Thomas Jefferson. Hamilton would have agreed with Jefferson's sentiments when the Secretary of State wrote that with debates on funding and assumption "out of the way" there was now room to hope that "nothing else may be able to call up local principles." National principles and "respectable" government seemed assured.

Chapter **9**

Public Affairs and a Private One

The spirit of conciliation and nationalism that flowered in the summer of 1790 was short-lived. In fact the compromise of 1790 may have been far less significant than Jefferson believed. There is considerable evidence that many of the senators and representatives who changed their votes on assumption and the location of the capital had made their decisions before the Secretary of State assumed the role of arbitrator. Perhaps the most important aspect of the compromise was that Jefferson believed that it had taken place. In later years, he complained that Hamilton had "duped" him into cooperating in the arrangement, and his sense of betrayal made him an increasingly bitter foe of the Treasury Secretary. Actually, Jefferson had perhaps duped himself by assuming that funding and assumption were the last of Hamilton's innovations. Hamilton had made no secret of the fact that these measures were only the beginning of a new financial system. Indeed, his first *Report on Public Credit* had closed with the promise that he would submit a plan for a national bank — an institution that Jefferson denounced as unconstitutional when it became a reality in 1791.

After the Government moved to Philadelphia in the autumn of 1790 (a temporary move until the new Federal City could be built on the Potomac), Jefferson had ample opportunity to become better acquainted with the Hamiltonian system. The Virginia statesman realized that he had apparently cooperated in a plan completely at odds with his own vision of America's national destiny. At every point the heads of the departments of State and of the Treasury now seemed certain to collide. In foreign policy, Hamilton was working for closer political and commercial ties with Britain, whose profitable trade could benefit the American mercantile community and swell the import duties assigned to funding the domestic debt; Jefferson, who had spent six years as America's minister in Paris, favored France, America's Revolutionary ally and Britain's traditional enemy. In domestic matters, Hamilton's reports on public credit, the bank, and manufactures revealed his conception of a national economy that could take advantage of the Industrial Revolution that was beginning to transform Europe, and that could add commerce and industry to its sources of wealth. Jefferson, however, clung to an almost mystical belief in the virtue of farming as an economic base, and to a Virginia planter's distrust of merchants.

It was a miracle of American political history that Jefferson and Hamilton avoided open conflict as long as they did. In the eighteen months after the passage of assumption, they learned to know each other better and to like each other less, but they managed to confine themselves to private expressions of mutual distrust and growing hostility. For much of this period, Hamilton was too involved in personal problems and with the routine of the Treasury to notice the depth of Jefferson's opposition. Like Jefferson, Hamilton was guilty of some self-delusion concerning the implications of the passage of assumption. His triumph in establishing the funding program made him overconfident. Success did entail a degree of personal inconvenience, for he now had to move his family and office to Philadelphia. But the task was made easier by a friend, to whom Hamilton wrote shortly after his victory in Congress.

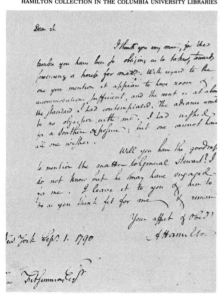

Hamilton's September note thanking Congressman Thomas FitzSimons of Pennsylvania for locating a house for the Hamilton family in Philadelphia

[New York] Augt. 5. 1790

I thank you for the interest you are so obliging as to take in procuring for me a house. My wish has been to have it first ascertained what arrangement would be made, if any, by your Magistracy or other public Men, in regard to *offices* for the accommodation of the department. If any public buildings should be destined to that purpose, my next wish would be to have a house as near my destined office as possible. A cool situation & exposure will of course be a very material point to a New Yorker. The house must have at least six rooms. Good dining and drawing rooms are material articles. I like elbow room in a yard. As to the rent the lower the better consistently with the acquisition of a proper house. But I must leave that to what is practicable.

When Judge [James] Wilson was in Town he obligingly offered to look out for me. Without adverting to your friendly undertaking I requested him to do so. I mention this that you may have the goodness to communicate with him: For *two houses* would be more than I shall *probably* have occasion for.

Congress had authorized the President to open two loans to implement the funding program: one for twelve million dollars, which would pay the foreign debt; and one that would raise two million dollars for the reduction of the domestic debt by purchases of government securities. At last Hamilton could employ the overenthusiastic Dutch bankers who had taken subscriptions for a loan to the United States without his approval. In a letter to Washington, Hamilton outlined his suggestions for using the funds available in Holland.

[New York, August 26, 1790]

The Minister of the Finances of France has ... *solicited* that the money arising from the Loan in question, of which he has been apprised, might be applied in part payment of the Debt due to that nation. Its peculiar situation at the present juncture contains an appeal to the sensibility, as well as to the policy and honor of this Country in favor of that requisition.

If these reasons appear to the President sufficient to induce his sanction to the loan in question, it will remain to consider, under what act, it will be most expedient to authorise its being made, whether that of the 4th. or that of the 12th. of the present month, or whether it may not be advisable to authorise it partly under one & partly under the other.

... the business may easily take the latter form ... and this is recommended by the consideration that it will contribute in a degree to all the purposes which require to be promoted.

If two thirds of the sum should be borrowed on account of the twelve millions and the remaining third on account of the two millions, the next half years interest in Holland may be discharged, the arrears of Interest on the Debt due to Spain may be paid off, a respectable payment may be made to France as a prelude to more considerable ones, and a sum of consequence to the operation, would remain towards the reduction of our Debt and supporting our funds in conformity to the intention of the last mentioned Act.

HISTORICAL SOCIETY OF PENNSYLVANIA

Philadelphia's Walnut Street, as it looked about 1790, when Hamilton took up residence there

Shortly thereafter, Elizabeth Hamilton took her children to Albany to visit her parents. Her husband, the only member of the Administration left in New York City, went about his official duties. In mid-September, he wrote to his wife.

[New York] Sep 15. 1790

You do not hope in vain My very Dear love that I am tired of living alone. I was so the very hour after you left me. But I am not sure for all this that it will be possible for

A miniature of Hamilton attributed to Charles Shirreff, circa 1790

me to come to you. . . . I am the only one of the Administration now here, and . . . it might be very awkward for me to be absent also. In this situation, I would press you to come down with your father, who writes me that he must be here by the 27th, if I did not believe that your health may be benefitted by your continuance where you are somewhat longer. . . . But I leave the matter to yourself. If you feel anxious or uneasy you had better come down. If you can prolong your stay with satisfaction it may be of service to you to do it and in that case I would endeavour to return with your father.

If you know My beloved wife how delightful it is to me to have you with me you need not be told how irksome it is to be separated from you & how much I desire to receive you again to my bosom.

Alone in Manhattan, Hamilton pursued one of the plans that would soon put him at odds with Jefferson. In October, 1789, Hamilton had begun a series of conferences with George Beckwith, Britain's unofficial representative in America. Beckwith's report of their first conversation revealed Hamilton's position clearly.

[New York, October, 1789]
[Hamilton:] I have requested to see you on this occasion from a Wish to Explain Certain points, relative to our situation, and from a desire to suggest a measure, which I conceive to be both for the interest of Great Britain, and of this Country to adopt. We have lately Established a Government upon principles, that in my opinion render it safe for any Nation to Enter into Treaties with us, Either Commercial or Political, which has not hitherto been the Case; I have always preferred a Connexion with you, to that of any other Country, *We think in English,* and have a similarity of prejudices, and of predilections. . . . We are a young and a growing Empire, with much Enterprize and vigour, but undoubtedly are, and must be for years, rather an Agricultural, than a manufacturing people. . . .

I am free to say, that Although France has been indulgent to us, in certain points, yet, what she can furnish, is by no means so Essential or so suited to us as Your productions, nor do our raw Materials suit her so well as they do you. . . .

We wish to form a Commercial treaty with you to Every

Extent, to which you may think it for Your interest to go....I am of opinion, that it will be better for Great Britain to grant us admission into her [West Indian] Islands...than by a rigid adherence to Your present plan to produce a system of warfare in Commercial matters, which however Encouraged by France in this Country... with a view to promote coldness and animosity between the two Countries, I have Ever viewed with much regret, as being directly opposed to that system, which upon Mature reflexion, I have thought it most Eligible for us to pursue.

New problems brought Beckwith back to New York in July, 1790, when the threat of war with Spain made Britain fear that America might seize her posts in the West. Beckwith was anxious to learn if such "hostile designs" existed, and Washington ordered Hamilton to treat the English agent "very civilly" and "to extract as much as he could" from Beckwith. Hamilton's readiness to court Britain's good will and profitable trade became apparent in September after the President left for Virginia. In one conversation with Beckwith, for example, Hamilton "candidly examined" American foreign policy in the event of an Anglo-Spanish war.

[New York, September 26–30, 1790]

You know we have two parties with us; there are gentlemen, who think we ought to be connected with France in the most intimate terms, and that the Bourbon compact [between France and Spain] furnishes an example for us to follow; there are others who are at least as numerous, and influential, who decidedly prefer an English connexion, but the present condition of Great Britain and the States is favorable to the former party, and they are zealous to improve it; the present therefore is the moment to take up the matter seriously and dispassionately, and I wish it done without loss of time.

We consider ourselves perfectly at liberty to act with respect to Spain in any way most conducive to our interests, even to the going to war with that power, if we shall think it advisable to join You.

There would be nothing to criticize in Hamilton's conferences with Beckwith if he had been equally candid with his own Government. It was certainly to the interest of the United States to have at least one Cabinet member at work in the fall of 1790 during this dangerous period in European diplomacy. When the British agent called to investigate reports that America's minister in London, Gouverneur Morris, was on overfriendly terms with the French ambassador, Anne César, Marquis de La Luzerne, and Charles James Fox, the leader of the opposition party in the House of Commons, Hamilton sent this description of his reply to George Washington at Mount Vernon.

New York Sepr. 30. 1790

Charles James Fox

My answer [to Beckwith] was nearly as follows —

I have never heared a syllable Sir, about the matter you mention. It appears to me however very possible [that] an intimacy with both the persons you mention may exist: With the first [La Luzerne], because the situation of the parties had naturally produced such an intimacy, while both were in this Country; and to have dropped and avoided it there would not have been without difficulty, on the score of politeness, and would have worn an extraordinary and mysterious aspect: With the last [Fox], from the patronage of American affairs, which is understood to have been uniformly the part of that Gentleman, and in some degree, from a similarity of dispositions and characters; both brilliant men, men of wit and genius; both fond of the pleasures of society. It is to be hoped that appearances, which admit of so easy a solution will not prove an obstacle to any thing which mutual interest dictates. It is impossible that there can be any thing wrong.

Judging from Beckwith's version of the same conversation, Hamilton had been far more frank with the English agent than his report to Washington indicated, and he had not hesitated to criticize Morris's "prudence" and "fancy."

[New York, September 25–30, 1790]

[Hamilton:] Yes...I believe it in some measure to be true; I am the more inclined to be of this way of thinking from extracts of letters, which I have seen of [Gouverneur Morris], in which he throws out, that such and such were Mr. Fox's opinions on particular subjects, and from the former intimacy, which subsisted here between [Morris] and Monsieur de la Luzerne, as well as from Mr. Fox's line of politics during the war, his general character, and from my knowledge of [Morris] himself.

I do not question this gentleman's sincerity in following up those objects committed to his charge, but to deal frankly with You, I have some doubts of his prudence; this is the point in which he is deficient, for in other respects he is a man of great genius, liable however to be occasionally influenced by his fancy, which sometimes outruns his discretion.

These private conferences in New York were unknown to Jefferson. After the Treasury had moved to Philadelphia in the last week of October, Hamilton began work on a series of reports to Congress—reports that Jefferson could neither endorse nor ignore. These reports, submitted to the House of Representatives on December 13, contained Hamilton's "further provision" for the establishment of public credit, including, first of all, a proposal for paying interest on the state debts assumed by the Union.

Treasury Department December 13th. 1790

The object, which appears to be most immediately essential to the further support of public credit, in pursuance of the plan adopted during the last session of Congress, is, the establishment of proper and sufficient funds, for paying the interest which will begin to accrue, after the year one thousand seven hundred and ninety one, on the amount of the debts of the several States, assumed by the United States; having regard at the same time, to the probable, or estimated deficiency in those already established, as they respect the original debt of the Union. . . .

. . . the sums requisite for those purposes . . . Making together Dollars. 826,624.73.

For procuring which sum, the reiterated reflections of the Secretary have suggested nothing so eligible and unexceptionable, in his judgment, as a further duty on foreign distilled spirits, and a duty on spirits distilled within the United States. . . .

HISTORICAL SOCIETY OF PENNSYLVANIA

The offices of the Secretaries of State and the Treasury were housed in the matching two-story buildings just off the corner of Third and Chestnut streets in Philadelphia.

Hamilton's second report consisted of the plan for a national bank, which he had promised at the conclusion of his first report on the public credit a year earlier. Americans had argued the virtues and evils of banks for decades, and Hamilton knew he would have to meet the criticism of those who disliked the idea of banks and the moneyed power that banks seemed to represent. To him, there was nothing to fear from such institutions if they were properly regulated and made to serve the interests of the society in which they operated. In this famous report he outlined the creation of a national bank that could be as much a "servant" of the people as were the men who held office in the Republic. He opened with this declaration.

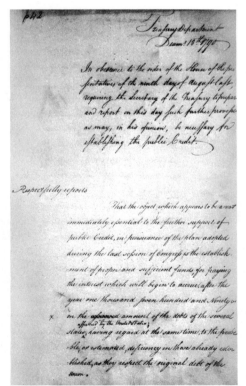

*Hamilton's original draft (above)
and a fair copy (below) of his
proposal for a national bank*

Treasury Department December 13th 1790
That from a conviction... That a National Bank is an
Institution of primary importance to the prosperous administration of the Finances, and would be of the greatest
utility in the operations connected with the support of
the Public Credit, his [the Secretary of the Treasury's]
attention has been drawn to devising the plan of such an
institution...

There are at present three banks in the United States.
That of North America, established in the city of Philadelphia; that of New York, established in the city of
New York; that of Massachusetts, established in the city
of Boston. Of these three, the first is the only one, which
has at any time had a direct relation to the Government
of the United States.

The Bank of North America originated in a resolution
of Congress of the 26th of May 1781, founded upon a
proposition of the Superintendant of finance....

The Directors of this Bank, on behalf of their constitu-
ents, have since *accepted* and *acted* under a new charter
from the State of Pennsylvania, materially variant from
their original one; and which so narrows the foundation
of the institution, as to render it an incompetent basis
for the extensive purposes of a National Bank....

The order of the subject leads next to an inquiry into
the principles, upon which a national Bank, ought to
be organised....

[First, however, Hamilton explained what the Bank
ought *not* to be: it would have no "plurality of branches"
nor would land form part of its capital.]

Considerations of public advantage suggest a further
wish, which is, that the Bank could be established upon
principles, that would cause the profits of it to redound
to the immediate benefit of the State. This is contemplated
by many, who speak of a National Bank, but the idea
seems liable to insuperable objections. To attach full
confidence to an institution of this nature, it appears to
be an essential ingredient in its structure, that it shall
be under a *private* not a *public* Direction, under the
guidance of *individual interest,* not of *public policy;*
which would be supposed to be...liable to being too
much influenced by *public necessity.* The suspicion of

this would most probably be a canker, that would continually corrode the vitals of the credit of the Bank....

The keen, steady, and, as it were, magnetic sense, of their own interest, as proprietors, in the Directors of a Bank, pointing invariably to its true pole, the prosperity of the institution, is the only security, that can always be relied upon, for a careful and prudent administration....

[Now Hamilton described what the bank *ought* to be: an institution whose capital would be limited to ten million dollars, of which two million dollars would be subscribed by the Federal Government. Only one fourth of each share would need to be paid in gold or silver; the rest would be in certificates of the public debt.]

The combination of a portion of the public Debt in the formation of the Capital, is the principal thing, of which an explanation is requisite. The chief object of this is, to enable the creation of a capital sufficiently large to be the basis of an extensive circulation, and an adequate security for it.... to collect such a sum in this country, in gold and silver, into one depository, may, without hesitation, be pronounced impracticable. Hence the necessity of an auxiliary which the public debt at once presents.

This part of the fund will be always ready to come in aid of the specie. It will more and more command a ready sale; and can therefore expeditiously be turned into coin if an exigency of the Bank should at any time require it....

The debt composing part of the capital... will produce a direct annual revenue of six per centum from the Government, which will enter into the half yearly dividends received by the Stockholders.

A 1799 engraving by William Birch shows the Bank of the United States on Third Street in Philadelphia.

In January, 1791, Hamilton wrote his sister-in-law that the success of his financial program meant that the time was "not *very* distant" when he could retire from office. During the following month, however, there were indications that his policies would not be implemented as quickly or as easily as he had hoped. In Congress, James Madison campaigned for commercial restrictions that would favor France at Britain's expense. While Hamilton assured George Beckwith that this was of little consequence, he may have realized that it was a sign of broader, more consistent opposition. Beckwith reported the Secretary's remarks to his superiors in London.

*Hamilton's certificate of election
to the American Philosophical
Society cited his "distinguished
Eminence" and "literary merit."*

Philadelphia January 19th.[–20] 1791

You know perfectly, that we have different opinions with us, as I have frequently told you; there is a Party which retaining those prejudices that were produced by the civil war, think nothing good can come from Great Britain, and that our obligations to France are never to be forgotten.... There are also worthy individuals with us, who are led to believe that by going into regulations which might cramp your trade to this country, that is, by advocating a system for a discrimination of duties, in favor of nations with whom we have treaties, it would lead to the attainment of a commercial treaty with England which they wish; and there is likewise a party, who ... are convinced, that you are the nation with whom we can trade to the greatest advantage: from these discordant sentiments it is difficult not to do something on this subject, and I think in the course of the present Sessions we shall adopt in a degree the idea furnished by your Navigation Act, the effect of which will be to restrain your shipping from being the carriers to our Markets of other produce or manufacture than that of your own dominions... or of carrying from hence, excepting to your possessions...: from the returns in my office, these regulations will not be of any consequence to the shipping of Great Britain.

While Madison was causing problems for Hamilton in the congressional debate on trade policies, Hamilton also found himself increasingly at odds with Jefferson in the Cabinet. When Gouverneur Morris's dispatches from London indicated that it would be impossible to conclude an Anglo-American commercial treaty, Jefferson advised the President to inform Congress of the failure of Morris's mission. Hamilton objected, but Washington made the disclosure to the House and Senate in February, 1791. When George Beckwith demanded the reasons for this decision, Hamilton offered him an explanation.

[Philadelphia, February 16, 1791]

I cannot bring myself to believe that The President's mind is the least influenced by any set of prejudices whatever; he indeed is of opinion from Mr. Morris's letters, *that no commercial treaty is attainable with England,* but I am sure he is not led to make these communications to the Legislature at this time, from any idea of assimilating this with other questions, yet I do not pretend to say that such views may not have struck the minds of certain persons, who have recommended this measure....

In the present state of things, nothing has happened between us and France, to give a tolerable pretence, for breaking off our treaty of Alliance with that Power and immediately forming one with you. A regard for National decorum, puts such a decisive step as this, out of our reach, but I tell you candidly as an individual, that I think the formation of a treaty of commerce, would by degrees have led to this measure, which undoubtedly that Party with us, whose remaining animosities and French partialities influence their whole political conduct, regard with dissatisfaction.

The same day that he commiserated with Beckwith on Anglo-American relations, Hamilton received a letter from Washington enclosing the written opinions of Jefferson and Edmund Randolph, the Attorney General, on the act of Congress establishing a Bank of the United States. Both Virginians had declared the measure to be unconstitutional, and Washington asked for the views of the Secretary of the Treasury. Hamilton replied in a document that must be considered one of the major state papers of the Federal period.

[Philadelphia, February 23, 1791]
It will naturally have been anticipated that, in performing this task he [the Secretary of the Treasury] would feel uncommon solicitude. Personal considerations alone arising from the reflection that the measure originated with him would be sufficient to produce it.... But the chief solicitude arises from a firm persuasion, that principles of construction like those espoused by the Secretary of State and the Attorney General would be fatal to the just & indispensible authority of the United States.

... the objections of the Secretary of State and Attorney General are founded on a general denial of the authority of the United States to erect corporations....

Now it appears to the Secretary of the Treasury, that this *general principle* is *inherent* in the very *definition* of *Government* and *essential* to every step of the progress to be made by that of the United States; namely — that every power vested in a Government is in its nature *sovereign,* and includes by *force* of the *term,* a right to employ all the *means* requisite, and fairly *applicable* to the attainment of the *ends* of such power; and which are not precluded by restrictions & exceptions specified in the constitution; or not immoral, or not contrary to the essential ends of political society....

It is not denied, that there are *implied,* as well as *express* powers, and that the former are as effectually delegated as the latter....

Then it follows, that as a power of erecting a corporation may as well be *implied* as any other thing; it may as well be employed as an *instrument* or *mean* of carrying into execution any of the specified powers, as any other instrument or mean whatever....

[Incorporation, Hamilton argued, was only a means to an end. If that end was "necessary and proper" for an object of the Government described by the Constitution, then incorporation of a bank would be valid. He also quarreled with Jefferson's narrow definition of the word "necessary."]

...the Secretary of State maintains, that no means are to be considered as *necessary,* but those without which the grant of the power would be *nugatory....*

It is certain, that neither the grammatical, nor popular sense of the term requires that construction. According to both, *necessary* often means no more than *needful, requisite, incidental, useful,* or *conducive to.* It is a common mode of expression to say, that it is *necessary* for a government or a person to do this or that thing, when nothing more is intended or understood, than that the interests of the government or person require, or will be promoted, by the doing of this or that thing. The imagination can be at no loss for exemplifications of the use of the word in this sense.

And it is the true one in which it is to be understood as used in the constitution. The whole turn of the clause containing it, indicates, that it was the intent of the convention, by that clause to give a liberal latitude to the exercise of the specified powers.... To understand the word as the Secretary of State does, would be to depart from its obvious & popular sense, and to give it a *restrictive* operation; an idea never before entertained. It would be to give it the same force as if the word *absolutely* or *indispensibly* had been prefixed to it.

A page from Hamilton's memo to Washington that defended the national bank's constitutionality

William Short

Washington accepted Hamilton's opinion of the bank's constitutionality as he had previously taken Jefferson's advice on diplomatic policy. The act incorporating the bank became law on February 25. A few weeks later the President left on a tour of the southern states. The informal, almost makeshift, nature of American government in 1791 was shown by the arrangements made for conducting business in his absence. The Cabinet and the Vice President were to "hold conversations" on "any serious and important cases" that might arise. This procedure was put to the test when Hamilton received a letter from William Short, the American chargé d'affaires in Paris, who had been named the official agent for supervising borrowing in Europe. Short's dispatch announced that a new loan had been obtained in Amsterdam. The Secretary of the Treasury explained his dilemma to the President.

Historic Carpenter's Hall in Philadelphia, first headquarters of the Bank of the United States

Treasury Department April 10 1791.
You will recollect that by a particular instruction from you to me, no succeeding *Loan* is to be opened, until *that* preceding has been submitted to you, and received your approbation. As it is very desireable that no delay may attend the progress of the business... to which the loans may be applied, I have concluded to submit Mr. Shorts letter tomorrow to the Vice President, and the heads of Departments, that they may consider, how far the case is within the purview of your letter; and whether it will not be expedient to authorise Mr. Short to proceed upon a further loan to the amount of three millions of guilders....

I request nevertheless to receive your instruction as soon as possible upon the subject. And I submit whether it will not be adviseable to change the restriction above mentioned so as to leave Mr. Short at liberty to open his loans successively for three millions of Dollars each; no new one to commence till after the preceding one has been filled; but without waiting for a ratification from this Country; provided the terms be not in any case less advantageous than those now announced. There is always danger of considerable delay in waiting for approbation from hence, before a new loan can be undertaken; and favourable *moments* may be lost.

Even though the Cabinet approved his plan for a new Dutch loan, Hamilton hesitated to send Short new instructions without Washington's personal authorization. While awaiting the President's instructions, Hamilton explained the gravity of the situation to Jefferson. France's precarious political position had caused her currency to depreciate, while Holland's remained stable in value. Thus a Dutch florin was worth more French livres than had been the case a few years earlier. Hamilton wrote to the Secretary of State, quoting William Short's description of a scheme by which speculators hoped literally to buy the American debt from the hard-pressed French Government.

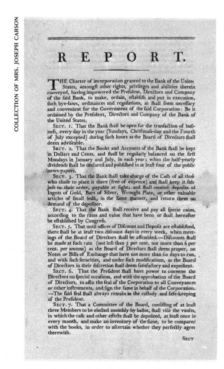

REPORT.

THE Charter of incorporation granted to the Bank of the United States, amongst other rights, privileges and abilities therein conveyed, having impowered the President, Directors and Company of the said Bank, to make, ordain, establish and put in execution, such bye-laws, ordinances and regulations, as shall seem necessary and convenient for the Government of the said Corporation: Be it ordained by the President, Directors and Company of the Bank of the United States,

SECT. 1. That the Bank shall be open for the transaction of business, every day in the year (Sundays, Christmas-day and the Fourth of July excepted) during such hours as the Board of Directors shall deem adviseable.

SECT. 2. That the Books and Accounts of the Bank shall be kept in Dollars and Cents, and shall be regularly balanced on the first Mondays in January and July, in each year; when the half-yearly dividends shall be declared and published in at least four of the public news-papers.

SECT. 3. That the Bank shall take charge of the Cash of all those who chuse to place it there (free of expence) and shall keep it subject to their order, payable at sight; and shall receive deposits of Ingots of Gold, Bars of Silver, Wrought Plate, or other valuable articles of small bulk, in the same manner, and return them on demand of the depositor.

SECT. 4. That the Bank shall receive and pay all specie coins, according to the rates and value that have been or shall hereafter be established by Congress.

SECT. 5. That until offices of Discount and Deposit are established, there shall be at least two discount days in every week, when meetings of the Board of Directors shall be assembled.—Discounts shall be made at such rate (not less than 5 per cent. nor more than 6 per cent. per annum) as the Board of Directors shall deem proper, on Notes or Bills of Exchange that have not more than 60 days to run, and with such securities, and under such modifications, as the Board of Directors in their discretion shall deem satisfactory and expedient.

SECT. 6. That the President shall have power to convene the Directors on special occasions, and with the approbation of the Board of Directors, to affix the seal of the Corporation to all Conveyances or other instruments, and sign the same in behalf of the Corporation.—The seal shall always remain in the custody and safe-keeping of the President.

SECT. 7. That a Committee of the Board, consisting of at least three Members to be elected monthly by ballot, shall visit the vaults, in which the cash and other effects shall be deposited, at least once in every month, and make an inventory of the same, to be compared with the books, in order to ascertain whether they perfectly agree therewith.

SECT

The bylaws of the Bank of the United States, printed in 1791 by Hamilton's protégé, John Fenno

Treasury Department, 15 April 1791

"The object of this company is, as you will see, to pay livres tournois [French currency] in their present depreciated State & to receive from the United States florins [Dutch currency] at the usual exchange—by this means France would receive from them *as much as she is entitled to receive from us,* but we should be obliged to pay the Company *much more than we are obliged to pay France.*"... "I must also add that the house which makes these propositions is *entirely unknown* here & that I never heared even their names at Paris, which proves that *it must be an inconsiderable one.*" Consequently the credit of the United States would be in imminent danger of suffering in their hands....

I take it for granted that the Court of France will not attempt any operation with the debt, without the consent of the United States. Any thing of this sort, considering the efforts which are making on our part, to discharge the debt, would certainly be very exceptionable. Indeed I do not see how any valid disposition of the debt of a sovereign power can be made without its consent; but it would be disagreeable to have to use this argument. I trust it will never be rendered necessary.

France's political and financial picture changed quickly, but the United States, hampered by long delays in the exchange of dispatches, could only react slowly. Hamilton did not receive Washington's approval of Short's new instructions until the last week of May—almost six months after Short had written to announce the Dutch loan. With this problem solved, however, Hamilton turned to other business. That summer, Jefferson and Madison found time for a leisurely tour of New York and New England, engaging in conferences along the way with leading northern "republicans" (that is, anti-Hamiltonians). In the meantime, Hamilton remained hard at work at the Treasury Office. Early in June, he undertook the satisfying task of issuing instructions to the captains of the new revenue cutters, who had been given the thankless job of ending a time-honored American occupation —smuggling.

Treasury Department June 4 1791.
While I recommend in the strongest terms to the respective Officers, activity, vigilance & firmness, I feel no less solicitude that their deportment may be marked with prudence, moderation & good temper. Upon these last qualities not less than upon the former must depend the success, usefulness, & consequently *continuance* of the establishment in which they are included. They cannot be insensible that there are some prepossessions against it, that the charge with which they are entrusted is a delicate one, & that it is easy by mismanagement to produce serious & extensive clamour, disgust & odium.

They will always keep in mind that their Countrymen are Freemen & as such are impatient of every thing that bears the least mark of a domineering Spirit.... They will endeavour to overcome difficulties, if any are experienced, by a cool and temperate perseverance in their duty, by address & moderation rather than by vehemence or violence. The former stile of conduct will recommend them to the particular approbation of the president of the United states, while the reverse of it, even a single instance of outrage, or intemperate or improper treatment of any person with whom they have any thing to do in the course of their duty, will meet with his pointed displeasure, & will be attended with correspondent consequences.

SMITHSONIAN INSTITUTION

The key to the first United States Treasury Building in Philadelphia

On learning that Washington had returned to his home at Mount Vernon after his tour of the South, Hamilton sent him this cheerful and confident note.

Philadelphia June 19th. 1791.
I am very happy to learn that the circumstances of your journey have been in all respects so favourable. It has certainly been a particularly fortunate one, and I doubt not it will have been of real utility.

There is nothing which can be said to be new here worth communicating, except generally that all my Accounts from *Europe*, both private & official, concur in proving that the impressions now entertained of our government and its affairs (I may say) *throughout* that quarter of the Globe are of a nature the most flattering & pleasing.

...warmest wishes for your health & happiness...

With these "flattering & pleasing" reports to lighten his labors, the Secretary of the Treasury began work on a plan "for the encouragement and promotion of...manufactures" assigned him by the House. In June, he sent this request to the Supervisors of the Revenue in the various states.

> Treasury Department, June 22, 1791.
>
> I request...that you will give me as accurate Information as it shall be in your Power to obtain, *of the Manufactures of every Kind carried on within the Limits of your District, whether incidentally in the domestic Way, or as regular Trades—of the respective Times of their first Establishment—of the Degree of Maturity they have obtained—of the Quantities periodically made—of the Prices at which they are sold—of their respective Qualities—of the impediments, if any, under which they labour—of the Encouragements, if any, which they enjoy under the Laws of the State—whether they are carried on by Societies, Companies, or Individuals.*
>
> It would also be acceptable to me, to have Samples in Cases in which it could be done with Convenience, and without Expence.

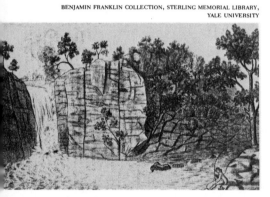

One of America's first industrial centers grew up around the Falls of the Passaic in New Jersey.

Hamilton's public interest in manufactures paralleled a private concern. In the spring, he and William Duer, a former Treasury Department official, had discussed the prospect of organizing a "manufacturing Society." Over the summer, Hamilton worked with the organizers of the Society for Establishing Useful Manufactures, a private corporation that was to establish such a "manufactory" in New Jersey. By the end of August, Hamilton had completed this prospectus for the society.

> [Philadelphia, August, 1791]
>
> What is there to hinder the profitable prosecution of manufactures in this Country, when it is notorious, that ...provisions and various kinds of raw materials are even cheaper here than in the Country from which our principal supplies come?
>
> The dearness of labour and the want of Capital are the two great objections to the success of manufactures in the United States.
>
> The first objection ceases to be formidable when it is recollected how prodigiously the proportion of manual labour in a variety of manufactures has been decreased by the late improvements in the construction and application of Machines—and when it is also considered to

*The journey to the Schuyler
summer home at Schuylerville
(above) meant a trip across the
Hudson at McNeal's Ferry (below).*

what an extent women and even children in the populous parts of the Country may be rendered auxiliary to undertakings of this nature. It is also to be taken into calculation that emigrants may be engaged on reasonable terms in countries where labour is cheap, and brought over to the United States.

The last objection disappears in the eye of those who are aware how much may be done by a proper application of the public Debt. Here is the resource which has been hitherto wanted. . . .

To remedy this defect an association of the Capitals of a number of Individuals is an obvious expedient — and the species of Capital which consists of the public Stock is susceptible of dispositions which will render it adequate to the end. . . .

To effect the desired association an incorporation of the adventurers must be contemplated as a mean necessary to their security. This can doubtless be obtained. There is scarcely a state which could be insensible to the advantage of being the scene of such an undertaking. But there are reasons which strongly recommend the state of New Jersey for the purpose. It is thickly populated — provisions are there abundant and cheap. The state having scarcely any external commerce and no waste lands to be peopled can feel the impulse of no supposed interest hostile to the advancement of manufactures.

Despite the demands of the Treasury Department and his work on the *Report on Manufactures,* Hamilton found time to maintain an affectionate correspondence with his wife Elizabeth in the summer of 1791, when she and their children were visiting her parents in Albany. Early in August, Hamilton wrote anxiously on learning that their three-year-old son, James, was ill.

> [Philadelphia] Aug. 2, 1791
> I thank you my beloved Betsey for your letter announcing your safe arrival; but my satisfaction at learning this has been greatly alloyed by the intelligence you give me of the indisposition of my darling James. Heaven protect and preserve him! I am sure you will lose no time in advising me of any alteration which may happen. I trust he will not be in danger.
> Remember the flannel next his skin, and If he should not be better when this reaches, try the bark-waiscoat.

Remember also the benefit he received from Barley water with a dash of brandy. Be very attentive to his diet. Indulge him with nothing that will injure him. Not much fruit of any kind. Be sure that he drinks no water which has not been first boiled in some iron vessel. I hope he will have had some rhubarb or antimonial wine. Paregoric at night in moderation will do him good & a little bark [quinine] will not do him harm.

Take good care of my Lamb; but I need not recommend. . . .

I am myself in good health & will wait with all the patience I can the time for your return. But you must not precipitate it. I am so anxious for a perfect restoration of your health that I am willing to make a great sacrifice for it.

Alexander Hamilton's "sacrifice" in insisting that his wife remain in Albany for her health was not as great as it seemed. Years later, he recounted his experiences during Elizabeth's absence—a personal adventure so bizarre that some of his later critics have suggested that he invented the tale to conceal official misconduct.

[August 31, 1797]

Some time in the summer of the year 1791 a woman called at my house in the city of Philadelphia and asked to speak with me in private. I attended her into a room apart from the family. With a seeming air of affliction she informed that she was a daughter of a Mr. Lewis, sister to a Mr. G. Livingston of the State of New-York, and wife to a Mr. Reynolds whose father was in the Commissary Department during the war with Great Britain, that her husband, who for a long time had treated her very cruelly, had lately left her, to live with another woman, and in so destitute a condition, that though desirous of returning to her friends she had not the means— that knowing I was a citizen of New-York, she had taken the liberty to apply to my humanity for assistance.

I replied, that her situation was a very interesting one —that I was disposed to afford her assistance to convey her to her friends, but this at the moment not being convenient to me (which was the fact) I must request the place of her residence, to which I should bring or send a small supply of money. She told me the street and the number of the house where she lodged. In the evening I put a bank-bill in my pocket and went to the house. I inquired for Mrs. Reynolds and was shewn up stairs, at the head of which she met me and conducted me into a bed room. I took the bill out of my pocket and gave it to her. Some conversation ensued from which it was quickly apparent that other than pecuniary consolation would be acceptable.

After this, I had frequent meetings with her, most of them at my own house; Mrs. Hamilton with her children being absent on a visit to her father.

In the midst of his liaison with Maria Reynolds, Hamilton was faced with a new crisis for the Treasury. In March, Congress had acted on his suggestion that distilled liquors be taxed. By the end of the summer, opposition to this excise had appeared in Pennsylvania. In a report prepared for President Washington three years later, Hamilton recalled incidents in the four westernmost counties of that state in 1791.

Hamilton wrote this tender letter to his "beloved Betsey" in the midst of his affair with Mrs. Reynolds.

Treasury Department [August 5] 1794
The opposition first manifested itself in the milder shape of the circulation of opinions unfavourable to the law & calculated by the influence of public disesteem to discourage the accepting or holding of Offices under it or the complying with it, by those who might be so disposed; to which was added the show of a discontinuance of the business of distilling. These expedients were shortly after succeeded by private associations to *forbear* compliances with the law. But it was not long before these more negative modes of opposition were perceived to be likely to prove ineffectual....

The officers now began to experience marks of contempt and insult. Threats against them became frequent and loud; and after some time, these threats were ripened into acts of ill-treatment and outrage.

These acts of violence were preceded by certain Meetings of malcontent persons who entered into resolutions calculated at once to confirm inflame and systematize the spirit of opposition.

The first of these Meetings was holden at a place called Red Stone Old Fort, on the 27 of July 1791 where it was concerted that county committe[e]s should be convened in the four Counties at the respective seats of Justice therein. On the 23 of August following one of these committees assembled in the County of Washington.... This Meeting passed some intemperate resolutions... containing a strong censure on the law, declaring that any person *who had accepted or might accept an office under Congress in order to carry it into effect should be considered as inimical to the interests of the Country; and recommending to the Citizens of Washington County to treat every person who had accepted or might thereafter accept any such office with contempt, and absolutely to refuse all kind of communication or intercourse with the Officers and to withold from them all aid support or comfort....*

[These meetings, "conducted without moderation or prudence," were not the worst displays of opposition to the excise law in Pennsylvania. Hamilton recounted the experience of one unfortunate revenue collector.]

A party of men armed and disguised way-laid him at a place on Pidgeon Creek in Washington county — seized tarred and feathered him cut off his hair and deprived him of his horse, obliging him to travel on foot a considerable distance in that mortifying and painful situation.

The case was brought before the District Court of Pensylvania out of which Processes issued against John Robertson John Hamilton & Thomas McComb: three of the persons concerned in the outrage.

The serving of These processes was confided by the then Marshall Clement Biddle to his Deputy Joseph Fox, who... went into Alleghany County for the purpose of serving them.

The appearances & circumstances which Mr. Fox observed himself in the course of his journey, & learnt afterwards upon his arrival at Pittsburgh, had the effect of deterring him from the service of the processes...

A page from Washington's letter authorizing Hamilton to set up a system for collecting a whiskey tax

A nother complication in Hamilton's official life appeared in early August, when France's new minister to the United States, Jean Baptiste de Ternant, presented his credentials to the American Government. After a conversation with Hamilton, Beckwith recorded the Secretary's remarks on the future of Franco-American relations.

Philadelphia August 12th [1791]

Since I saw you, we have got Mr. Ternant, the minister pleniopotentiary from France; I have seen him for a few

Philip Freneau

minutes only. You will find him a man of easy, pleasing manners, and very fit for the objects of his appointment. There has been a sort of alarm in France, and a degree of jealousy of *your* having lately turned your attention more towards this Country than formerly. [Britain had recently named a minister to the United States.]

From the nature of our government foreign affairs are totally in the department of the Secretary of State; we have no Cabinet, and the heads of Departments meet on very particular occasions only, therefore I am a stranger to any special views, that may be in the contemplation of the French government from the appointment of this Minister, but I think it probable, that a revision of their whole commercial condition with *us* may be in agitation, in the Hope of acquiring thereby some share in the trade and consumption of this country; he is a fit man in many respects for such purposes.

That same month, Jefferson and Madison completed arrangements for a young New York newspaperman named Philip Freneau, whom they had recruited during their summer tour of the northern states, to move to Philadelphia to serve as a State Department translator and as publisher of a "republican" newspaper. In August, too, Jefferson angrily denounced Vice President Adams for a series of letters signed "Publicola," which he believed Adams had written. In trying to soothe the Secretary of State, Hamilton only damned himself further in the Virginian's eyes. Jefferson made these notes of Hamilton's remarks—remarks that must have made Philip Freneau's venture as a publicist for republicanism seem all the more necessary.

[Philadelphia, August 13, 1791]

A. H. condemning mr A's writings...as having a tendency to weaken the present govmt declared in substance as follows. "I own it is my own op[inio]n, tho' I do not publish it in Dan & Bersheba, that the present govmt is not that which will answer the ends of society by giving stability & protection to it's rights, and that it will probably be found expediente to go into the British form. However, since we have undertaken the experiment, I am for giving it a fair course, whatever my expect[atio]ns may be. The success indeed so far is greater than I had expected, & therefore at present success seems more possible than it had done heretofore, & there are still other & other stages of improvemt which, if the present

Hamilton's certificate of election to the American Academy of Arts and Sciences, signed and sealed by the Academy's president, John Adams

does not succeed, may be tried & ought to be tried before we give up the republican form altogether for that mind must be really depraved which would not prefer the equality of political rights which is the found[atio]n of pure republicanism, if it can be obtained consistently with order. Therefore whoever by his writings disturbs the present order of things, is really blameable, however pure his intent[io]ns may be, & he was sure mr Adams's were pure."

Increasingly, Jefferson saw Hamilton as the representative of "monarchical" thinking in politics and of the "monied" interest in financial policies. This moneyed interest, which was supposed to have benefited by Federal assumption of state debts and by the establishment of the national bank, was indulging in irresponsible speculation in government securities and bank stock in August, 1791. Activities in the New York stock market were compared to the legendary "South Sea Bubble," which had caused a crash in the British market a half century earlier. Hamilton's natural concern for the New York market was increased by the fact that William Duer, his former assistant in the Treasury Department and cosponsor of the Society for Establishing Useful Manufactures, was the most notorious of these speculators. In mid-August, the Secretary wrote to Duer.

Philadelphia Aug 17 1791

The conversation here was—"Bank Script is getting so high as to become a bubble" in one breath—in another, "'tis a South Sea dream," in a third, "There is a combination of knowing ones at New York to raise it as high as possible by fictitious purchases in order to take in the credulous and ignorant"—In another "Duer [William] Constable and some others are mounting the balloon as fast as possible—If it dont soon burst, thousands will rue it" &c &c.

As to myself, my friend, I think I know you too well to suppose you capable of such views as were implied in those innuendoes, or to harbour the most distant thought that you could wander from the path either of public good or private integrity. But I will honestly own I had serious fears for you—for your *purse* and for your *reputation,* and with an anxiety for both I wrote to you in earnest terms. . . . My friendship for you & my concern for the public cause were both alarmed. If the infatuation had continued progressive & any extensive mischiefs had ensued you would certainly have had a large portion

William Duer

of the blame. Conscious of this I wrote to you in all the earnestness of apprehensive friendship.

Hamilton's comment that "the Stocks are all too high" was repeated in New York, and the Secretary found it necessary to defend himself to Senator Rufus King.

Rufus King, by C. W. Peale

[Philadelphia, August 17, 1791]

I observe what you say respecting the quotation of my opinion. I was not unaware of the delicacy of giving any & was sufficiently reserved 'till I perceived the extreme to which Bank Script and with it other stock was tending. But when I saw this I thought it adviseable to speak out, for a bubble connected with my operations is of all the enemies I have to fear, in my judgment, the most formidable—and not only not to promote, but as far as depends on me, to counteract delusions, appears to me to be the only secure foundation on which to stand. I thought it therefore expedient to risk something in contributing to dissolve the charm.

The "charm" of Hamilton's affair with Maria Reynolds was also dissolving in late August. This relationship cannot be described as any classic tale of romantic love. A restless married man had taken advantage of his wife's absence to have an extramarital fling. By the time he wrote this letter to Elizabeth, Alexander Hamilton had begun to regret his venture in adultery.

[Philadelphia, August 21, 1791]

You said that you would not stay longer at Albany than twenty days which would bring it to the first of September. How delighted shall I be to receive you again to my bosom & to embrace with you my precious children. And yet much as I long for this happy moment, my extreme anxiety for the restoration of your health will reconcile me to your staying longer where you are upon condition that you really receive benefit from it, and that your own mind is at ease. But I do not believe that I shall permit you to be so long absent from me another time.

By the first week of September, some of the complications in Hamilton's public and private life had begun to disappear. The New

York market had recovered, and Hamilton had persuaded Maria Reynolds to return to her husband. Elizabeth Hamilton was on her way to Philadelphia, and Hamilton sent this apologetic note when he realized he could not meet her in New Jersey.

A view of the Palisades along the Hudson—a prospect enjoyed by Elizabeth Hamilton en route south.

[Philadelphia, September 4, 1791]
I hoped with the strongest assurance to have met you at Eliz Town; but this change of weather has brought upon me an attack of the complaint in my kindneys, to which you know I have been sometimes subject in the fall. So that I could not with safety commit myself to so rude a vehicle as the stage for so long a journey....

But dont alarm yourself nor hurry so as to injure either yourself or the children. I am not *ill* though I might make myself so by the jolting of the carriage were I to undertake the journey. I am indeed better than I was, this Evening, and if I can get a proper machine I shall make use of a warm bath to which I am advised and from which I am persuaded I shall receive benefit.

A month later, Hamilton received word from William Short that American credit in Europe seemed shaky. Having dealt with a troubled stock market and a demanding mistress, Hamilton showed little alarm in writing to the Government's bankers in Amsterdam.

Treasury Department October 3d. 1791.
I have learnt with some surprise, through Mr. Short, that the price of the effects of the United States had undergone a sudden depression in the market of Amsterdam.

This is so different from the tenor of the hopes I had built upon those expressed by you, and so contrary to all the calculations I can form on the *natural course* of the thing, that I cannot but be curious for a particular develloppment of its cause.

It will therefore be satisfactory to me to receive from you, as early as may be, a full explanation of the circumstances which shall appear to you to have occasioned so unexpected a turn of the thing.

Logo of the National Gazette

A s the day approached when he would submit the last of his famous reports to Congress, Hamilton seemed as confident as ever. "Republican" criticism of his programs did not appear serious, and although Philip Freneau's *National Gazette* began publication in Philadelphia in October, its contents seemed harmless enough. There was, however, one sign that Hamilton's "arrangements" for American finances were not progressing as he had wished. Without his knowledge, the directors of the new Bank of the United States had voted to establish branches in the major commercial cities. Nevertheless, after learning of the development, Hamilton wrote reassuringly to William Seton of the Bank of New York.

A letter from Hamilton to William Seton of the Bank of New York

[Philadelphia] November 25. 1791

Strange as it may appear to you, it is not more strange than true, that the whole affair of branches was *begun*, *continued* and *ended*; not only without my participation but *against my judgment*. When I say against my judgment, you will not understand that my opinion was given and overruled, for I never was consulted, but that the steps taken were contrary to my private opinion of the course which ought to have been pursued.

I am sensible of the inconveniences to be apprehended and I regret them; but I do not know that it will be in my power to avert them.

Ultimately it will be incumbent upon me to place the public funds in the keeping of the branch; but *it may be depended upon* that I shall *precipitate nothing*, but shall so conduct the transfer as not to embarrass or distress your institution.

In retrospect, the incident did not appear particularly significant. Meanwhile, Hamilton does not seem to have doubted that his *Report on Manufactures* would be as successful as his earlier recommendations to Congress had been. The report, which is now recognized as one of the most imaginative and innovative aspects of his Treasury program, demonstrates that Hamilton saw his proposals as much more than a means of preserving America's credit or of furnishing badly needed capital in the young nation. Important as these goals were, they were but part of a larger program, under which Hamilton dreamed of giving the American people, through careful government planning, an opportunity to take advantage of all the nation's resources. His report showed flexibility, foresight, and common sense in outlining the methods that could be used to develop a strong, balanced economy that would make the United States as independent of European trade policies as it was now free of foreign rule.

In presenting his report to the House, the Secretary did not ignore the fact that many members felt that it was unwise to encourage manufactures at the expense of agriculture; but he opened his proposals with the assumption that this idea had been "pretty generally" discarded.

[Philadelphia, December 5, 1791]

The embarrassments, which have obstructed the progress

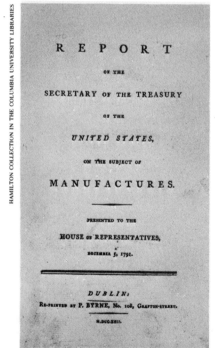

Title pages from Hamilton's draft (top) and from a published edition of his Report on Manufactures

of our external trade, have led to serious reflections on the necessity of enlarging the sphere of our domestic commerce: the restrictive regulations, which in foreign markets abrige the vent of the increasing surplus of our Agricultural produce, serve to beget an earnest desire, that a more extensive demand for that surplus may be created at home: And the complete success, which has rewarded manufacturing enterprise, in some valuable branches, conspiring with the promising symptoms, which attend some less mature essays, in others, justify a hope, that the obstacles to the growth of this species of industry are less formidable than they were apprehended to be....

[Using the arguments employed in the prospectus for the Society for Establishing Useful Manufactures, Hamilton said both land and factories could be productive. Further, he pointed out that America put herself at the mercy of "foreign demand" by concentrating on agriculture.]

The consequence of it is, that the United States are to a certain extent in the situation of a country precluded from foreign Commerce. They can indeed, without difficulty obtain from abroad the manufactured supplies, of which they are in want; but they experience numerous and very injurious impediments to the emission and vent of their own commodities....

In such a position of things, the United States cannot exchange with Europe on equal terms; and the want of reciprocity would render them the victim of a system, which should induce them to confine their views to Agriculture and refrain from Manufactures. A constant and encreasing necessity, on their part, for the commodities of Europe, and only a partial and occasional demand for their own, in return, could not but expose them to a state of impoverishment, compared with the opulence to which their political and natural advantages authorise them to aspire....

[At this time, American factories had a great disadvantage in competing with foreign goods, since European governments subsidized their native industries. America, too, could aid her manufacturers, and the new financial system would end the scarcity of capital for investment.]

In order to a better judgment of the Means proper to be resorted to by the United States, it will be of use to Advert to those which have been employed with success in other Countries. The principal of these are.

I Protecting duties—or duties on those foreign articles which are the rivals of the domestic ones, intended to be encouraged . . .

II. Prohibitions of rival articles or duties equivalent to prohibitions . . .

III Prohibitions of the exportation of the materials of manufactures . . .

IV Pecuniary bounties . . .

V. Premiums . . .

VI The Exemption of the Materials of manufactures from duty . . .

VII Drawbacks of the duties which are imposed on the Materials of Manufactures . . .

VIII The encouragement of new inventions and discoveries, at home, and of the introduction into the United States of such as may have been made in other countries; particularly those, which relate to machinery . . .

IX Judicious regulations for the inspection of manufactured commodities . . .

X The facilitating of pecuniary remittances from place to place is a point of considerable moment to trade in general, and to manufactures in particular. . . . A general circulation of Bank paper . . . will be a most valuable mean to this end. . . .

XI The facilitating of the transportation of commodities.

. . . There is perhaps scarcely any thing, which has been better calculated to assist the manufactures of Great Britain, than the ameliorations of the public roads of that Kingdom, and the great progress which has been of late made in opening canals. Of the former, the United States stand much in need; and for the latter they present uncommon facilities.

Shares of stock in the Society for Establishing Useful Manufactures, signed by William Duer

His official duty done, Hamilton found time for more personal business, such as writing to his eldest son, Philip, who had been sent to a boarding school in Trenton, New Jersey.

Philadelphia December 5 1791

Your Mama and myself were very happy to learn that you are pleased with your situation and content to stay as long as shall be thought for your good. . . .

Your Master also informs me that you recited a lesson the first day you began, very much to his satisfaction. I expect every letter from him will give me a fresh proof of your progress. For I know that you can do a great deal, if you please, and I am sure you have too much spirit not to exert yourself, that you may make us every day more and more proud of you. . . .

You remember that I engaged to send for you next Saturday and I will do it, unless you request me to put it off. For a promise must never be broken; and I never will make you one, which I will not fulfil as far as I am able. But it has occurred to me that the Christmas holidays are near at hand, and I suppose your school will then break up for some days and give you an opportunity of coming to stay with us for a longer time than if you should come on Saturday. Will it not be best for you, therefore, to put off your journey till the holidays? But determine as you like best and let me know what will be most pleasing to you.

A good night to my darling son. Adieu

A HAMILTON

As he looked forward to the Christmas holidays in December, 1791, Hamilton must have congratulated himself on having made several narrow escapes in that year. Gouverneur Morris's mission in London had failed, but Britain's new minister to the United States might have better luck in improving Anglo-American ties. He had betrayed his wife with Maria Reynolds, but his mistress had returned to her husband and seemed to be losing interest in her former lover. The New York stock market had shaken public confidence in the "funds," but no disastrous "bubble" had burst over the head of the Secretary of the Treasury.

With the *Report on Manufactures* in the hands of Congress, the last of the major pieces in the Hamiltonian system had been submitted. Its implementation, he hoped, would crown the success of his plan for America's economic development and permit Hamilton to retire. His successes in 1790 and 1791 had required hard work, skill, and foresight. Difficult as his tasks had been, he could consider himself a fortunate and contented man. Before the end of winter, however, Hamilton would meet a series of misfortunes that threatened to offset his earlier triumphs.

Chapter **10**

Crisis in the Cabinet

The fate of his *Report on Manufactures* may have warned Hamilton that his policies would no longer win support so easily. Its recommendations were simply ignored by Congress. There were new issues and new divisions in the House in 1791–92 that left little time to consider subsidies for American industry or protective tariff policies. In that session, the "factions" that were supposed to have been banished under constitutional government reappeared. In the *Federalist* essays, James Madison had argued eloquently against the potential dangers of these divisive political groups. With ratification, so the theory went, Antifederalists would disappear and all Americans would unite in support of the new Administration. But new controversies, centering on the Department of the Treasury, created new factions, although Jefferson and Madison would have denied that they had inaugurated a party system. When they began to speak and write of a "republican interest" or "republican party," they saw themselves as defenders of American liberties who had to mount a counterattack against an alleged "monarchical party." There is no evidence that such a party ever existed, but fear of this shadowy force was a powerful motive for Republicans.

In some ways Hamilton's attitude toward this new faction was as unfair and unrealistic as the Republican fear of monarchy. To him it was not a political movement by men who honestly disagreed with his policies, but a plot to destroy "good government." When American Democratic-Republicans allied themselves with the cause of the new French Republic in early 1793, the "plot" seemed all the more threatening. The French Revolution had progressed through a period of constitutional monarchy to a republican regime that guillotined the former monarch and quarreled with all of Europe. Hamilton could not imagine that any man with a due regard for "proper" or "respectable" government could support such a nation.

The joint threat of French and American republicanism developed swiftly in 1792 and early 1793. The eighteen months after the completion of his *Report on Manufactures* must have seemed among the most discouraging in Hamilton's life. Everything that could have gone amiss with his "system" had occurred. Had he been a superstitious man, Hamilton might have taken a warning from the events of December 15, 1791. He later remembered how the day had begun with a note from Maria Reynolds.

[August, 1798]

One day, I received a letter from her...intimating a discovery by her husband. It was matter of doubt with me whether there had been really a discovery by accident, or whether the time for the catastrophe of the plot was arrived.

The same day, being the 15th of December 1791, I received from Mr. Reynolds the letter...by which he informs me of the detection of his wife in the act of writing a letter to me, and that he had obtained from her a discovery of her connection with me, suggesting that it was the consequence of an undue advantage taken of her distress....

[Then, as Hamilton recalled, he sent Reynolds a note asking him to call at the Treasury office. Reynolds complied immediately.]

He in substance repeated the topics contained in his letter, and concluded as he had done there, that he was resolved to have satisfaction.

I replied that he knew best what evidence he had of the alleged connection between me and his wife, that I neither admitted nor denied it—that if he knew of any injury I had done him, intitling him to satisfaction, it lay with him to name it.

He travelled over the same ground as before, and again concluded with the same vague claim of satisfaction, but without specifying the kind, which would content him. It was easy to understand that he wanted money, and to prevent an explosion, I resolved to gratify him. But willing to manage his delicacy, if he had any, I reminded him that I had at our first interview made him a promise of service, that I was disposed to do it as far as might be proper, and in my power, and requested him to consider in what manner I could do it, and to write to me. He withdrew with a promise of compliance.

Two days after, the 17th of December, he wrote me.

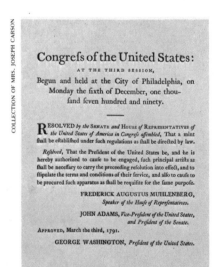

Congrefs of the United States:

AT THE THIRD SESSION,

Begun and held at the City of Philadelphia, on Monday the fixth of December, one thoufand feven hundred and ninety.

RESOLVED *by the* SENATE *and* HOUSE *of* REPRESENTATIVES *of the United States of America in Congrefs affembled,* That a mint fhall be eftablifhed under fuch regulations as fhall be directed by law.

Refolved, That the Prefident of the United States be, and he is hereby authorized to caufe to be engaged, fuch principal artifts as fhall be neceffary to carry the preceeding refolution into effect, and to ftipulate the terms and conditions of their fervice, and alfo to caufe to be procured fuch apparatus as fhall be requifite for the fame purpofe.

FREDERICK AUGUSTUS MUHLENBERG,
Speaker of the Houfe of Reprefentatives.

JOHN ADAMS, *Vice-Prefident of the United States, and Prefident of the Senate.*

APPROVED, March the third, 1791.

GEORGE WASHINGTON, *Prefident of the United States.*

Above, the act of Congress that established the United States Mint; below, the first Mint building

Suspecting a plot against himself, Hamilton alerted a friend to the impending danger prior to his "rendezvous" with James Reynolds.

... The evident drift of this letter is to exaggerate the injury done by me, to make a display of sensibility and to magnify the atonement, which was to be required. It however comes to no conclusion, but proposes a meeting at the *George Tavern,* or at some other place more agreeable to me, which I should name....

I called upon Reynolds, and assuming a decisive tone, told him, that I was tired of his indecision, and insisted upon his declaring to me explicitly what it was he aimed at—He again promised to explain by letter.

On the 19th, I received the promised letter ["Sir I have Considered on the matter Serously. I have This preposial to make to you. give me the Sum Of thousand dollars and I will leve the town and take my daughter with me and go where my Friends Shant here from me and leve her to Yourself to do for as you [think] proper."] the essence of which is that he was willing to take a thousand dollars as the plaister of his wounded honor.

I determined to give it to him, and did so in two payments ... dated the 22d of December and 3d of January.

Assured that Reynolds's injured feelings could be "plaistered" with cash, Hamilton returned to work. Britain's new minister, young George Hammond, had come to Philadelphia to conduct formal negotiations with Thomas Jefferson. In private, Hammond found Hamilton as "candid" as had George Beckwith. Reporting to his superiors in London in the first week of 1792, Hammond recorded the Secretary's comments on a list, prepared by Jefferson, of British infractions of the peace treaty of 1783.

[Philadelphia, January 1–8, 1792]

Mr. Hamilton expressed his conviction that the surrender of the posts was the only one which could produce any lengthy or difficult investigation. Upon this head he intimated that although he did not imagine this country could be easily induced to consent to a dereliction of any part of its territory acquired by the Treaty, it might perhaps still be possible to grant to his Majesty's subjects such privileges and immunities in the respective posts as would protect and secure them in the undisturbed prosecution of the Fur Trade....

... Upon the subject of the British Creditors, which he considered as the chief ground of complaint on the part of Great Britain, he assured me that in all cases of this kind, which had been brought before the federal Courts,

Patterns for the first U.S. half dollar; the House found the image of Washington too "monarchical" and substituted the figure "Liberty."

their determinations had been uniformly founded upon the treaty of peace, and had been consequently favorable to the British Creditors....

In treating of the commercial arrangements between the two countries, Mr Hamilton readily admitted the importance of the British Commerce to the United States, and expressed his sanguine hopes that some system might be established mutually satisfactory to both countries. He did not fail to urge with much force and emphasis the anxiety of this country to obtain a small participation in the carrying trade with the West Indies, and the expediency of granting it.

A few days later, Hamilton received the flattering news that a group of New York merchants had commissioned John Trumbull to execute his portrait. The merchants suggested that a part of his "Political Life" would be an appropriate setting for the picture, but Hamilton demurred.

Philadelphia January 15 1792

The mark of esteem on the part of fellow Citizens, to whom I am attached by so many ties, which is announced in your letter...is intitled to my affectionate acknowlegements.

I shall chearfully obey their wish as far as respects the taking of my Portrait; but I ask that they will permit it to appear unconnected with any incident of my political life. The simple representation of their fellow Citizen and friend will best accord with my feelings.

Although pleased with the compliment from his friends in the business community, Hamilton well knew that they could damage the Treasury's programs if left to their own devices. Memories of the speculative fever of August, 1791, were still fresh at the end of February, 1792, when the "superstructure of Credit" collapsed completely. Worst of all, from Hamilton's point of view, the crash was triggered by the failure of his friend and former aide, William Duer. Prices of government securities fell sharply, and Hamilton did his best to save the market with purchases for the Sinking Fund. Too impatient to wait for the commissioners of the fund to argue legal technicalities before giving him formal authorization to act, he wrote to William Seton at the end of March asking him to buy securities in the New York stock market—with the following proviso.

Phila. 25th March 1792

You will not however declare on whose account you act,

John Trumbull, by S. L. Waldo

because tho there is, as to a purchase on that principle, no difference of opinion among the Trustees, the thing is not formally aranged and this is Sunday.

It will be very probably conjectured that you appear for the Public; and the conjecture may be left to have its course but without confession. The purchase ought in the present state of things to be at Auction and not till tomorrow evening. But if the purchase at Auction will not tend as well to the purpose of relief as a different mode — it may be departed from. . . . I have just received a Letter from Mr. Short . . . by which he informs me that he has effected a loan for Three Millions of Florins at 4 [Per] Cent Interest on account of the United States. This may be announced; and as in the present moment of suspicion some minds may be disposed to consider the thing as a mere expedient to support the Stocks, I pledge my honor for its exact truth.

The commissioners of the Sinking Fund met the next day and gave Hamilton the powers to make these purchases. But the Secretary now faced new problems. Philip Freneau's *National Gazette* had declared war on the Treasury. Attacks on Hamilton began in mid-March, and on April 2, the paper carried an essay by "Brutus" (James Madison) assailing those who "pampered the spirit of speculation." The next day, at a meeting of the commissioners, Thomas Jefferson objected that the prices being offered for purchases were unrealistically high and would favor the hated speculators. Such criticisms may have prompted Hamilton to make these comments in the instructions he sent to William Seton.

Philadelphia April 4th 1792

I am pained, beyond expression, at the picture you and others give me of the situation of my fellow Citizens — especially as an ignorance of the extent of the disorder renders it impossible to judge whether any adequate remedy can be applied.

You may apply another 50 000 Dollars to purchases at such time as you judge it can be rendered most useful. . . .

I have doubt however whether it will be best to apply this immediately or wait the happening of the crisis which I fear is inevitable. If as is represented a pretty extensive explosion is to take place — the depression of the funds at such a moment will be in the extreme and then it may be more important than now to enter the market in force. I can in such case without difficulty add

William Seton

a hundred thousand Dollars probably a larger Sum....

How vexatious that imprudent speculations of Individuals should lead to an alienation of the National property at such under rates as are now given!

Still another of Hamilton's projects suffered as a result of the market crisis. He had envisioned government securities as a means of furnishing capital for investment at home. The failure of William Duer and other leaders in the Society for Useful Manufactures brought the society's operations to a halt. Hamilton gave the directors firm, sensible advice on salvaging what they could from the situation.

Philadelphia April 14. 1792

The following appears to me to be the course proper to be pursued.

1 To appoint the principal Officers of the Institution and regulate their duties. I mean a Superintendant, an Accountant, and a Cashier, especially the first. Tis impossible that any thing can proceed with vigour or efficiency till this is done....

The Cashier ought...to be of a character and *in a situation* to inspire the most thorough confidence.

No time ought to be lost in determining upon the place and contracting for the land and commencing the buildings. Under present circumstances I would advise that the latter be begun upon a moderate scale yet so as to be capable of extension.

I would also advise that the Society confine themselves at first to the cotton branch.... A complication of objects will tend to weaken still further a confidence already too much impaired.

If a loan should be wanted I would if requisite cooperate to endeavour to procure one on favourable terms.

Means should be taken to procure from Europe a *few essential* workmen; but in this too there ought to be *measure* and circumspection. Nothing should be put in jeopardy....

...I will only add this general observation that nothing scarcely can be so injurious to the affairs of the Society as a much longer suspension of operation.

William Duer published this notice to his creditors the day after being imprisoned for his debts.

The validity of Hamilton's views on promoting industry in America would have to be proved by the success of such private undertakings as the Society for Useful Manufactures, since Congress had shown less interest in adopting the *Report on Manufactures* than in harassing its author. Nor did Hamilton's trials end when Congress adjourned. His plans for reconciliation with Britain continued to be thwarted by Jefferson, who insisted on giving George Hammond a strongly worded statement of American grievances—despite Hamilton's pleas that he modify his tone. Hammond, after a meeting with Hamilton at the end of May, described the Secretary's attempts to minimize the importance of Jefferson's letter.

[Philadelphia, May 29–June 2, 1792]

The conflict between Federalists and Republicans erupted in a brawl on the floor of the House in 1798.

This Gentlemen treated me (as he has done upon every occasion) with the strictest confidence and candour. After lamenting the intemperate violence of his colleague Mr Hamilton assured me that this letter was very far from meeting his approbation, or from containing a faithful exposition of the sentiments of this government. He added that at the time of our conversation the President had not had an opportunity of perusing this representation: For having returned from Virginia in the morning only on which it had been delivered to me, he had relied upon Mr Jefferson's assurance, that it was conformable to the opinions of the other members of the executive government.

The outraged Hamilton lashed out at his enemies in a letter to his old friend Edward Carrington of Virginia. He concluded with a lengthy indictment of Madison and Jefferson.

Philadelphia May 26th, 1792

It was not 'till the last session that I became unequivocally convinced of the following truth—*"That Mr. Madison cooperating with Mr. Jefferson is at the head of a faction decidedly hostile to me and my administration, and actuated by views in my judgment subversive of the principles of good government and dangerous to the union, peace and happiness of the Country."* . . .

This conviction in my mind is the result of a long train of circumstances; many of them minute. To attempt to detail them all would fill a volume. I shall therefore confine myself to the mention of a few.

First—As to the point of opposition to me and my administration.

Mr. Jefferson with very little reserve manifests his dislike of the funding system generally; calling in question the expediency of funding a debt at all. Some expressions which he has dropped in my own presence...will not permit me to doubt on this point, representations, which I have had from various respectable quarters....

In various conversations with *foreigners* as well as citizens, he has thrown censure on my *principles* of government and on my measures of administration. He has predicted that the people would not long tolerate my proceedings & that I should not long maintain my ground. Some of those, whom he *immediately* and *notoriously* moves, have *even* whispered suspicions of the rectitude of my motives and conduct. In the question concerning the Bank he not only delivered an opinion in writing against its constitutionality & expediency; but he did it *in a stile and manner* which I felt as partaking of asperity and ill humour towards me. As one of the trustees of the sinking fund, I have experienced in almost every leading question opposition from him. When any turn of things in the community has threatened either odium or embarrassment to me, he has not been able to suppress the satisfaction which it gave him....

With regard to Mr. Madison—the matter stands thus. I have not heard, but in...one instance...of his having held language unfriendly to me in private conversation. But in his public conduct there has been a more uniform & persevering opposition than I have been able to resolve into a sincere difference of opinion. I cannot persuade myself that Mr. Madison and I, whose politics had formerly so much the *same point of departure,* should now diverge so widely in our opinions of the measures which are proper to be pursued. The opinion I once entertained of the candour and simplicity and fairness of Mr. Madisons character has, I acknowledge, given way to a decided opinion that *it is one of a peculiarly artificial and complicated kind....*

In respect to our foreign politics the views of these Gentlemen are in my judgment equally unsound & dangerous. *They have a womanish attachment to France and a womanish resentment against Great Britain.* They would draw us into the closest embrace of the former & involve us in all the consequences of her politics, & they would risk the peace of the country in their endeavours to keep us at the greatest possible distance from the latter. This disposition goes to a length particularly in

A share of stock and a certificate of ownership issued by the U.S. Loan Office and signed by Hamilton

In a Federalist cartoon of 1790, Washington leads troops against French "cannibals," while Gallatin, Genêt, and Jefferson (right) try to hold back the Federal chariot.

Hamilton's promise to contribute money for a "water engine" to keep down the dust on Walnut Street

Mr. Jefferson of which, till lately, I had no adequate Idea. Various circumstances prove to me that if these Gentlemen were left to pursue their own course there would be in less than six months *an open War between the U States & Great Britain....*

Mr. Jefferson, it is known, did not in the first instance cordially acquiesce in the new constitution for the U States; he had many doubts & reserves. He left this Country before we had experienced the imbicillities of the former....

Mr. Madison had always entertained an exalted opinion of the talents, knowledge and virtues of Mr. Jefferson. The sentiment was probably reciprocal. A close correspondence subsisted between them during the time of Mr. Jefferson's absence from this country. A close intimacy arose upon his return.

Whether any peculiar opinions of Mr. Jefferson concerning the public debt wrought a change in the sentiments of Mr. Madison (for it is certain that the former is more radically wrong than the latter) or whether Mr. Madison seduced by the expectation of popularity and possibly by the calculation of advantage to the state of Virginia was led to change his own opinion—certain it is, that a very material *change* took place, & that the two Gentlemen were united in the new ideas. Mr. Jefferson was indiscreetly open in his approbation of Mr. Madison's principles, upon his first coming to the seat of Government. I say indiscreetly, because a Gentleman in the administration in one department ought not to have taken sides against another, in another department....

Another circumstance has contributed to widening the breach. 'Tis evident beyond a question, from every movement, that Mr Jefferson aims with ardent desire at the Presidential Chair. This too is an important object of the party-politics. It is supposed, from the nature of my former personal & political connexions, that I may favour some other candidate more than Mr. Jefferson when the Question shall occur by the retreat of the present Gentleman. My influence therefore with the Community becomes a thing, on ambitious & personal grounds, to be resisted & destroyed...

In such a state of mind, both these Gentlemen are prepared to hazard a great deal to effect a change. Most of the important measures of every Government

269

A broadside reporting on the hurricane that struck Philadelphia and New York on July 1, 1792

are connected with the Treasury. To subvert the present head of it they deem it expedient to risk rendering the Government itself odious; perhaps foolishly thinking that they can easily recover the lost affections & confidence of the people. . . .

[To this end, rumors had been spread in Virginia that Hamilton headed a "Monarchical party meditating the destruction of State & Republican Government." Denying the existence of such a party, Hamilton ended his letter to Carrington with this observation.]

If I were disposed to promote Monarchy & overthrow State Governments, I would mount the hobby horse of popularity—I would cry out usurpation—danger to liberty &c. &c—I would endeavour to prostrate the National Government—raise a ferment—and then "ride in the Whirlwind and direct the Storm." That there are men acting with Jefferson & Madison who have this in view I verily believe. I could lay my finger on some of them. That Madison does *not* mean it I also verily believe, and I rather believe the same of Jefferson; but I read him upon the whole thus—"A man of profound ambition & violent passions."

Hamilton's battle with his enemies paralleled his campaign to persuade the most important agent of "proper" government to remain in office. George Washington dreaded the prospect of another four years as President. Hamilton, Jefferson, and Madison had all urged him to accept a second term, but retirement was tempting to the sixty-year-old soldier, plagued with bad health and failing hearing. When the President left Philadelphia for Mount Vernon in mid-July, 1792, he was still undecided, and Hamilton pleaded with him in this letter.

Philadelphia July 30th [–August 3] 1792
I received the most sincere pleasure at finding in our last conversation, that there was some relaxation in the disposition you had before discovered to decline a reelection. Since your departure, I have lost no opportunity of sounding the opinions of persons, whose opinions were worth knowing, on these two points—1st the effect of your declining upon the public affairs, and upon your own reputation—2dly. the effect of your continuing, in reference to the declarations you have made of your

disinclination to public life—And I can truly say, that I have not found the least difference of sentiment, on either point. The impression is uniform—that your declining would be to be deplored as the greatest evil, that could befall the country at the present juncture, and as critically hazardous to your own reputation—that your continuance will be justified in the mind of every friend to his country by the evident necessity for it. Tis clear, says every one, with whom I have conversed, that the affairs of the national government are not yet firmly established—that its enemies, generally speaking, are as inveterate as ever—...that if you continue in office nothing materially mischievous is to be apprehended—if you quit much is to be dreaded—...and, in fine, that on public and personal accounts, on patriotic and prudential considerations, the clear path to be pursued by you will be again to obey the voice of your country; which it is not doubted will be as earnest and as unanimous as ever.

Much of Washington's distaste for office stemmed from the growing spirit of "party" opposition, for Hamilton was now doing his best to counter Republican criticism. The day after he wrote to the President, the *Gazette of the United States* carried the first of Hamilton's letters as "An American" exposing the history of Philip Freneau's appearance in Philadelphia.

[Philadelphia, August 4, 1792]

Mr. Freneau before he came to this City to conduct the National Gazette was employed by Childs & Swaine Printers of the Dayly Advertiser in the City of New York in capacity of editor or superintendant. A paper more devoted to the views of a certain party of which Mr. Jefferson is the head than any to be found in this City was wanted. Mr. Freneau was thought a fit instrument. ...A negotiation was opened with him, which ended in the establishment of the National Gazette under his direction. There is good ground to believe that Mr. Madison while in New York...was the medium of that Negotiation.

Mr. Freneau came here at once Editor of the National Gazette and Clerk for foreign languages in the department of Mr. Jefferson....

Mr. Freneau is not then, as he would have supposed,

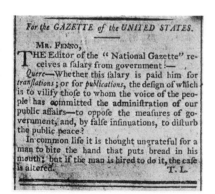

One of Hamilton's letters attacking Philip Freneau, the Antifederalist editor of the National Gazette

the Independent Editor of a News Paper, who, though receiving a salary from Government has firmness enough to expose its maladministration. He is the faithful and devoted servant of the head of a party, from whose hand he receives the boon. The whole complexion of his paper is an exact copy of the politics of his employer foreign and domestic, and exhibits a decisive internal evidence of the influence of that patronage under which he acts.

The need to defend the principles of constitutional government must have seemed even more pressing to Hamilton when he received a letter from Washington concerning public criticism of the Administration. The President sent Hamilton a list of "a variety of matters" for which the Government had been attacked and asked for his "ideas upon the discontents." Many of the "objections" were old arguments against a national bank, funding, and the Federal assumption of state debts. But Hamilton's opponents now claimed that these programs were part of a scheme in which "barren & useless speculation" was being used to corrupt Congress and nourish "vice & Idleness" in the people. Hamilton defended himself in a letter to Washington.

Philadelphia Aug 18. 1792

To uphold public credit and to be friendly to the Bank must be presupposed to be *corrupt things* before the being a proprietor in the funds or of bank Stock can be supposed to have a *corrupting influence*. The being a proprietor in either case is a very different thing from being ... a Stock jobber. On this point of the corruption of the Legislature one more observation of great weight remains. Those who oppose a *funded* debt and mean any provision for it contemplate an *annual* one. Now, it is impossible to conceive a more fruitful source of legislative corruption than this. All the members of it who should incline to speculate would have an annual opportunity of speculating upon their influence in the legislature to promote or retard or put off a provision. Every session the question whether the annual provision should be continued would be an occasion of pernicious caballing and corrupt bargaining. In this very view when the subject was in deliberation, it was impossible not to wish it declared upon once for all & out of the way....

[The intent of the speculators and "corrupt" legislators, so the whispering campaign went, was to overthrow the

Portrait of Alexander Hamilton by John Trumbull painted in 1792

Republic and to establish a monarchy. Hamilton knew that some of his own "theoretical" remarks had been responsible for this charge.]

A letter from the president of Harvard informing Hamilton that he had been awarded an honorary Doctor of Laws degree

This is a palpable misrepresentation. No man, that I know of, contemplated the introducing into this country of a monarchy. A very small number (not more than three or four) manifested theoretical opinions favourable in the abstract to a constitution like that of Great Britain, but every one agreed that such a constitution except as to the general distribution of departments and powers was out of the Question in reference to this Country. The Member [of the Philadelphia Convention] who was most explicit on this point (a Member from New York) declared in strong terms that the republican theory ought to be adhered to in this Country as long as there was any chance of its success—that the idea of a perfect equality of political rights among the citizens, exclusive of all permanent or hereditary distinctions, was of a nature to engage the good wishes of every good man, whatever might be his theoretic doubts—that it merited his best efforts to give success to it in practice—that hitherto from an incompetent structure of the Government it had not had a fair trial, and that the endeavour ought then to be to secure to it a better chance of success by a government more capable of energy and order.

There is not a man at present in either branch of the Legislature who, that I recollect, had held language in the Convention favourable to Monarchy.

The wide range of "discontents" that Washington had pointed out may have caused Hamilton to suspend temporarily his newspaper campaign against the Republicans. For the rest of August, local papers carried no articles that can definitely be attributed to him. By the end of the month, the Treasury had more than enough business to occupy the Secretary. The distillers and farmers of western Pennsylvania were obstructing the excise law more vigorously than ever. Congress had revised the tax in May, 1792, but opposition continued. Two years later, when the crisis came to a head, Hamilton gave the President a history of the affair.

[Philadelphia, August 5, 1794]

The first Law had left the number and positions of the Offices of Inspection, which were to be established in each District . . . to the discretion of the Supervisor. The

273

second [of May, 1792], to secure a due accommodation to Distillers, provides peremptorily that there shall be one in each County.

The idea was immediately embraced, that it was a very important point in the scheme of opposition to the law to prevent the establishment of Offices in the respective Counties. For this purpose, the intimidation of well disposed inhabitants was added to the plan of molesting and obstructing the Officers by force or otherwise, as might be necessary. So effectually was the first point carried, (the certain destruction of property and the peril of life being involved) that it became almost impracticable to obtain suitable places for Offices in some of the Counties—and when obtained, it was found a matter of necessity in almost every instance to abandon them.

After much effort The Inspector of the Revenue succeeded in procuring the house of William Faulkner a captain in the army for an Office of Inspection in the County of Washington. This took place in August 1792. The office was attended by the Inspector of the Revenue in person, till prevented by the following incidents.

Capt Faukner, being in pursuit of some Deserters from the troops, was encountered by a number of people ...who reproached him with letting his house for an Office of Inspection—drew a knife upon him, threatened to scalp him, tar and feather him, and reduce his house and property to Ashes, if he did not solemnly promise to prevent the further use of his House for an Office.

A copy of the controversial act of 1792 imposing duties on spirits distilled within the United States

Captain Faulkner made the promise demanded of him. Hamilton, who sent a revenue officer to investigate the situation, at first advised the President to use any means necessary to suppress "the spirit of disobedience." But conferences with the Secretary of War and the Attorney General persuaded him that the Government could afford to show moderation. Meanwhile, Washington had learned of the newspaper war in Philadelphia and had written to Hamilton, Jefferson, and Randolph on the painful subject of dissension in the Cabinet. To his Secretary of the Treasury, the President suggested that the "irritating charges" in "some of our Gazettes" might "tare the Machine asunder" and must give way to "mutual forebearances and temporising yieldings *on all* sides." Hamilton promptly replied.

Philadelphia September 9 1792

The feelings and views which are manifested in that

letter are such as I expected would exist. And I most sincerely regret the causes of the uneasy sensations you experience. It is my most anxious wish, as far as may depend upon me, to smooth the path of your administration, and to render it prosperous and happy. And if any prospect shall open of healing or terminating the differences which exist, I shall most chearfully embrace it; though I consider myself as the deeply injured party. The recommendation of such a spirit is worthy of the moderation and wisdom which dictated it; and if your endeavours should prove unsuccessful, I do not hesitate to say that in my opinion the period is not remote when the public good will require *substitutes* for the *differing members* of your administration. The continuance of a division there must destroy the energy of Government, which will be little enough with the strictest Union. On my part there will be a most chearful acquiescence in such a result.

...I cannot conceal from you that I have had some instrumentality of late in the retaliations which have fallen upon certain public characters and that I find myself placed in a situation not to be able to recede *for the present.*

I considered myself as compelled to this conduct by reasons public as well as personal of the most cogent nature. I *know* that I have been an object of uniform opposition from Mr. Jefferson, from the first moment of his coming to the City of New York to enter upon his present office. I *know,* from the most authentic sources, that I have been the frequent subject of the most unkind whispers and insinuating from the same quarter. I have long seen a formed party in the Legislature, under his auspices, bent upon my subversion. I cannot doubt... that the National Gazette was instituted by him for political purposes and that one leading object of it has been to render me and all the measures connected with my department as odious as possible....

As long as I saw no danger to the Government, from the machinations which were going on, I resolved to be a silent sufferer of the injuries which were done me....

But when I no longer doubted, that there was a formed party deliberately bent upon the subversion of measures, which in its consequences would subvert the Government ...I considered it as a duty, to endeavour to resist the

A page from Washington's letter to Hamilton admonishing against the dissension he found in the Cabinet

torrent, and as an essential mean to this end, to draw aside the veil from the principal Actors. To this strong impulse, to this decided conviction, I have yielded. And I think events will prove that I have judged rightly.

Nevertheless I pledge my honor to you Sir, that if you shall hereafter form a plan to reunite the members of your administration, upon some steady principle of cooperation, I will faithfully concur in executing it during my continuance in office. And I will not directly or indirectly say or do a thing, that shall endanger a feud.

Hamilton's promise to do nothing "that shall endanger a feud" apparently did not include retirement from the public press. Three days after he wrote to Washington, a letter from "Civis" (Hamilton's current pen name) was published in the *National Gazette* in reply to "Mercator."

[Philadelphia, September 11, 1792]

The actual benefits or actual evils of the measures connected with the Treasury Department present and future would be cheerfully submitted to the *Test* of *Experience.* Happy would it be for the country, honorable for human nature, if the experiment were permitted to be fairly made.

But the pains which are taken to misrepresent the tendency of those measures, to inflame the public mind, to disturb the operations of Government are a decided proof, that those to whom they are attributable dare not trust the appeal to such a *Test.* Convinced of this, they have combined all their forces and are making one desperate effort to gain an ascendancy, in the public councils, by means of the ensuing election, in order to precipitate the laudable work of destroying what has been done.

The importance of the "ensuing election" would not permit Hamilton to keep silent. Washington had not yet announced that he would run for reelection, and George Clinton appeared to be making progress in his campaign for John Adams's office. Aaron Burr, the junior Senator from New York, was also making a bid for the Vice Presidency, and although Hamilton at first viewed the Senator as no more than "a diversion in favour of Mr. Clinton," to be safe he began moving against Burr's candidacy. While both Burr and Clinton were Republicans in politics, to Hamilton the Governor was far preferable in his morals and ethics. Adding "Fact" to his list of pen names, Hamilton began attacking the Senator in the public press; in private, he sent letters like this one to friends unacquainted with Burr.

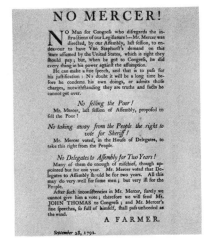

Hamilton published this broadside in 1792 to refute charges that he had engaged in financial speculation while he was Treasury Secretary.

Philadelphia September 21. 1792

Mr. Clinton's success I should think very unfortunate. I am not for trusting the Government too much in the hands of its enemies. But still Mr. C— is a man of property, and, in private life, as far as I know of probity. I fear the other Gentleman is unprincipled both as a public and private man. When the constitution was in deliberation, his conduct was equivocal; but its enemies, who I believe best understood him considered him as with them. In fact, I take it, he is for or against nothing, but as it suits his interest or ambition. He is determined, as I conceive, to make his way to be the head of the popular party and to climb... to the highest honors of the state; and as much higher as circumstances may permit. Embarrassed, as I understand, in his circumstances, with an extravagant family—bold enterprising and intriguing, I am mistaken, if it be not his object to play the game of confusion, and I feel it a religious duty to oppose his career.

It was not long before another possibility occurred to Hamilton: the Burr and Clinton candidacies might be part of a plot to elect Jefferson, as he warned Charles Cotesworth Pinckney, a leading South Carolina Federalist.

Philadelphia October 10th 1792

A particular attention to the election for the next Congress is dictated by the vigorous and general effort which is making by factious men to introduce every where and in every department persons unfriendly to the measures, if not the constitution, of the National Government.

Either Governor Clinton or Mr. Burr of New York, both decidedly of the description of persons, I have mentioned, is to be run in this quarter as Vice President in opposition to Mr. Adams.... It will be a real misfortune to the Government if either of them should prevail. Tis suspected by some that the plan is only to divide the votes of the N & Middle States to let in Mr. Jefferson by the votes of the South. I will not scruple to say to you in confidence that this also would be a serious misfortune to the Government. That Gentleman whom I once very much esteemed, but who does not permit me to retain

A broadside, found among Hamilton's papers, opposing the reelection of Congressman John Mercer, who had charged Hamilton with malfeasance that sentiment for him, is certainly a man of sublimated and paradoxical imagination—entertaining & propagating notions inconsistent with dignified and orderly Government. Mr. Adams whatever objections may be against some of his theoretic opinions is a firm honest independent politician.

Hamilton's fears of Jefferson's vice-presidential ambition proved groundless. The Secretary of State wanted nothing so much as to resign and retire to Monticello at the end of Washington's term in office. Still, even though the President had decided to serve for four more years—and was, of course, reelected—and even though John Adams also won a second term, there was not much to cheer the Secretary of the Treasury. A new revolutionary government in France had "suspended" the King, and Republicans had made gains in congressional races. Hamilton scarcely needed more troubles, but more were on the way. On the morning of December 15, 1792, exactly a year after his meeting with James Reynolds, he welcomed three visitors to the Treasury office: Frederick Muhlenberg, former Speaker of the House, Senator James Monroe, and Representative Abraham Venable of Virginia. Later, Hamilton told the story.

Hamilton's letters to congressmen Muhlenberg, Monroe, and Venable, demanding copies of all documents relating to the Reynolds affair

[August, 1798]

Mr. Muhlenberg... introduced the subject by observing to me, that they *had discovered a very improper connection* between me and a Mr. Reynolds: extremely hurt by this mode of introduction, I arrested the progress of the discourse by giving way to very strong expressions of indignation. The gentlemen explained, telling me in substance that I had misapprehended them—that they did not intend to take the fact for established—that their meaning was to apprise me that unsought by them, information had been given them of an improper pecuniary connection between Mr. Reynolds and myself; that they had thought it their duty to pursue it and had become possessed of some documents of a suspicious complexion—that they had contemplated the laying the matter before the President, but before they did this, they thought it right to apprise me of the affair and to afford an opportunity of explanation; declaring at the same time that their agency in the matter was influenced solely by a sense of public duty and by no motive of personal ill will....

I replied, that the affair was now put upon a different footing—that I always stood ready to meet fair inquiry with frank communication—that it happened, in the present instance, to be in my power by written documents to remove all doubt as to the real nature of the business, and fully to convince, that nothing of the kind imputed to me did in fact exist. The same evening at my house was...appointed for an explanation.

Some weeks before this meeting, James Reynolds and Jacob Clingman had been arrested for bribing a witness so that they could win a financial claim against the Treasury. In their desperate attempts to escape prosecution, Clingman had hinted to Muhlenberg (a former employer) that Reynolds could prove that Hamilton had advanced him money to be used for speculation. It was this tale that brought Muhlenberg and the two members of Congress to see Hamilton, but at his home that evening Hamilton told them his version of the story—an account that reflected on his private, not his public, morality.

[August, 1798]

I stated in explanation, the circumstances of my affair with Mrs. Reynolds and the consequences of it and in confirmation produced the documents....One or more of the gentlemen...was struck with so much conviction, before I had gotten through the communication that they delicately urged me to discontinue it as unnecessary. I insisted upon going through the whole and did so. The result was a full and unequivocal acknowlegement on the part of the three gentlemen of perfect satisfaction with the explanation and expressions of regret at the trouble and embarrassment which had been occasioned to me. Mr. Muhlenberg and Mr. Venable, in particular manifested a degree of sensibility on the occasion. Mr. Monroe was more cold but intirely explicit.

One of the gentlemen, I think, expressed a hope that I also was satisfied with their conduct in conducting the inquiry. I answered, that they knew I had been hurt at the opening of the affair—that this excepted, I was satisfied with their conduct and considered myself as having been treated with candor or with fairness and liberality.

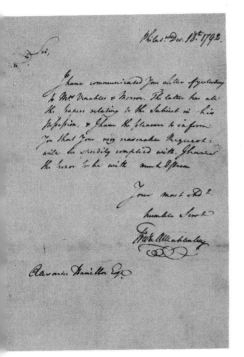

Muhlenberg's reply assuring Hamilton that his request (opposite) would be "speedily complied with"

Three days later, Hamilton belatedly replied to letters from his old friend John Jay. It was clear that his usual self-confidence had been badly shaken.

Frederick A. Muhlenberg

Philadelphia Decembr 18, 1792

Tis not the load of proper official business that alone engrosses me; though this would be enough to occupy any man. Tis not the extra attentions I am obliged to pay to the course of legislative manoevres that alone add to my burthen and perplexity. Tis the malicious intrigues to stab me in the dark, against which I am too often obliged to guard myself, that distract and harrass me to a point, which rendering my situation scarcely tolerable interferes with objects to which friendship & inclination would prompt me.

In the first months of 1793, Hamilton's enemies attacked again—not with "intrigues . . . in the dark," but with public charges to which Hamilton could respond. William Branch Giles of Virginia introduced a series of resolutions in the House calling for extensive investigation of Treasury operations. The resolutions were worded more as accusations than as requests for information, and Giles doubtless believed that Hamilton could never answer the charges before the end of the session. The challenge of hard work seemed to revive the Secretary's morale, and early in February Hamilton submitted his first reply.

William Branch Giles

Treasury Department, February 4th, 1793.

The resolutions, to which I am to answer, were not moved without a pretty copious display of the reasons, on which they were founded. These reasons are before the public through the channel of the press. They are of a nature, to excite attention, to beget alarm, to inspire doubts. Deductions of a very extraordinary complexion may, without forcing the sense, be drawn from them.

I feel it incumbent on me to meet the suggestions, which have been thrown out, with decision and explicitness. And, while I hope, I shall let fall nothing inconsistent with that cordial and unqualified respect, which I feel for the House of Representatives, while I acquiesce in the sufficiency of the motives, that induced, on their part, the giving a prompt and free course to the investigation proposed—I cannot but resolve to treat the subject, with a freedom, which is due to truth, and to the consciousness of a pure zeal for the public interest.

Soon the House was flooded with Hamilton's tables, accounts, and exhibits. There seemed no end to his reports, and one has the sense that he relished the hard work necessary to confound Giles. But during the congressional debate a new issue arose—one that would occupy more and more of Hamilton's time and energy. The Secretary was asked to justify his decision to suspend payments on the French debt in October, 1792, when he learned that Louis XVI had been deposed in favor of a new government. The fate of the French Republic soon became a focal point of party differences and helped persuade Jefferson to remain in the Cabinet. Hamilton, who had long doubted the possibility of orderly, democratic government in the Bourbon kingdom, had grown even more skeptical when the Revolution changed from a movement for a limited monarchy to one for a republic. In November, 1792, the French minister, Ternant, applied for funds to be used in the French colony of Santo Domingo. Hamilton warned Washington that it might be unwise to oblige Ternant because of the situation in France.

The rebellious mob that marched on Versailles on October 5, 1789

Treasury Department November 19th 1792

If a restoration of the King should take place, I am of opinion, that no payment which might be made in the Interval would be deemed regular or obligatory. The admission of it to our credit would consequently be considered as a matter of discretion, according to the opinion entertained of its merit and utility. A payment to the newly constituted power, as a reimbursement in course, or in any manner, which would subject it to be used in support of the change, would doubtless be rejected.

Granting aid to France was an especially delicate matter, since the new Republic was on the point of war with all her neighbors. Among members of the Cabinet, Hamilton stood alone in his determination to maintain American neutrality and to do as little as possible for the new French Government. When he finally learned that Louis XVI had been executed and that France had declared war on England, Holland, and Spain, Hamilton immediately set to work devising policies for meeting the crisis. The "continuance of peace" was essential to his program and could not be left to chance; and the imminent arrival of the new French minister, Edmond Genêt, made the American position even more delicate. Seeking the advice of a friend, Hamilton wrote two letters to John Jay in the same day.

Philadelphia April 9 1793

When we last conversed together on the subject we were both of opinion that the Minister expected from France should be received.

Subsequent circumstances have perhaps induced an

One American broadside depicts the
fate of France's Louis XVI (above);
another (below) laments the death
of the King, America's former ally.

additional embarrassment on this point and render it
adviseable to reconsider the opinion generally and to
raise this further question—Whether he ought to be
received *absolutely* or with *qualifications?*

The King has been decapitated. Out of this will arise a
Regent, acknowleged and supported by the Powers of
Europe almost universally—in capacity to Act and who
may himself send an Ambassador to the United States.
Should we in such case receive both? If we receive one
from the Republic & refuse the other, shall we stand
on ground perfectly neutral?

If we receive a Minister from the Republic, shall we
be afterwards at liberty to say—"We will not decide
whether there is a Government in France competent to
demand from us the performance of the existing treaties.
What the Government in France shall be is the very
point *in dispute.* 'Till that is decided the *applicability*
of the Treaties is suspended. When that Government is
established we shall consider whether such changes have
been made as to render their continuance incompatible
with the interest of the U States." If we shall not have
concluded ourselves by any Act, I am of opinion, that
we have at least a right to hold the thing suspended till
the point in dispute is decided. I doubt whether we could
bona fide dispute the ultimate obligation of the Treaties.
Will the unqualified reception of a Minister conclude us?

If it will ought we so to conclude ourselves?

Ought we not rather to refuse receiving or to receive
with qualification—declaring that we receive the person as the representative of the Government *in fact* of
the French Nation reserving to ourselves a right to consider the applicability of the Treaties to the *actual situation* of the parties?

Philad April 9. 1793
I have already written you by this Post. A further Question occurs. Would not a proclamation prohibiting our
citizens from taking Com[missio]ns. &c on either side
be proper?

Would it be well that it should include a declaration of Neutrality?

If you think the measure prudent could you draft such
a thing as you would deem proper? I wish much you
could.

With debate heating up over the French crisis, Washington returned hastily to Philadelphia. On April 18, the Cabinet members met to give their opinions on "a general plan of conduct for the Executive," and, the next day, agreed to a Proclamation of Neutrality. This by no means settled American policy toward France, however. Hamilton and Secretary of War Henry Knox, who still differed sharply with Jefferson and Randolph over the reception to be given Genêt on his arrival, presented the President with their joint opinion (drafted by Hamilton) that the French minister should be received "with qualification." After discoursing at length on international law and the obligations of treaties, Hamilton came to the crucial point of his argument.

Philadelphia May 2. 1793

Are the United States bound, by the principles of the laws of nations, to consider the Treaties heretofore made with France, as in present force and operation between them and the actual Governing powers of the French Nation? or may they elect to consider their operation as suspended, reserving also a right to judge finally, whether any such changes have happened in the political affairs of France as may justify a renunciation of those Treaties?...

The conclusion from the whole is, that there is an option in the United States to hold the operation of the Treaties suspended—and that in the event, if the form of Government established in France shall be such as to render a continuance of the Treaties contrary to the interest of the United States, they may be renounced.

If there be such an option, there are strong reasons to shew, that the character and interest of the United States require, that they should pursue the course of holding the operation of the Treaties suspended.

Their character—because it was from Louis the XVI, the then sovereign of the Country, that they received those succours, which were so important in the establishment of their independence and liberty—It was with him his heirs and successors, that they contracted the engagements by which they obtained...succours....

To throw their weight into the scale of the New Government, would it is to be feared be considered by Mankind as not consistent with a decent regard to the relations which subsisted between them and Louis the XVI....

The character of the United States may be also con-

Silhouette of Edmond Charles Genêt

cerned in keeping clear of any connection with the Present Government of France in other views.

A struggle for liberty is in itself respectable and glorious. When conducted with magnanimity, justice and humanity it ought to command the admiration of every friend to human nature. But if sullied by crimes and extravagancies, it loses its respectability. Though success may rescue it from infamy, it cannot in the opinion of the sober part of Mankind attach to it much positive merit or praise. But in the event of a want of success, a general execration must attend it.

It appears thus far but too probable, that the pending revolution of France has sustained some serious blemishes. There is too much ground to anticipate that a sentence uncommonly severe will be passed upon it, if it fails.

The Cabinet had plenty of time to consider Genêt's reception, since the new minister had landed at Charleston, South Carolina, and seemed in no hurry to reach Philadelphia. Washington accepted Jefferson's advice to receive Genêt unconditionally, but even before the French diplomat arrived in the capital, there seemed to be good reason to regret the decision. George Hammond protested Genêt's activities in Charleston, and Hamilton presented this "state of facts" to Washington.

[Philadelphia, May 15, 1793]

Mr. Jenet Minister Plenipotentiary from the Republic of France arrives at charsletown. There he causes two privateers to be fitted out, to which he issues Commissions, to cruise against the enemies of France. There also, the Privateers are manned and partly with citizens of the United States, who are inlisted or engaged for the purpose, without the privity or permission of the Government of this Country; before even Mr Jenet has delivered his credentials and been recognized as a public Minister. One or both these Privateers make captures of British Vessels, in the neighbourhood of our Coasts, and bring or send their prizes into our Ports.

The British Minister Plenipotentiary among other things demands a restitution of these prizes. Ought the demands to be complied with?

I am of opinion that it ought to be complied with, and for the following reasons.

The proceedings in question are highly exceptionable

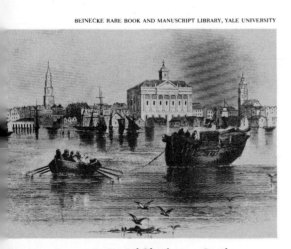

A view of Charleston, South Carolina, as it appeared in 1780

both as they respect our rights and as they make us an instrument of hostilities against Great Britain.

The jurisdiction of every *Independent* Nation, within its own territories, naturally excludes all exercise of authority, by any other Government, within those Territories, unless by its own consent, or in consequence of stipulations in Treaties. . . .

The equipping manning and commissioning of Vessels of War, the inlisting, levying or raising of men for military service, whether by land or sea—all which are essentially of the same nature—are among the highest and most important exercises of sovereignty.

It is therefore an injury and affront of a very serious kind, for one Nation to do acts of the above description, within the territories of another, without its consent or permission.

History of Philadelphia BY THOMPSON WESTCOTT

Genêt's house in Philadelphia

Hamilton's suspicions of a Republican "plot" were multiplied when Genêt reached Philadelphia on May 16. As soon as the French minister presented his credentials, he demanded advances on payments of the debt to France. Washington overruled Hamilton's suggestion that the request be declined abruptly; Genêt was refused, but he was refused as Jefferson wished, with courtesy. Taking heart, Genêt then refused to pay bills drawn by the Santo Domingo authorities under an agreement between his predecessor, Ternant, and the United States. Hamilton was furious and poured out his anger to George Hammond, who afterward wrote an account of the Secretary's remarks.

[Philadelphia, June 10–July 6, 1793]
A very influential member of the American administration . . . informed me . . . that Mr. Genêt's conduct was a direct violation of a formal compact, originally entered into with Mr. Ternant and subsequently confirmed by himself both in conversation and in writing, and on the faith of which the last payment of the installment due had been made: but notwithstanding the precise conditions of the contract, Mr. Genêt had not only refused payment of the bills in question, but had treated all the remonstrances of the government on the subject, with the utmost arrogance, and contempt. My informant farther said that this circumstance was extremely embarassing to the government, as it stood pledged to its own citizens that these bills should be paid. In consequence of which it would be under the necessity of

anticipating as much of the installment due next September as would discharge these bills.

The unpaid bills were forgotten temporarily as the privateers commissioned at Charleston sent in more captured British prizes. Washington chose a middle course in dealing with these ships: the privateers were to leave American ports, although their prizes could remain, and Genêt was warned to cease commissioning privateers. The Frenchman simply disregarded the order. His privateers were seized in New York and Philadelphia, but George Hammond protested that two more ships were being armed in Baltimore. The Cabinet responded with limp assurances that it would consider "whether any practicable arrangement can be adopted to prevent the augmentation of the [privateer] force..." The Cabinet's attitude helped Hamilton to make a difficult decision: on June 21, he notified Washington that he would resign as Secretary of the Treasury.

> Philadelphia June 21. 1793
>
> Considerations, relative both to the public Interest and to my own delicacy, have brought me, after mature reflection, to a resolution to resign the office, I hold, towards the close of the ensuing session of Congress.
>
> I postpone the final act to that period, because some propositions remain to be submitted by me to Congress, which are necessary to the full developement of my original plan, and, as I suppose, of some consequence to my reputation — and because, in the second place, I am desirous of giving an opportunity, while I shall be still in office, to the revival and more deliberate prosecution of the Inquiry into my conduct, which was instituted during the last session.
>
> I think it proper to communicate my determination, thus early, among other reasons, because it will afford full time to investigate and weigh all the considerations, which ought to guide the appointment of my successor.

In September, 1792, Hamilton had warned Washington that the "public good" would soon "require *substitutes* for the differing members of your administration." He had remarked, as well, that "on my part there will be a most chearful acquiescence in such a result." By June, 1793, he was convinced that he was the member who would have to be replaced. The fortunes of party politics and war had gone against Hamilton for eighteen months, and he had good reason to feel that his presence in the Cabinet would only weaken the precious union he had so long defended.

A Picture Portfolio

Shaping the Young Republic

ODE
FOR THE
FEDERAL PROCESSION,
Upon the Adoption of the NEW GOVERNMENT.

Composed by Mr. L.

I.

EMERGING from Old Ocean's bed,
　When fair Columbia rear'd her awful head
To his* enraptur'd view, whose dauntless soul
Heav'n had impell'd t' explore the unknown goal;
The Genius of the solitary waste,
With extacy the god-like man embrac'd,
　Prophetic of her future state:
And smil'd serene, and bless'd th' approaching day,
When older Nations, envious, should survey
　Our Wisdom, Virtue, Pow'r how great!
　But still she sigh'd and dropt a tear,
　And still she entertain'd a fear,
Anticipating what she knew too well;
And what, this memorable day, the Muse
With retrospective ken reluctant views,
And this blest Epocha forbids to tell.†

II.

Distress'd she saw—but, with predictive eyes,
Through scenes of horror future bliss descrys;
Sees greater good from partial evil rise.
She knew how Empires rise and fall;
That all the changes on this terrene ball
　Revolve by Heav'n's command,
　Nor can its will withstand—
Submissive she that Pow'r ador'd,
　The Sovereign Universal Lord,
　Almighty, wise and good!
Whose eye omniscient saw 'twas right,
We should attain that glorious height,
　Through Seas of kindred blood.

II.

And, lo! the all-important period's nigh,
　And swells the mighty theme—
An Æra, greater than the golden age
　Of which the Poets dream;
And adds a wond'rous, an illustrious page
To this terrestial Globe's vast history.
　Begin oh Muse,
　And far diffuse
　Th' inspiring news
　To Earth's remotest bound:
Throughout the world let joy like ours be found,
And Echo catch the animating sound,
　Now all our highest hopes are crown'd.
　Through time's incessant round,
　Fame shall resound
　This long desir'd event,
And tell what mighty blessings Heav'n has sent;
　Immortal Fame,
　Whose loud acclaim
　Is deathless as the Poet's song,
To countless ages shall the theme prolong.

IV.

Ten Sovereign States, in Friendship's league combin'd,
Blest with a G verament, which does embrace
The dearest Interests of the human race,
　This festive day, to joy refign'd,
　This signal day we celebrate—
　Let ev'ry patriot heart dilate,
　Let ev'ry care be banish'd far,
Nor aught the honors of this solemn season mar.
Behold th' admir'd Procession move along,
Our sister States, the happy ten, to greet—
What animation in the crouded Street!
　What buzzing eclat from each tongue!
　In beautiful arran ement lo!
　Majestically flow,
　Some thousand souls, a federal band,
　Advancing hand in hand—
Heart-cheering fight! not half so much applause
Did Alexander's pompous entries crown;
Nor did he ever gain such true renown—
This grand display can boast a nobler cause.

* Columbus.　† Alluding to the late war.

V.

Hail Liberty, thou heav'n-born child!
Young, smiling Cherub, virtuous, mild!
We feel, we feel thy pow'r divine!
These solemnities are thine!
　Our hearts o'erflow,
　Our bosoms glow,
　Sorrow fades,
　Joy pervades
Th' intoxicated senses!
Floods of Transport fill the soul,
And Melancholy's haggard train controul,
For now our Country's happiness commences!

VI.

Joy to the Union! Fair Columbia hail!——
Distraction in our Councils now shall fail,
And Strength, Respect and Wisdom join'd, prevail:
　Justice shall lift her well-poiz'd Scale.
With placid aspect, Peace her wand extend,
And white rob'd Virtue from the Sky descend;
Genius shall mount a glorious tow'ring height,
By genial Science foster'd and refin'd,
And never-dying wreaths our Offspring's temples bind—
While dwindled Europe sickens at the sight.
Arts, still encreasing, shall our clime adorn,
Success and Wealth crown millions yet unborn,
Glorious and smiling as the op'ning Morn!
And, if fair Industry but prompt the hand,
The cultur'd Earth shall teem at their command,
And Health and Plenty glad Heav'n's fav'rite land;
Pomona's charge shall grow luxuriant here,
And bounteous Ceres crown the blissful year;
Commerce shall raise her languid head——
The Nation's dignity, which with her fled,
Triumphant shall her place resume,
And Navies start from the tall forest's gloom.

VII.

Joy to our far-fam'd Chief! whose peerless worth
Makes Monarchs sicken at their royal birth;
And thou, grown dim with honorable age,
Whose Lore shall grace the scientific page,
Franklin, the patriot, venerable Sage,
Of philosophic memory! And thou,*
Our City's boast, to whom so much we owe;
In whom, tho' last and youngest of the three,
No common share of excellence we see:
In ev'ry grateful heart thou hast a place,
Nor Time, nor Circumstance can e'er erase.
All hail, ye Champions in your Country's cause!
Soon shall that Country ring with your applause—
With such, and with ten thousand Patriots more,
To what vast Fame this Western World shall soar!
Discord shall cease, and perfect Union reign,
And all confess that sweetly-pow'rful chain,
The Fed'ral System, which, at once, unites
The Thirteen States, and all the people's rights.
Oh, may those rights be sacred to the end,
And to our vast posterity descend;
That beauteous Structure flourish and expand,
And ceaseless Blessings crown our native Land!

Alexander Hamilton, Esquire.

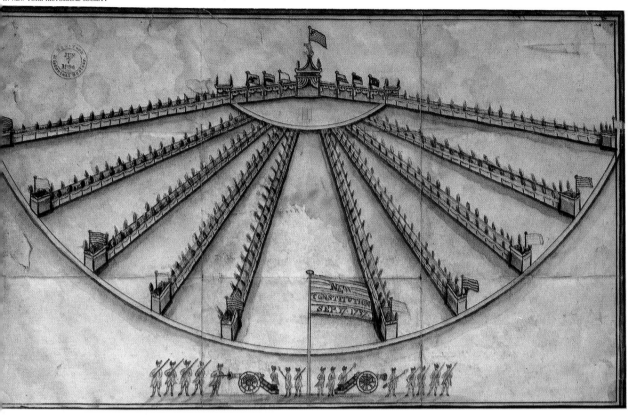

HAMILTONIANA

During the war one of George Washington's other military aides had dubbed Hamilton "the Little Lion," and it proved a sobriquet that suited him well during the difficult political battles he was to fight in the years ahead. When the New York Convention met at Poughkeepsie in June, 1788, to vote on ratification of the Constitution, Hamilton was by then its determined champion. A major voice at the Annapolis Convention of 1786 and the only New York delegate to the Constitutional Convention who had signed what he considered an acceptable compromise, Hamilton was also the author—with John Jay and James Madison—of *The Federalist*. During the tense summer of 1788, he helped sway the heavily Antifederalist New York Convention by his eloquent arguments. When the final vote was taken on July 26, ratification won by a slim vote of 30 to 27. In celebration of ratification by the necessary nine states, New York City had staged a huge federal procession three days earlier. A commemorative ode was written for the occasion (left) calling Hamilton "Our City's boast, to whom so much we owe...." A great float drawn by six white horses carried a ship marked "Hamilton," and L'Enfant designed a banquet pavilion (above) that would seat six thousand people for a celebratory feast. Hamilton at the age of thirty-three was the toast of his adopted town, and someone even suggested calling the city Hamiltoniana.

HAMILTON'S NEW YORK

Following New York's ratification of the Constitution, Hamilton returned to the Continental Congress, to which he had been elected in February, 1788, and successfully campaigned to keep the temporary seat of government in his own New York City. The view below shows the lower tip of Manhattan Island from the Hudson River in Hamilton's day. Just to the right of the ship's mast is the dome of the old City Hall, a block away from Trinity Church on Wall Street. Modernized and renamed Federal Hall, it became the first Capitol of the United States (right); Washington took his oath as first President on the balcony in 1789. Hamilton lived and had his law office at 56 and 57 Wall Street, which became known as Bank Row in 1792 when the first Bank of the United States opened at 52 Wall. At the northeast corner of Wall and William streets (right, below) stood the Bank of New York, founded in 1784 by Hamilton. All these water colors were done in the 1790's by Archibald Robertson of the British Army's Royal Engineers.

At the corner of Wall and Water streets was the Tontine Coffee House (left), which housed the New Yo

tock Exchange. At far right is the Merchant's Coffee House, a gathering place for merchants and brokers.

THE

REPORT

OF THE

SECRETARY OF THE TREASURY,

(ALEXANDER HAMILTON,)

ON THE SUBJECT OF A

NATIONAL BANK.

Read in the House of Representatives, Dec. 13th, 1790.

NEW-YORK:

PUBLISHED BY S. WHITING & CO.
No. 118, Pearl-street.
J. Seymour, print.

1811.

HIGH FINANCE

Two of Hamilton's mentors in the world of finance were Robert Morris and Gouverneur Morris. Robert Morris commissioned Charles Willson Peale to paint the double portrait at left of himself and Gouverneur (seated), his assistant in the Office of Finance, in 1783 — the year after he had appointed Hamilton as his financial agent in New York State. As Secretary of the Treasury in 1790, Hamilton — in order to get approval for his fiscal programs — compromised with southerners who wished to move the capital from New York to a site on the Potomac River. The cartoon at lower left shows Robert Morris moving the Capitol to its interim location in Philadelphia. Hamilton himself moved his whole family, which by this time included four children, to Philadelphia and opened the Treasury office just around the corner from his house at 226 Walnut Street. In December, 1790, he submitted to Congress his report (left) urging that a national bank be established. After considerable debate, Congress enacted it into law; and a handsome building on Third Street (below) was built to house the first Bank of the United States.

FIRST SECRETARY OF THE TREASURY

The handsome portrait of Alexander Hamilton at right was painted for the New York Chamber of Commerce by John Trumbull in 1792 — a reflection of the pride that New York took in its illustrious resident. The indefatigable Secretary of the Treasury, by that time, had already issued four of his famous series of state papers, concerning public credit, a national bank, the mint, and manufactures. On most of these important questions Hamilton was opposed, often bitterly, by Thomas Jefferson. Washington's Secretary of State said of Hamilton that he "was not only a monarchist, but for a monarchy bottomed on corruption.... Hamilton was, indeed, a singular character. Of acute understanding, disinterested, honest, and honorable in all private transactions...yet so bewitched and perverted by the British example, as to be under thorough conviction that corruption was essential to the government of a nation." Indeed, about the only issue he and Hamilton agreed on was the decimal system of currency. Jefferson proposed it and Hamilton acted on it. The coins above show a selection issued between 1793 and 1796, including copper half cents and cents; silver half dimes, dimes, twenty-five cents, fifty cents, and dollars; and two and a half, five, and ten dollar gold pieces.

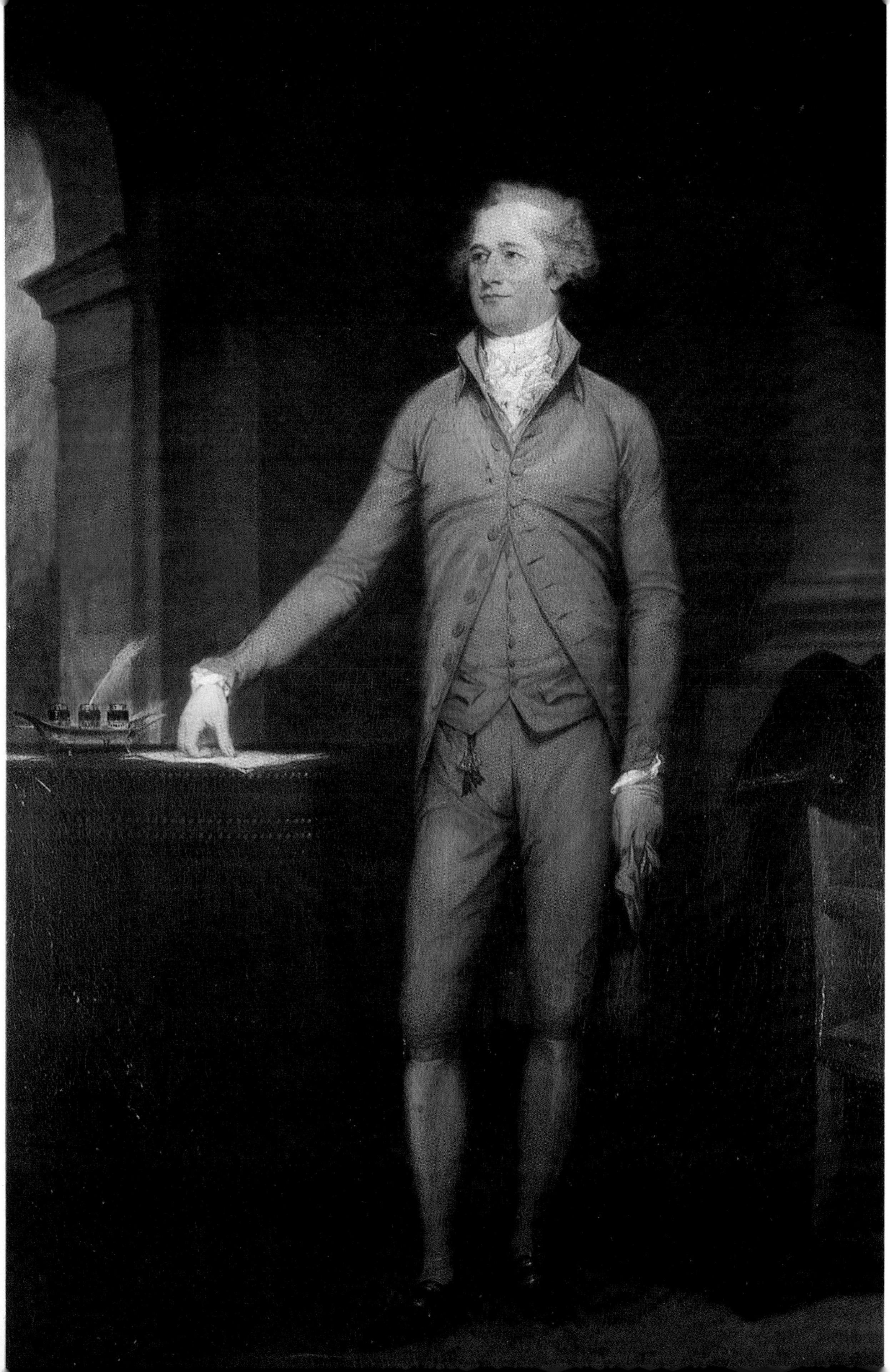
NEW YORK CHAMBER OF COMMERCE

USEFUL MANUFACTURES

In addition to writing his notable *Report on The Subject of Manufactures,* which urged the Government to encourage manufacturing, as well as "the cultivation of the earth, as the primary and most certain source of national supply," Hamilton helped found the Society for Establishing Useful Manufactures. The venture was located in Paterson, New Jersey, alongside the beautiful Falls of the Passaic (below), which furnished the necessary water power for the mills that were built. At right is a lottery ticket issued to raise funds for the project. Unfortunately, the early experiment in American industrialization failed.

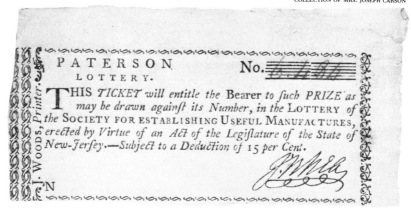

Nº XXXVII. Nº XXXVIII.

The subtle Seducer. *The American Financier.*

London, Publish'd by A.Hamilton Jun?, Fleet Street, Jan?ºc, 1782.

OBSERVATIONS

ON

CERTAIN DOCUMENTS

CONTAINED IN NO. V & VI OF

" THE HISTORY OF THE UNITED STATES
FOR THE YEAR 1796,"

IN WHICH THE

CHARGE OF SPECULATION

AGAINST

ALEXANDER HAMILTON,

LATE SECRETARY OF THE TREASURY,

IS FULLY REFUTED.

WRITTEN BY HIMSELF.

PHILADELPHIA:
PRINTED FOR JOHN FENNO, BY JOHN BIOREN.
1797.

HOME LIFE

Although Hamilton's married life appeared to be a happy one, he asserted under political pressure in 1797 that he had had an affair with Maria Reynolds, which began six years earlier in Philadelphia while Betsey and the children were in Albany. An English publisher inserted stock engravings labeled "The Subtle Seducer" and "The American Financier" as frontispieces to Hamilton's published confession (below, left). He managed to salvage his marriage, however, and built the Grange (left) in the countryside of upper Manhattan as a permanent home for his family. Cerrachi's fine bust (below) was placed in the entrance hall.

301

A FATAL ENCOUNTER

In 1804, Alexander Hamilton and Aaron Burr, by then bitter political enemies, started down a path from which there would be, for Hamilton, no return. When Burr challenged Hamilton to the fatal duel, Hamilton wrote "some remarks explanatory" of his conduct and motives. "...it is not to be denied that my animadversions on the political principles, character, and views of Col. Burr have been extremely severe.... He may have supposed himself under a necessity of acting as he has done...." The spot chosen for the dueling ground (right foreground) was in Weehawken, New Jersey, just across the Hudson River from New York City.

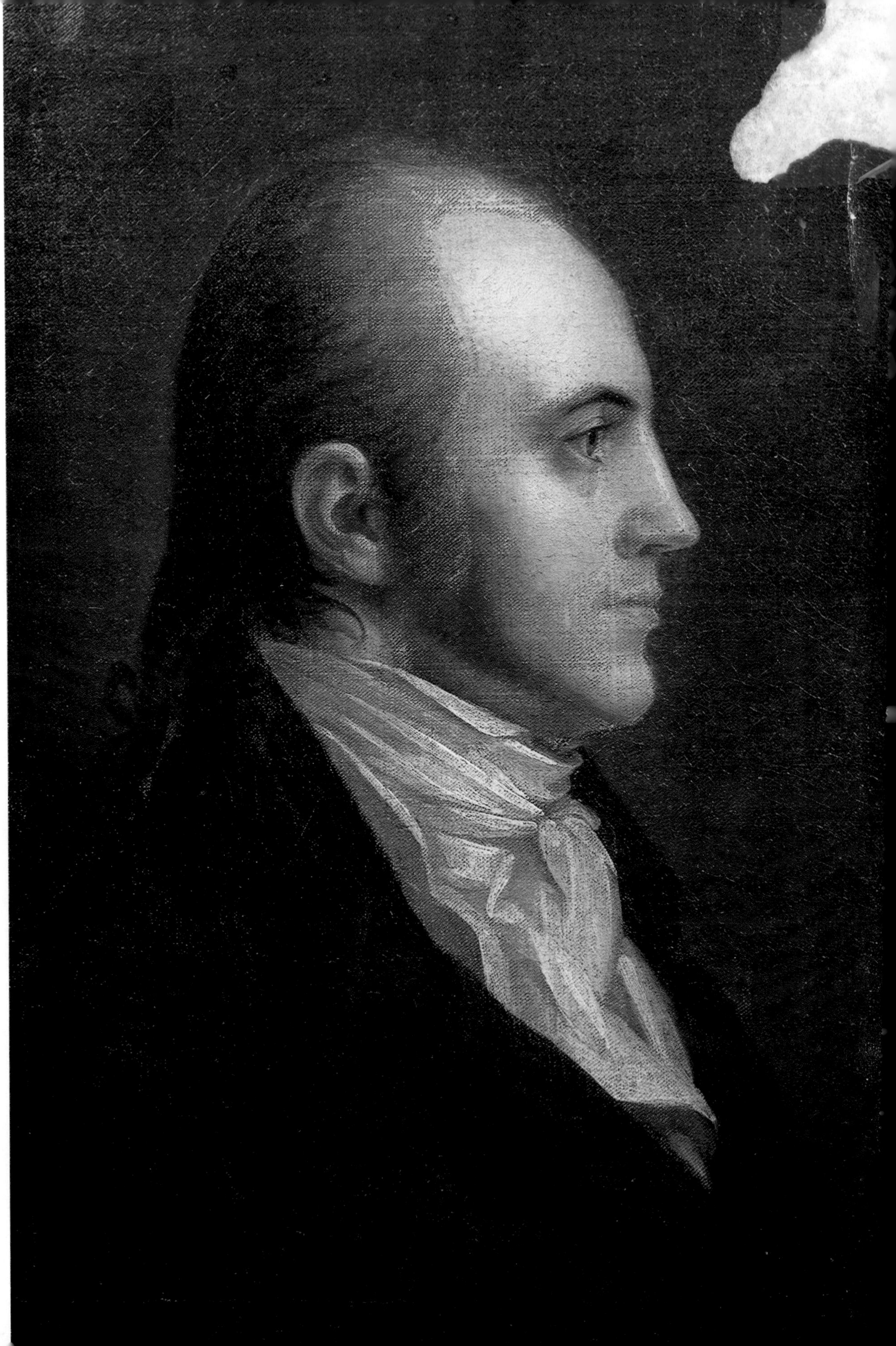

BY JOHN VANDERLYN, 1802; NEW-YORK HISTORICAL SOCIETY

A LIFE CUT TRAGICALLY SHORT

Hamilton had good reason to abhor the practice of dueling. Only a few years earlier his eldest son, Philip, had been killed in a duel, and he never recovered from that terrible shock. But his deep-seated sense of "what men of the world denominate honor, imposed on me...a peculiar necessity not to decline the call." He had made up his mind not to shoot to kill Burr (left), but Burr's first bullet found its mark in Hamilton's left side. Dr. David Hosack (bottom left), whom both men had chosen as their attending physician, rushed Hamilton back across the river to the house of William Bayard (bottom right) and informed Betsey, who hastened to the bedside from the Grange. Hamilton's last letter to her, "not to be delivered to you, unless I shall first have terminated my earthly career," reassured her of his "love for you and my precious children." He enjoined her to "Fly to the bosom of your God and be comforted.... Adieu best of wives and best of Women." Hamilton died on the afternoon of July 12, 1804. New York and the country mourned him, and among expressions of their grief was the detail below from a memorial handkerchief, "In memory of the lamented Hamilton."

Chapter **11**

Creating a Legacy

At the end of June, 1793, Alexander Hamilton was determined to leave the Cabinet and return to his legal practice in New York. But within a month, the tables were turned: it was Jefferson whose policies were questioned. Shortly thereafter, the Secretary of State announced his own plans for retirement, leaving Hamilton to dominate the Cabinet without serious opposition. His coming months in office would be attended by new hostilities in Europe and by armed resistance to the revenue laws on the Pennsylvania frontier. On the whole, Hamilton was to meet these challenges to America's neutrality and her national honor with considerable success and good sense. But in July, 1793, it was Edmond Genêt and his intrigues that most concerned the Treasury Secretary. In the first week of that month, local authorities learned that Genêt had begun to arm another vessel in the port of Philadelphia. Hamilton sent a detailed account of the incident to Senator Rufus King of New York, as he and Henry Knox had heard it from Governor Thomas Mifflin of Pennsylvania.

> Philadelphia August 13th 1793
> On Saturday the 6th of July last, the warden of this Port reported to Governor Mifflin that the Brig Little Sarah since called The Petit Democrat (an English merchant vessel mounting from two to four Guns taken off our coast by the French Frigate The Ambuscade and brought into this Port) had very materially augmented her Military equipments; having then fourteen Iron Cannon and six swivels mounted; and it being understood that her crew was to consist of one hundred & twenty men.
>
> Governor Mifflin, in consequence of this information sent Mr [Alexander J.] Dallas to Mr Genet to endeavour to prevail upon him to enter into an arrangement for

detaining the vessel in Port without the necessity of employing for that purpose military force.

Mr Dallas reported to Governor Mifflin that Mr Genet had absolutely refused to do what had been requested of him—that he had been very angry and intemperate—that he had complained of ill treatment from the Government and had declared that "he would appeal from the President to the People"—mentioned his expectation of the arrival of three Ships of the line; observing that he would know how to do justice to his country or at least he had a Frigate at his command and could easily withdraw himself from this—said that he would not advise an attempt to take possession of the vessel as it would be resisted.

The refusal was so peremptory that Governor Mifflin in consequence of it ordered out 120 men for the purpose of taking possession of the vessel....

Mr Jefferson on sunday went to Mr Genet to endeavour to prevail upon him to detain the Petit Democrat till the President could return and decide upon the case; but, as Mr Jefferson afterwards communicated, he absolutely refused to give a promise of the kind saying only that she would not probably be ready to depart before the succeeding wednesday, the day of the Presidents expected return. This however Mr Jefferson construed into an intimation that she would remain. Mr Jefferson also informed that Mr Genet had been very unreasonable and intemperate in his conversation....

Mud Island, located in the Delaware River just below Philadelphia, was caricatured as a formidable lady in this British cartoon of 1777.

On Monday, July 8, the Cabinet met to consider the events of the weekend. Hamilton and Knox demanded that Mud Island be fortified to prevent the *Little Sarah* from putting out to sea. Jefferson disagreed strongly, and Hamilton prepared a written list of "reasons" for his and Knox's position. In the fifth section of this document, he presented the basis for all his fears and arguments.

[Philadelphia, July 8, 1793]

It is impossible to interpret such conduct into any thing else than a *regular plan to force the United States into the War.* Its tendency to produce that effect cannot be misunderstood by the Agents of France. The direct advantage of the measure to her is obviously too inconsiderable to induce the persisting in it, contrary to the remonstrances of the Government—if it were not with a

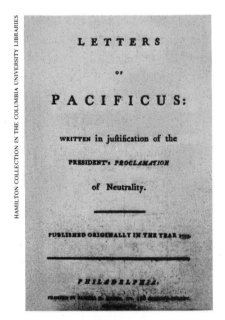

The title page of Hamilton's collected Letters of Pacificus

view to the more important end just mentioned: a conduct the more exceptionable because it is accompanied with the fallacious disavowal of an intention to engage us in the War.

...there is satisfactory evidence of a *regular system,* in pursuit of that object, *to endeavour to controul the Government itself, by creating, if possible, a scism between it and the people* and inlisting them on the side of France....

The declaration of the Minister of France to Mr. Dallas, Secretary of the Commonwealth of Pensylvania ...is a further confirmation of the same system. That Declaration, among other exceptionable things, expressed *"That he* (the Minister of France) *would appeal from the President of the United States to the People."* It would be a fatal blindness, not to perceive the spirit, which dictates such language, and an ill-omened passiveness not to resolve to withstand it with energy.

Even before Washington returned to Philadelphia on July 11, Hamilton's carefully drafted "reasons" had lost any practical interest. Genêt, breaking his vague promise to Jefferson, had sent the *Little Sarah* down the Delaware River out of reach of the guns on Mud Island. Since the vessel was still in American waters, her activities were a continued object of concern, and on July 12, the Cabinet referred the problem to the Supreme Court. While he waited for the justices' opinion, Hamilton issued his sixth "Pacificus" letter. Recent proclamations of the French Republic, he wrote, bore an "instructive lesson to the people of this country."

[Philadelphia, July 17, 1793]

It ought to teach us not to over-rate *foreign friendships* — to be upon our guard against *foreign attachments.* The former will generally be found hollow and delusive; the latter will have a natural tendency to lead us aside from our own true interest, and to make us the dupes of foreign influence. They introduce a principle of action, which in its effects, if the expression may be allowed, is *anti-national.* Foreign influence is truly the GRECIAN HORSE to a republic. We cannot be too careful to exclude its entrance. Nor ought we to imagine, that it can only make its approaches in the gross form of direct bribery. It is then most dangerous, when it comes under the patronage of our passions, under the auspices of national prejudice and partiality.

Foreign friendships" seemed even less reliable when Genêt put the *Little Sarah* out to sea before the Supreme Court could take action. Jefferson, his cause betrayed, informed Washington that he would resign in the fall, and on August 1, the Cabinet voted to demand the French minister's recall. But Genêt's disgrace and the prospect of Jefferson's departure did not end Hamilton's concern that America might be dragged into war. Peace was endangered again at the end of the summer, when Philadelphians learned of a new British directive, issued in London on June 8, ordering English naval commanders to seize all ships carrying provisions to France or to French-occupied ports, and all ships trying to enter a port under British blockade. Hamilton proved more "neutral" than any of his political enemies expected him to be when he reacted to the British infraction of American commercial rights almost as angrily as he had to Genêt's attempts to make the United States a party to France's wars. George Hammond, in a dispatch to his superiors in London, reported Hamilton's reaction to the British maneuver.

NEW YORK ACADEMY OF MEDICINE

MEETING of the Corporation of the city of Burton, Auguft 30th, 1793, the following recommendation to the citizens was unanimoufly agreed to.

EREAS there is great reafon for caution againft the malignant Fever or conbiforder, which prevails in Philadelphia, and it is our duty to ufe every proleans to prevent the fame in the city of Burlington; the Corporation of gton after collecting every advice which could be obtained,

RECOMMEND to the Citizens of Burlington,

at all unneceffary intercourfe be avoided with Philadelphia, that no dry ollen cloths, woollens, cottons or linens, or any packages where ftraw, ings are ufed, be imported within twenty days.

the mafters of the boats which ply to and from Burlington to Philadelry careful that they do not receive on board their veffels, or bring to ridin twenty days, any perfon or perfons but thofe who appear in

no animal or vegetable fubftances be thrown or permitted to lay in the eys, but that all offals, water-melon rinds and fubftances that putrefy to the delaware or buried.

o water be permitted to ftagnate about the pumps, in the ftreets or les; but that the wharves, ftreets, alleys and gutters, ditches, houfe, ds, be kept as clean as poffible.

Phyficians in Burlington are requefted to make report to the Mayor or foon as poffible, after they fhall have been called to and vifited any perfon, who fhall have the faid malignant Fever.

Signed by order of the Corporation,

BOWES REED, *Mayor.*

his broadside was posted in urlington, New Jersey, to warn 2 town's citizens of the yellow er epidemic in Philadelphia.

[Philadelphia, August 21–30, 1793]

Mr. Hamilton ... regarded it as a very harsh and unprecedented measure, which not only militated against the principal branch of the present American exports but ... appeared to be peculiarly directed against the commerce and navigation of the United States. For these reasons it would be incumbent upon this government, to make a representation on the subject to the Court of London. In the mean time, he earnestly desired me, if I received any exposition of it from your Lordship, to state it to the American administration, as a timely explanation might remove the unfavorable impressions it had made. In my answer I defended it, as well as I was able, on the ground of expediency, and of its not being contrary to the Law of nations. ... I however perceived that he was not convinced by *my* reasoning.

Instructions went out to Thomas Pinckney, the American minister to the Court of St. James's, to make appropriate "representations." Toward the end of September, meanwhile, Hamilton and his wife contracted the yellow fever that was then sweeping Philadelphia. During the next two months, more than five thousand Philadelphians would die of the disease, and Hamilton was convinced that he was saved only by the treatment ministered by his boyhood friend from St. Croix, Dr. Edward Stevens. When the Hamiltons recovered, they set off for Albany, where their children had been sent for safekeeping during the epidemic. In October, they returned to their summer home outside Philadelphia. Their children, however, remained in Albany with their grandparents, and there Hamilton sent a bit of fatherly advice to his daughter Angelica.

[Philadelphia, November, 1793]

I was very glad to learn, my dear daughter, that you were going to begin the study of the French language. We hope you will in every respect behave in such a manner as will secure to you the good-will and regard of all those with whom you are. If you happen to displease any of them, be always ready to make a frank apology. But the best way is to act with so much politeness, good manners, and circumspection, as never to have occasion to make any apology. Your mother joins in best love to you. Adieu, my very dear daughter.

Health conditions in Philadelphia were improving, but Hamilton had new worries when he learned that John Fenno, the Philadelphia printer of the Federalist *Gazette of the United States,* faced financial ruin. After an appeal to Rufus King to raise funds in New York, he wrote to John Kean, cashier of the Bank of the United States.

[Philadelphia] Friday Novr. 29 [1793]

Poor *Fenno* is ruined by his Patriotism. His weekly paper is at an end — and he cannot begin again without a loan of at least 1500 Dollars. As I think he deserves assistance from the goodness of his motives and that it is of consequence to the Foederal cause that he should be enabled to prosecute a paper — I have set on foot a subscription to a loan for his use. The inclosed will shew its progress. Do me the favour to present it to The President [of the Bank of the United States] & such others as you may think adviseable between this & two oClock & then send it to me.

Logo of Philadelphia's Federalist Gazette of the United States

In Cabinet meetings in November, Hamilton and Jefferson continued their quarrel. When Washington and his officers discussed the annual message the President would deliver to Congress on December 3, there were sharp differences on the kind of statement that should be made on foreign policy and American neutrality. Hamilton suggested this paragraph.

[November, 1793]

It is greatly to be lamented, for the sake of humanity, that the flame of War, which had before spread over a considerable part of Europe has within the present year extended itself much further; implicating all those

CULVER PICTURES, INC.

This Federalist cartoon of 1793 portrays Republicans as a gang of anarchists consorting with Satan.

powers with whom the United States have the most extensive relations. When it was seen here, that almost all the maritime Nations either were, or were likely soon to become parties to the War, it was natural that it should excite serious reflections about the possible consequences to this Country. On the one hand, it appeared desireable, that no impressions in reference to it should exist with any of the powers engaged, of a nature to precipitate arrangements or measures tending to interrupt or endanger our peace. On the other, it was probable, that designing or inconsiderable persons among ourselves might from different motives embark in enterprizes contrary to the duties of a nation at peace with nations at war with each other; and, of course, calculated to invite and to produce reprisals and hostilities. Adverting to these considerations, in a situation both new and delicate, I judged it adviseable to issue a Proclamation.... The effects of this measure have, I trust, neither disappointed the views which dictated it, nor disserved the true interests of our Country.

Washington ignored Hamilton's draft and accepted the advice of the Secretary of State. The annual message was scrupulously "neutral" in the Jeffersonian sense. Hamilton still planned to leave office in the spring of 1794, but he first wished to attend to a piece of unfinished business: replying to the questions raised in Congress about his administration of the Treasury Department. In mid-December, in a letter to the Speaker, he boldly invited the House of Representatives to begin its investigations.

Treasury Department December 16, 1793. It is known that in the last Session certain questions were raised respecting my Conduct in Office, which, though decided in a manner the most satisfactory to me, were nevertheless, unavoidably from the lateness of the period when they were set on foot, so accelerated in their issue, as to have given occasion to a Suggestion that there was not time for due examination. Unwilling to leave the Matter upon such a footing, I have concluded to request of the House of Representatives, as I now do, that a new Inquiry may be without delay instituted, in some mode most effectual for an accurate and thorough investigation—And I will add, that the more comprehensive it is, the more agreeable it will be to me.

311

More than two months passed before Congress responded to Hamilton's challenge to investigate his department. In the meantime, Jefferson resigned from the Cabinet (he was succeeded by Edmund Randolph), and Genêt was recalled by his Government. Nevertheless, when Congress finally named a special committee to investigate the Treasury in late February, 1794, there was ample evidence that Hamilton had many enemies left in Philadelphia. This committee was more successful than earlier investigators had been in finding an issue with which to embarrass the Secretary of the Treasury. The legislators showed particular interest in the history of the European loans obtained under the statutes of August, 1790, and in the use that had been made of the proceeds. Replying to their request for the "authorities" under which these funds had been allocated, Hamilton insisted that Congress had only a limited right of inquiry into executive affairs.

Treasury department, 24th. March 1794

I ask the Committee... to decide, whether they expect from the Secretary of the Treasury, the production of any other authorities from the President to him, in reference to the loans made under the Acts of the 4th. and 12th. of August 1790, except such as regard merely the making of the said loans and the application or disbursement of such part of the proceeds of those loans, as were to be disbursed in foreign countries?

I object to the being required to produce any other authorities, than those excepted, for the following reasons, Viz:

1st   Because it results from the constitution of the Treasury department, that all the receipts and expenditures of public money within the United States, must pass through that department,... consequently, whenever a loan is made either abroad, or at home, on account of the United States, destined for disbursement within the United States, it becomes, *ex officio,* the province of the Treasury department, to draw the proceeds of such loan into the treasury, and to disburse them thence, according to law.

2nd   Because, when it once appears, that the President has constituted the head of a department, his agent, for any general purpose entrusted to him by law, all intermediate authorities from the President to the Agent, being conformable with law, are to be presumed. The proper enquiry for the Legislature must be, "whether the laws have been duly executed or not." If they have been duly executed, the question of sufficiency or deficiency of authority from the President to his Agent, must be, to the Legislature, immaterial and irrelevant.

Hamilton knew that this matter would give his enemies political ammunition. He sent Washington a copy of his letter to the committee, voicing the hope that his opinion on "the proper limits of a Legislative enquiry" would discourage the congressmen. But he asked that the President support his version of the Treasury's transactions should the committee persist in its demands.

Treasury Dept. Mar. 24. 1794.
In the event of a determination that the enquiry should be general it becomes proper to fix with the President the true view of facts.

The real cause of the transaction has been this. Before I made the disposition of any Loan I regularly communicated to the President my ideas of the proper disposition, designating how much it would be expedient to pay to France—how much to draw to the United States—and always received his sanction for what was adopted & afterwards carried into execution. The communication & the sanction were verbal whenever the President was at the seat of Government. In a case of absence they were in writting. . . .

The sanctions of the President were sometimes expressly and always, as I conceived in their spirit, founded in a material degree on the confidence, that the measures proposed were guided by a just estimate on my part of circumstances, which from situation must have been best known to me—and that they would be always in conformity to the Law.

From GREENLEAF's PRESS.
New-York, January 16, 1794.
GLORIOUS NEWS *from* FRANCE.

ABOUT noon this day an express arrived from Citizen Genet, at Philadelphia, to the French Consul in this City, informing, that the vessel which was expedited by the President of the United States to France some time since, returned yesterday to Philadelphia, after a very short passage from thence. The purport of the express is as follows:

" The DUKE of YORK, with ALL HIS ARMY, are TAKEN.— TOULON is RE-TAKEN, with ALL THE VESSELS which were in the port and in the road. This is the news which has just been announced to Congress, *not officially*, but as *certain*, and Congress could not continue their *sitting*. All the city is in the heights of joy, and my lodgings are crowded with felicitating friends.

" *This news was brought by the return of the advice boat of the President.—* *Share with me, my dear Citizens, and let all our friends, assembled, re-echo—* *VIVE LA REPUBLIC.*"

We learn, that all the bells of Philadelphia, on this occasion, re-echoed the glorious sound of—*downfall to tyrants—the Rights of Man forever.*

A Republican broadside heralding recent victories of revolutionary France in its war against the First Coalition of European powers

As Hamilton feared, the select committee was not easily satisfied. Madison gloated to Jefferson that the inquiry "begins to pinch where we most expected"—the occasions when Hamilton had deposited proceeds of the European loans in the Bank of the United States. The committee demanded Hamilton's authority for these decisions. In his reply the Secretary declared that the Treasury had full power to dispose of "all public monies, once obtained." Washington, who had no desire to become involved in the controversy, did furnish Hamilton with a noncommital "certificate" stating that he could not "charge" his "memory with all the particulars" of these transactions. Writing again to the President, Hamilton pointed out the need for a firmer statement.

These nineteenth-century copies of earlier prints contrast the French and American versions of liberty

Philadelphia April 8 1794

I . . . find, with regret, that the terms used are such as will enable those, who are disposed to construe every thing to my disadvantage, to affirm "That the Declaration of The President has intirely waved the main point and does not even manifest an *opinion* that the representation of the Secretary of the Treasury is well founded."

To this it would be added, that the reserve of The President is a proof that he does not think that representation true—else his justice would have led him to rescue the officer concerned even from suspicion on the point. . . .

Under all that has happened Sir, I cannot help entertaining and frankly expressing to you my apprehension, that false and insidious men, whom you may one day understand, taking advantage of the want of recollection, which is natural, where the mind is habitually occupied with a variety of important objects, have found means by artful suggestions to infuse doubts and distrusts very injurious to me.

James Madison remarked that Washington's certificate was "inexpressibly mortifying" to Hamiltonians. Equally annoying was a new British order in council that permitted the capture of neutral ships carrying goods to and from the French colonies. The order, which was dated November 6, but which did not reach America until March, gave added support to Madison's fight for an anti-British commercial policy. Hamilton sent the President a plan for meeting the British challenge to American trade.

March 8th 1794.

The present situation of the United States is undoubtedly critical and demands measures vigorous though prudent. We ought to be in a respectable military posture, because war may come upon us, whether we choose it or not and because to be in a condition to defend ourselves and annoy any who may attack us will be the best method of securing our peace. If it is known that our principal maritime points are out of the reach of any but formal serious operations—and that the government has an efficient active force in its disposal for defence or offence on an emergency—there will be much less temptation to attack us and much more hesitation to provoke us. . . .

In addition to this, the Legislature ought to vest the President of the United States with a power to lay an embargo partial or general and to arrest the exportation of commodities partially or generally.

It may also deserve consideration whether the Executive ought not to take measures to form some concert of the Neutral Powers for common Defence.

On March 26, the President approved Congress's thirty-day embargo on vessels bound for foreign ports. With Anglo-American relations now strained more than ever, many Federalists believed that a permanent settlement of differences between the United States and Britain would come only if a special envoy were sent to London. Hamilton realized that Republicans distrusted such a plan for fear that he might be the appointee. He also realized that the plan would not succeed without Republican support. He tempered his remarks accordingly when he sent Washington his suggestions for measures to be taken should the President choose a policy of "preparation for war" and simultaneous negotiations of America's differences with Britain.

Philadelphia April [14] 1794

The mode of doing it which occurs is this—to nominate a person, who will have the confidence of those who think peace still within our reach, and who may be thought qualified for the mission as envoy extraordinary to Great Britain—to announce this to...Congress with an... earnest recommendation that vigorous and effectual measures may be adopted to be prepared for war should it become inevitable....

Knowing as I do Sir that I am among the persons who have been in your contemplation to be employed in the capacity I have mentioned, I should not have taken the present step, had I not been resolved at the same time to advise you with decision to drop me from the consideration and to fix upon another character. I am not unapprised of what has been the byass of your opinion on the subject. I am well aware of all the collateral obstacles which exist and I assure you in the utmost sincerity that I shall be completely and intirely satisfied with the election of another.

I beg leave to add that of the persons whom you would deem free from any constitutional objections—Mr. Jay is the only man in whose qualifications for success there would be a thorough confidence and him whom alone it would be adviseable to send. I think the business would have the best chance possible in his hands.

Even before he had received Hamilton's letter, the President had decided that John Jay would be the most suitable and popular choice for the mission to England. Meanwhile, the British minister, armed with the news that his Government had modified its order against neutral ships caught trading with the French colonies, tried to learn the intentions of the American Administration from the Secretary of the Treasury. George Hammond later described his vain efforts to extract information from Hamilton.

> [Philadelphia, April 15–16, 1794]
> I flattered myself that from communicating to him confidentially and informally the very conciliatory explanations, with which your Lordship [Lord Grenville] furnished me, of the instructions of the 6th of November and of the modifications of them on the 8th of January, I might derive the right of requiring an equal confidential communication on his part with relation to the special commission in question. I was however much surprized at perceiving that he did not receive those explanations with the cordiality I expected, but entered into a pretty copious recital of the injuries which the commerce of this country had suffered from British cruisers, and into a defense of the consequent claim which the American citizens had on their government to vindicate their rights.

Hammond and all of Philadelphia soon learned that Jay had been named to try to "settle all the grounds of dispute" with Britain. Federalist leaders now faced the task of deciding just what Jay's instructions should be. Hamilton urged that Jay should not only negotiate differences arising from Britain's wartime commercial codes and from the treaty of 1783, but should also negotiate a commercial treaty. Washington, however, bowed to Edmund Randolph's opinion that the matter should be left to Jay's "discretion" and was only to be considered if the more important problems were settled first. Hamilton nevertheless sent Jay a copy of his proposals for a trade agreement. In it, he admitted that the American public justly expected substantial reparations for British raids on American shipping; but he suggested that these reparations could be "more laxly dealt with if a truly beneficial treaty of Commerce" was concluded.

> Philadelphia May 6. 1794
> I see not how it can be disputed with you that this Country in a commercial sense is more important to G Britain than any other. The articles she takes from us are certainly precious to her, important perhaps essential to the ordinary subsistence of her Islands.... As a

Hamilton's draft of his instructions to John Jay on his peace mission to Great Britain, dated April 23, 1794

Consumer . . . we stand unrivalled. We now consume of her exports from a milion to [a] milion & a half Sterling more in value than any other foreign country & while the consumption of other countries from obvious causes is likely to be stationary that of this country is increasing and for a long, long, series of years, will increase rapidly. . . .

How unwise then in G Britain to suffer such a state of things to remain exposed to the hazard of constant interruption & derangement by not fixing on the basis of a good Treaty the principles on which it should continue? . . .

. . . But you will discover from your instructions that the opinion which has prevailed is that such a Treaty of commerce ought not to be *concluded* without previous reference here for further instruction. It is desireable however to push the British Ministry in this respect to a result that the extent of their views may be ascertained.

Hamilton did his best to see that Jay's mission went as smoothly as possible. One way to insure this was for Hamilton himself to remain in office. Although the select committee of the House had reported favorably on the Secretary's administration of the Treasury, and although Genêt's long-awaited successor, Jean Antoine Joseph Fauchet, seemed a marked improvement over the former French minister, the international situation still seemed too precarious for Hamilton to retire, as he informed Washington late in May.

Philadelphia May 27 1794

I some time since communicated an intention to withdraw from the office I hold, towards the close of the present session.

This I should now put in execution, but for the events, which have lately accumulated, of a nature to render the prospect of the continuance of our peace in a considerable degree precarious. I do not perceive, that I could voluntarily quit my post at such a juncture, consistently with considerations either of duty or character; and therefore I find myself relunctantly obliged to defer the offer of my resignation.

But if any circumstances should have taken place in consequence of the intimation of an intention to resign or should otherwise exist which serve to render my continuance in office in any degree inconvenient or ineligible, I beg leave to assure you Sir that I should yield to

John Jay by Trumbull

them with all the readiness naturally inspired by an impatient desire to relinquish a situation in which even a momentary stay is opposed by the strongest personal & family reasons & could only be produced by a sense of duty or Reputation.

Washington assured Hamilton that there was nothing "inconvenient" or "ineligible" in his decision to remain. Quite the contrary, the President wrote that he was pleased the Secretary would be staying "until the clouds over our affairs, which have come on so fast of late, shall be dispersed." Shortly after Jay sailed for London, the "clouds" broke a bit when the Senate defeated a House motion to extend the embargo. Congress adjourned on June 9, leaving the executive branch to guide America along the path of neutrality during the summer. But in July, family responsibilities began to absorb much of Hamilton's time. His two-year-old son John became seriously ill, and his wife Elizabeth was in the early months of a difficult pregnancy. It was decided to send her and the two youngest boys, James and the ailing John, to Albany. Hamilton took them as far as New York, then returned to Philadelphia on July 30 to look after his older children, Philip, Angelica, and Alexander. The next day he sent a note to Elizabeth.

> [Philadelphia] Thursday July 31. 1794
> I arrived here, My beloved Eliza, yesterday, too late to write by the Post—but am happy to be able to inform you that the precious little ones we left behind are well. As there is a vacation at this time, I propose sending the two youngest to Mrs. Morris's who has requested it, or to Mrs. Bradford's—I have not intirely determined which.
>
> I shall expect with infinite anxiety a letter from you & heaven Grant that it may bring me good tidings of the health of yourself & the dear Children with you. Alas my beloved Johnny—what shall I hear of you! This question makes my heart sink. Adieu.

With three lively youngsters demanding his attention in Philadelphia, Hamilton must have prayed for an uneventful summer in the Treasury Department. Instead, he was greeted by Francis Mentges, a colonel in the Pennsylvania militia, who had just returned from the disaffected western counties of that state. Mentges reported that a new "insurrection" was brewing on the Pennsylvania frontier, where there was violent opposition to the Federal Government's excise tax on whiskey. The tax, which had been imposed by Congress at Hamilton's urging in order to help pay for the Federal assumption of state debts, was especially hard on western farmers, who converted much of their grain into alcohol to cut down transportation costs. Hamilton carefully recorded Mentges's testimony concerning the rebellion.

[Philadelphia, August, 1794]

...Francis Mentges...maketh oath That he arrived at Pittsburgh in the County of Alleghanny on the 22 of July last past and continued there until the 25 of the same month. That it was there matter of public notoriety and general conversation that several collections of armed men had on the seventeenth of the same month successively made repeated attacks upon the house of General John Neville Inspector of the Revenue for and on account of his holding and exercising the said Office and to oblige him to relinquish the same...moreoever that David Lenox Marshall of the District had been taken into custody by some of the said armed collections in consequence of his having been there for the service of certain processes in relation to laws of the United States laying duties on distilled spirits and on stills but was afterwards released and that the said Marshall together with the said Inspector of the Revenue had descended the Ohio in a Boat to avoid personal violence or the being compelled by force to enter into engagements or do acts contrary to the duties of their respective Offices.... And the said Deponent further saith that on the twenty fourth of the same month of July he saw & conversed at Pittsburgh aforesaid with Hugh Brackenridge who informed him that he had been the day preceding at a Meeting...at Mingo Creek Meeting House in the County of Washington consisting generally of the most respectable people of that County...that it was there proposed that the Meeting should...pledge themselves to stand by each other until the Excise law was repealed and an Act of Oblivion passed—which proposition was not agreed to but instead of it it was proposed and agreed to that the four Western Counties of Pensylvania and the neighbouring counties of Virginia should be invited to assemble by delegates in a Convention to be holden on the fourteenth of this present Month of August in Mingo Creek...at Parkinson's [Ferry]...to take into consideration the situation of the Western Counties and adopt such measures as should appear suited to the

Orders issued by Hamilton as Secretary of the Treasury

exigency. And this Deponent further saith that from the general state of affairs in the said Western Counties of Pensylvania as they came under his observation he doth verily believe that it is intirely impracticable to execute the laws aforesaid by the means of civil process and Judiciary proceeding.

Events in western Pennsylvania were particularly disturbing to Hamilton. As a man concerned with governmental effectiveness and national honor, he found that resistance to Federal law (especially the law that helped finance his funding program) was a challenge that had to be met with prompt, decisive action. Along with other Cabinet members, Hamilton advised Washington to invoke a statute under which the President was empowered to call up the militia if he were "notified" by a member of the Supreme Court that military force was needed to enforce Federal law or suppress disorder. After forwarding the necessary documents to Associate Justice James Wilson, Washington and the Cabinet met with the Governor of Pennsylvania. During the conference, Hamilton responded to an assertion that the state judiciary could deal with the insurgents without the militia. The Secretary's remarks were reported in the minutes of the meeting.

[Philadelphia, August 2, 1794]
[The Secretary of the Treasury] insisted upon the propriety of an immediate resort to Military force. He said that it would not be sufficient to quell the existing riot to restore us to the state in which we were a few weeks back; for, before the present outrages, there was equal opposition to the laws of the U.S., though not expressed in the same manner; but that now the crisis was arrived when it must be determined whether the Government can maintain itself, and that the exertion must be made, not only to quell the rioters, but to protect the officers of the Union in executing their offices, and in compelling obedience to the laws.

Even as Justice Wilson was pondering the wisdom of "notifying" Washington that the militia was needed, Hamilton began planning troop movements. After the conference with Pennsylvania's Governor, he outlined his proposals to Washington.

Treasury Department August 2d. 1794
What force of Militia shall be called out, and from What State or States?

320

The force ought if attainable to be an imposing one, such if practicable, as will deter from opposition, save the effusion of the blood of Citizens and secure the object to be accomplished.

The quantum must of course be regulated by the resistance to be expected. Tis computed, that the four opposing Counties contain upwards of sixteen thousand males of 16 years and more, that of these about seven thousand may be expected to be armed. Tis possible that the union of the nieghbouring Counties of Virginia may augment this force. Tis not impossible, that it may receive an accession from some adjacent Counties of this state on this side of the Alleghany Mountains.

To be prepared for the worst, I am of opinion, that twelve thousand Militia ought to be ordered to assemble; 9000 foot and 3000 horse. . . .

The Law contemplates that the Militia of a State, in which an insurrection happens, if willing & sufficient shall first be employed, but gives power to employ the Militia of other States in the case either of refusal or insufficiency.

The Governor of Pennsylvania in an Official conference this day, gave it explicitly as his opinion to the President, that the Militia of Pennsylvania alone would be found incompetent to the suppression of the insurrection. . . .

I would submit then, that Pennsylvania be required to furnish 6000 men of whom 1000 to be horse, New-Jersey 2000 of whom 800 to be horse, Maryland 2000 of whom 600 to be horse, Virginia 2000, of whom 600 to be horse.

. . . The Militia called for to rendezvous at Carlisle in Pensylvania & Cumberland Fort in Virginia on the 10th of September next.

The law requires that previous to the using of force a Proclamation shall issue, commanding the Insurgents to disperse and return peaceably to their respective abodes within a limited time. This step must of course be taken.

NATIONAL COLLECTION OF FINE ARTS, WASHINGTON

James Wilson of Pennsylvania: a signer of the Declaration of Independence; Associate Justice of the Supreme Court, 1789–98

Two days later, Wilson gave the President the necessary "notification." As Washington began work on the proclamation that would precede military operations, Hamilton furnished the President with a history of the "insurrection," ending with an account of what happened when Marshal David Lenox attempted to serve writs on excise violators in July, 1794. Lenox and John Neville, the inspector of revenue in Allegheny County, were first attacked on the road. Then, on July 16, a band of one hundred men besieged Neville's house near Pittsburgh. Neville appealed to local courts, militia officers, and the county sheriff for protection, but was told that no aid could be given him because of the unpopularity of his office.

[Treasury Department, August 5, 1794]

The day following, the Insurgents reassembled with a considerable augmentation of numbers amounting as has been computed to at least 500 and on the 17th of July renewed their attack upon the House of the Inspector; who in the interval had taken the precaution of calling to his aid a small detachment from the garrison of Fort Pit which at the time of this attack consisted of 11 Men, who had been joined by Major Abraham Kirkpatrick a friend & connection of the Inspector.

There being scarcely a prospect of effectual defence against so large a body...and as the Inspector had every thing to apprehend for his person, if taken, it was judged adviseable that he should withdraw from the house to a place of concealment—Major Kirkpatrick generously agreeing to remain with the 11 men, in the intention if practicable to make a capitulation in favour of the property if not to defend it as long as possible.

A parly took place, under cover of a flag, which was sent by the Insurgents to the House to demand, that the Inspector should come forth, renounce his office and stipulate never again to accept an office under the same laws. To this it was replied, that the Inspector had left the house upon their first approach, and that the place to which he had retired was unknown. They then declared that they must have whatever related to his office....they insisted unconditionally, that the armed men who were in the house for its defence should march out & ground their arms; which Major Kirkpatrick peremptorily refused....This refusal put an end to the parley.

A brisk firing then ensued between the insurgents and those in the House, which it is said lasted for near an hour; 'till the assailants having set fire to all the neighbouring & adjacent buildings...the intenseness of the heat & the danger of an immediate communication of the fire to the house obliged Maj Kirk: & his small party to come out & surrender themselves.

Henry ("Light Horse Harry") Lee, cavalry officer in the Revolution and later Governor of Virginia

Henry Knox, the Secretary of War, having issued orders to the governors of New Jersey, Pennsylvania, Maryland, and Virginia to call out 12,950 militiamen, then left Philadelphia to look after his business interests in Maine. Hamilton, now Acting Secretary of War as well as head of the Treasury, still found time to write to his wife.

Henry Knox and Hamilton

[Philadelphia] August 12. 1794

If my darling child is better when this reaches you persevere in the plan which has made him so. If he is worse —abandon the laudanum & try the cold bath—that is abandon the laudanum by degrees giving it over night but not in the morning—& then leaving it off altogether. Let the water be put in the Kitchen over night & in the morning let the child be dipped in it head foremost wrapping up his head well & taking him again immediately out, put in flannel & rubbed dry with towels. Immediately upon his being taken out let him have two tea spoons full of brandy mixed with just enough water to prevent its taking away his breath.

Observe well his lips. If a glow succeeds continue the bath. If a chill takes place forbear it. If a glow succeeds the quantity of brandy may be lessened after the first experiment.

One burden was lifted from Hamilton's shoulders on August 21, when he learned that his wife and son were well enough to return to Philadelphia. But the news from western Pennsylvania was less encouraging. Three Federal commissioners sent to negotiate with the insurgents reported that they saw little hope for their mission and planned to return to the capital. Washington, Randolph, and Hamilton urged the commissioners to remain as long as possible, but on August 24, agreed to begin mobilizing the militia. To that end, Hamilton wrote to Governor Henry Lee of Virginia.

War Department August 25. 1794

In place of The Secretary at War, who is absent, I am instructed by The President to signify to you his wish and request that you will come forth in the command of the Militia, which is to be detached from Virginia against the Insurgents in the Western parts of Pensylvania; in which case You will have the command of the whole force that may be employed upon that Enterprise.

The President anticipates, that it will be as painful to you to execute, as it is to him to direct, measures of coertion against fellow citizens however misled. Yet he needed not the assurance you have already given him of the sense you entertain of their conduct and its consequences to be convinced that he might count ever on your zealous personal service, towards suppressing an example fatal in its tendency to every thing that is dear and valuable in political society.

In the next two weeks, the Federal commissioners sent encouraging reports of the insurgents' willingness to submit to the excise laws and accept an amnesty for earlier violations. But this did not satisfy the President, and Hamilton issued these orders to the governors involved in the militia call.

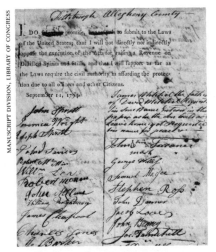

The participants in the Whisky Rebellion were allowed to go free after signing this oath to "submit to the Laws of the United States."

War Department Sepr 10th. 1794

This final resolution has been taken by the President in consequence of a very undecided state of things in the western Counties of this State when the last intelligence from thence came away. It appears that although the restoration of Order had gained powerful advocates & supporters; yet that there is a violent and numerous party which does not permit to count upon a submission to the laws without the intervention of force. Hence the advanced state of the Season considered, it became indispensable to put the force which had been provisionally called for in motion. I advise the appointment of a person in capacity of Quartermaster & Commissary of Military stores to the detachment with a competent Salary, I should think the pay & emoluments of a Major might suffice.

Although occupied with the supervision of troop movements and supply operations, Hamilton, who was still eager for military command, applied to the President for permission to accompany the expedition.

Philadelphia Sept 19 1794.

Upon full reflection I entertain an opinion, that it is adviseable for me, on public ground, considering the connection between the immediate ostensible cause of the insurrection in the Western Country and my department, to go out upon the expedition against the insurgents. In a government like ours, it cannot but have a good effect for the person who is understood to be the adviser or proposer of a measure, which involves danger to his fellow citizens, to partake in that danger: While, not to do it, might have a bad effect. I therefore request your permission for the purpose.

Pressed by the responsibilities of administering two departments, Hamilton rushed to put his affairs in order in time to join Washington when the President rode west to supervise the assembly of the militia. Finally, by the end of September, having authorized the comptroller, Oliver Wolcott, Jr., to act in his absence, Hamilton was ready to leave. But first he took a moment to write to his two sons at their school in New Jersey.

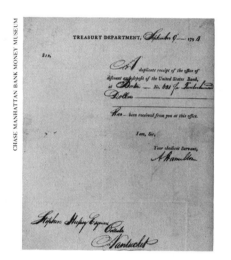

Hamilton signed this Treasury Department receipt for twelve hundred dollars received from a collector of revenue in Nantucket.

[Philadelphia, September 29, 1794]

Dear Children

We have been very sorry to hear that our dear Alexander has been unwell but thank God that he was better. We hope he will soon be quite well.

Your Mama will leave this place tomorrow or next day for Trenton to bring you herself to Town.

I expect to set out tomorrow for Carlisle. But you must not be uneasy about it. For by the accounts we have received there will be no fighting and of course no danger. It will only be an agreeable ride which will I hope do me good.

I give you both my best love & blessings as does your Mama. It will give me great pleasure when I come back to know that you have not neglected your studies & have been good boys during the vacation.

On September 30, Hamilton began his "agreeable ride" at Washington's side. When they reached Carlisle, Pennsylvania, on October 4, they found chastened delegates from the insurgents, who begged that the march be halted. Washington promised that there would be no bloodshed if the westerners submitted to Federal authority. The President continued his tour of other units of the militia and then, having set the campaign in motion, he prepared to return to Philadelphia, leaving Hamilton and the citizen-soldiers to continue the march under the command of Governor Lee of Virginia. Before riding east, however, Washington had Hamilton draft instructions for the Governor.

Bedford [Pennsylvania] 20th October 1794.

The objects of the military force are twofold.

1. To overcome any armed opposition which may exist.

325

*This painting by Kemmelmeyer shows
General Washington reviewing the
Western Army at Fort Cumberland
at the time of the Whisky Rebellion.*

2. To countenance and support the civil officers in the means of executing the laws.

With a view to the first of these two objects, you will proceed as speedily as may be, with the army under your command, into the insurgent counties to attack, and as far as shall be in your power subdue, all persons whom you may find in arms, in opposition to the laws above mentioned. You will march your army in two columns, from the places where they now are assembled...

When arrived within the insurgent Country, if an armed opposition appear, it may be proper to publish a proclamation, inviting all good citizens...to join the standard of the United States....

Of those persons in arms, if any, whom you may make prisoners; leaders, including all persons in command, are to be delivered up to the civil magistrate: the rest to be disarmed, admonished and sent home (except such as may have been particularly violent and also influential)....

The better to effect these purposes, the Judge of the District, Richard Peters Esquire, and the Attorney of the District, William Rawle Esquire, accompany the army.

You are aware that the Judge cannot be controuled in his functions. But I count on his disposition to cooperate in such a general plan as shall appear to you consistent with the policy of the case. But your method of giving a direction to legal proceedings, according to your general plan, will be by instruction to the District Attorney.

He ought particularly to be instructed, (with due regard to time and circumstance)—1st to procure to be arrested, all influential actors in riots and unlawful assemblies...and combinations to resist the laws... who shall not have complied with the terms offered by the Commissioners [the amnesty offered by the Federal commissioners at conferences with the insurgents on August 28 and 29]; or manifested their repentance in some other way, which you may deem satisfactory. 2dly. To cause process to issue for enforcing penalties on delinquent distillers. 3d. To cause *offenders*, who may be arrested, to be conveyed to goals where there will be no danger of rescue....4th. To prosecute indictable offences in the Courts of the United States—those for penalties on delinquents...in the courts of Pennsylvania.

To his wife, Hamilton sent this reassuring note on the eve of Washington's departure for Philadelphia.

Bedford [Pennsylvania] Oct 20 1794

I am very sorry that some of my sweet angels have been again sick. You do not mention my precious John. I hope he continues well.

The day after tomorrow I march with the army. Be assured that there is not the least appearance of opposition from the Insurgents & that I shall take the greatest care of myself & I hope by the Middle of November to return. Have patience my love & think of me constantly as I do of you with the utmost tenderness.

Kisses & blessings without number to You & my Children

As the militia marched from one tiny farmtown and crossroads village to another, it became obvious that the insurgents had given up any idea of armed resistance. Still, Hamilton was not convinced that the "disaffected country" had been pacified, and he made the following suggestion to Senator Rufus King.

Journalist Hugh H. Brackenridge became a justice of the supreme court of Pennsylvania in 1799.

Jones Mill [Pennsylvania] October 30. 1794

It is of great consequence that a law should if possible be expedited through Congress for raising 500 infantry & 100 horse to be stationed in the disaffected country. Without this the expence incurred will be essentially fruitless.

A law regulating a process of outlawry is also urgent; for the best objects of punishment will fly & they ought to be compelled by their outlawry to abandon their property houses & the UStates. This business must not be skinned over. The political putrefaction of Pensylvania is greater than I had any idea of. Without vigour every where our tranquillity is likely to be of very short duration & the next storm will be infinitely worse than the present one.

The prospect of seeing the insurgents punished kept Hamilton from returning to Philadelphia. On November 16, he reached Pittsburgh, where he confronted Hugh H. Brackenridge, a local journalist and politician who was suspected of having played a role in the insurrection. By the late summer of 1794, Brackenridge had seen the error of his ways and had assisted the Federal commissioners, but he had neglected to sign

327

the oath of submission to the excise laws before the time limit expired. Later, Brackenridge described his interview with Hamilton.

[Pittsburgh, November 18–19, 1794]

I was received by Hamilton, with that countenance, which a man will have, when he sees a person, with regard to whom his humanity and his sense of justice struggles;—he would have him saved, but is afraid he must be hanged;—was willing to treat me with civility, but was embarrassed with a sense, that, in a short time, I must probably stand in the predicament of a culprit, and be in irons. He began, by asking me some general questions, with regard to any system or plan, within my knowledge, of overthrowing the government. I had known of nothing of the kind. After a number of general questions, to which I had to answer in the negative, I proposed putting an end to that, by giving him a narrative of every thing I did know. It was agreed; and he began to write. I gave him the outlines of the narrative.... the secretary laid down his pen, and addressed himself to me; Mr. Brackenridge, said he, I observe one leading trait in your account, a disposition to excuse the principal actors; and before we go further, I must be candid, and inform you of the delicate situation in which you stand; *you are not within the amnesty; you have not signed upon the day;* a thing we did not know until we came... into the western country; and though the government may not be disposed to proceed rigorously, yet it has you in its power; and it will depend upon the candour of your account, what your fate will be....

[Brackenridge explained his actions to Hamilton all morning and at another conference that afternoon.]

After some time the secretary observed, "My breast begins to ach, we will stop to night; we will resume it tomorrow morning at 9 o'clock." I withdrew, but was struck with his last expression. I was at a loss to know whether his breast ached for my sake, or from the writing; but disposed to construe every thing unfavourable, I supposed it was for my sake, and that he saw I must be arrested....

Waiting on the secretary, at 9 o'clock [the morning of November 19], my examination recommenced. In the course of the narrative, his countenance began to

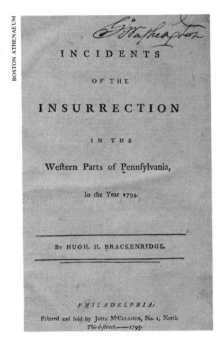

INCIDENTS

OF THE

INSURRECTION

IN THE

Weftern Parts of Pennfylvania,

In the Year 1794.

By HUGH H. BRACKENRIDGE.

PHILADELPHIA:

Printed and fold by JOHN M'CULLOCH, No. 1, North Third-ftreet.——1795.

The title page of Brackenridge's account of the Whisky Rebellion, from George Washington's library

brighten, and having finished the history, there was an end. "Mr. Brackenridge," said he, "in the course of yesterday I had uneasy feelings, I was concerned for you as for a man of talents; my impressions were unfavourable; you may have observed it. I now think it my duty to inform you, that not a single one remains. Had we listened to some people, I do not know what we might have done. There is a side to your account; your conduct has been horribly misrepresented, owing to misconception. I will announce you in this point to governor [Henry] Lee, who represents the executive. You are in no personal danger. You will not be troubled, even by a simple inquisition by the judge; what may be due to yourself with the public, is another question."

Later that day, Hamilton left Pittsburgh for Philadelphia, the insurrection having been suppressed without bloodshed. Feeling free at last to retire, Hamilton conferred with Washington, then informed Congress that he would resign from office at the end of January, 1795. When he wrote to his sister-in-law, Angelica Church, it was in a lighthearted vein.

Hamilton's draft of his last major report to Congress as Secretary of the Treasury, January, 1795

Philadelphia, December 8, 1794.

You say I am a politician, and good for nothing. What will you say when you learn that after January next, I shall cease to be a politician at all? So is the fact. I have formally and definitely announced my intention to resign at that period, and have ordered a house to be taken for me at New York.

My dear Eliza has been lately very ill. Thank God, she is now quite recovered, except that she continues somewhat weak. My absence on a certain expedition was the cause. . . .

Don't let Mr. Church be alarmed at my retreat—all is well with the public. Our insurrection is most happily terminated. Government has gained by it reputation and strength, and our finances are in a most flourishing condition. *Having contributed to place those of the Nation on a good footing, I go to take a little care of my own; which need my care not a little.*

On January 16, Hamilton submitted his last major report to Congress. Although James Madison complained that the Secretary had "got it in" by parliamentary trickery, the document was not the less valuable for the methods used to introduce it to the House. This, like his first great report, dealt with public credit and outlined the means by which the United States could erase the principal as well as the interest of the domestic debt. Perhaps its greatest virtue was not Hamilton's carefully considered recommendations, but the closing paragraphs, which captured the spirit of Hamilton's vision of the Treasury's role. Madison called the address a "valedictory," and indeed, it was a heartfelt, almost poetic, plea to Congress to guard the credit Hamilton had fought to establish for more than five years.

Treasury Department January 16. 1795

Credit public and private is of the greatest consequence to every Country. Of this, it might be emphatically called the invigorating principle. No well informed man, can cast a retrospective eye over the progress of the United States, from their infancy to the present period, without being convinced that they owe in a great degree, to the fostering influence of Credit their present mature growth....

There can be no time, no state of things, in which Credit is not essential to a Nation, especially as long as nations in general continue to use it, as a resource in war. It is impossible for a Country to contend on equal terms, or to be secure against the enterprises of other nations without being able equally with them to avail itself of this important resource. And to a young Country with moderate pecuniary Capital and not a very various industry, it is still more necessary than to Countries, more advanced in both; a truth not the less weighty for being obvious and frequently noticed....

But Credit is not only one of the main pillars of the public safety — it is among the principal engines of useful interprise and internal improvement. As a substitute for Capital it is little less useful than Gold or silver, in Agriculture, in Commerce, in the Manufacturing and mechanic arts....

If the individual Capital of this Country has become more adequate to its exigencies than formerly, 'tis because individuals have found new resources in the public *Credit*, in the funds to which *that* has given value and activity. Let Public Credit be prostrated, and the deficiency will be greater than before. Public and private Credit are closely allied, if not inseparable. There is perhaps no example of the one being in a flourishing, where the other was in a bad, state. A shock to public Credit would therefore not only take away the additional means

In this letter (above and opposite) Washington assures his retiring Treasury Secretary of his "sincere esteem, regard and friendship."

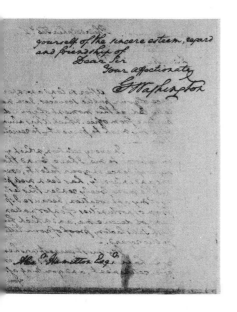

which it has furnished, but by the derangements, disorders distrusts and false principles, which it would engender and disseminate, would diminish the antecedent resources of private Credit. . . .

Credit is an *intire thing*. Every part of it has the nicest sympathy with every other part. Wound one limb, and the whole Tree shrinks and decays. The security of each Creditor is inseperable from the security of all Creditors. . . .

'Tis Wisdom in every case to cherish what is useful and guard against its abuse. 'Twill be the truest policy in the United States to give all possible energy to Public Credit, by a firm adherence to its strictest maxims, and yet to avoid the ills of an excessive employment of it, by true œconomy and system, in the public expenditures, by steadily cultivating peace, and by using sincere, efficient and persevering endeavors to diminish present debts, prevent the accumulation of new, and secure the discharge within a reasonable period of such as it may be matter of necessity to contract.

This, then, was the underlying theme of the seemingly unrelated incidents of Hamilton's years as Secretary of the Treasury. Funding, assumption, foreign relations, the defeat of recalcitrant distillers in the Pennsylvania mountains — all were part of a pattern that would give America firm public credit, which in turn would give the new nation a reputation for financial trustworthiness that would provide public security and an economic base for future expansion.

It was, too, Hamilton's best and most lasting legacy. While he often misunderstood the American people and their political leaders, Hamilton realized from the beginning that the young nation could not prosper without the "invigorating principle" of fiscal respectability. In part, he pursued this goal because of his concern for national honor. More practically, he knew that the United States could not preserve its independence or safety without the ability to borrow money in times of national emergency. Although Hamilton laid this foundation of credit for the "proper" government of his country, that foundation was solid enough to support the administrations of Federalists and Jeffersonian Republicans alike. Long after Hamilton's political theories and political allies had fallen into disrepute, that "pillar" he had described in his report of January 16, 1795, would stand.

Fifteen days after having made that report, Hamilton tendered his resignation and turned his office over to Oliver Wolcott, Jr. With the nation's credit assured, he could, at last, look to his own fortunes.

Chapter 12

A Man of Influence

When Hamilton left his post at the Treasury, he could feel confident that the administration was in good, if not brilliant, hands. Oliver Wolcott, although he might not be very imaginative, could supervise the progress of the programs Hamilton had inaugurated in capable fashion; and Henry Knox's successor in the War Department, Timothy Pickering, was an experienced military administrator. The government of Hamilton's home state, however, must have given him reason for dread. A New York "republican interest" had emerged in the gubernatorial campaign of 1792, just as it had on the national level that same year. While the New York Republicans were largely heirs to the Clintonian and Antifederalist factions, they had also recruited some of Hamilton's old friends and former allies. A variety of personal disappointments and ambitions had caused these defections from Federalist ranks. Chancellor Robert R. Livingston and his youngest brother, Edward, had led their family to the Republican side, and even Commodore James Nicholson, the naval hero who commanded the ship *Hamilton* in the 1788 ratification parade, worked for Clinton's election in 1792. But the fact that George Clinton had kept his office that year only by resorting to legalized election fraud demonstrated that the "republican interest" was not yet an effective Republican party.

Hamilton's policies in the Treasury gave New York's Republicans the incentive and issues they needed to create a meaningful organization after 1792. George Clinton embraced the French cause and even welcomed Edmond Genêt into his family as a son-in-law. British raids on neutral shipping gave Clinton's men a useful rallying point in a city that depended on trade, and in the spring of 1794, local Republicans were "clear for war." Although John Jay's mission to England had quieted them, they had still made large gains in local elections, and the Federal Government's suppression of the Whisky Rebellion that autumn may have helped Republicans win a majority of New York's congressional delegation.

Yet, although Hamilton had unwittingly helped the opposition "interest" become a strong "party," the state picture was not entirely dark when he returned to New York. In January, 1795, after Clinton announced that he would not seek another three-year term, the way was clear to run John Jay for office again despite his absence in London. If Jay returned to the United States with an agreement that settled Anglo-American differences and insured peace and prosperity for New York, the Republicans would lose their most important issue. With Jay in the governor's chair, the "friends of government," as the Federalists called themselves, could regain the congressional seats they had lost in 1794.

In general, then, Hamilton could congratulate himself on having discharged his public duties in such a way that he could at last concentrate on his obligations to his own family. His work in preserving America's credit and peace had forced him to neglect his wife and children too long. His sons would soon require the expensive educations necessary to fit them for their proper places in business and society. His wife had a special claim on his time and attention, since, when her sixth pregnancy ended in miscarriage, he had disregarded her pleas that he leave his militia command in western Pennsylvania to be with her in Philadelphia. Determined now to provide for his family's financial and emotional needs, Hamilton had, by mid-February, 1795, completed arrangements for moving his wife, sons, and daughter to New York. He and his family then traveled north to Albany for an extended visit with the Schuylers. Along the way, unable to forget his commitment to the maintenance of the public credit, Hamilton returned briefly to business matters. Having learned that Congress had rejected some minor proposals on the domestic debt, he wrote to Senator Rufus King.

> Kingston [New Jersey] Feby. 21. 1795
> The unnecessary capricious & abominable assassination of the National honor by the rejection of the propositions respecting the unsubscribed debt in the House ... haunts me every step I take, and afflicts me more than I can express. To see the character of the Government and the country so sported with, exposed to so indelible a blot puts my heart to the Torture. Am I then more of an American than those who drew their first breath on American Ground? Or What is it that thus torments me at a circumstance so calmly viewed by almost every body else? Am I a fool—a Romantic quixot—Or is there a constitutional defect in the American Mind?

There was little sign of a "Romantic quixot" in Hamilton's letter to his sister-in-law two weeks later, when he outlined very practical plans for his professional future.

[Albany, March 6, 1795]

Eliza & our children are with me here at your fathers house who is himself at New York attending the Legislature. We remain till June, when we become stationary at New York, where I resume the practice of the law. For My Dear Sister, I tell you without regret what I hope you anticipate, that I am poorer than when I went into office. I allot myself full five or six years of more work than will be pleasant though much less than I have had for the last five years.

The Federalist campaign to elect Jay was running smoothly in the spring of 1795, and Hamilton was able to concentrate on his own plans. Robert Troup, a New York attorney, suggested that he and Hamilton accept a retainer from a group of English and Dutch "Capitalists" who planned to buy lands in the Northwest Territory. Troup offered to arrange the transaction so that the former Secretary could invest in the speculation as well as serve as a legal adviser—and do so in complete secrecy. But Hamilton was determined to guard his reputation as carefully in private life as he had done while serving in the Treasury. Hamilton showed little interest in such ventures after his retirement, and profitable as this scheme might have been, he displayed no regrets when he wrote to Troup declining the offer.

Albany April 13. 1795

Tis not my Dear Friend that I think there is any harm or even indelicacy in the thing—I am now in no situation that restrains me—But 'tis because I think there is at present a great crisis in the affairs of [man]kind which may in its consequences involve this country in a sense most affecting to every true friend to it—because concerns of the nature alluded to, though very harmless in the *saints,* who may even fatten themselves on the opportunities or if you please spoils of office, as well as profit by every good thing that is going...[without] hazarding their popularity yet those who are not of the *regenerat*[*ing*] tribe may not do the most unexceptionable things without its being thundered in their ears—without being denounced as speculators peculators British Agents &c. &c. Because there must be some *public fools* who sacrifice private to public interest at the certainty of ingratitude and obloquy—because my *vanity* whispers I ought to be one of those fools and ought to keep myself in a situation the best calculated to render service....

Bust of John Jay by John Frazer

The game to be played may be a most important one. It may be for nothing less than true liberty, property, order, religion and of course *heads*. I will try Troupe if possible to guard yours and mine.

Hamilton was called upon to "render service" shortly after his family moved to New York City at the end of May. The treaty negotiated in London by John Jay was kept secret even after the Senate began debates on ratification in early June, but gossip about its provisions spread quickly. The twelfth article, limiting American trading privileges in the West Indies, was particularly controversial, and Hamilton made a shrewd suggestion to Rufus King.

In 1795 Hamilton was granted the "freedom of the city" by the mayor and aldermen of New York, in testimony of their high esteem.

New York June 11. 1795

It is to be observed that no time is fixed for the ratification of the Treaty. It may then be ratified with a collateral instruction to make a declaration that the UStates consider the article in question aggregately taken as intended by the King of G B as a privilege; that they conceive it for their interest to forbear the exercise of that privilege . . . till an explanation in order to a new modification of it shall take place on a more acceptable footing or *till an article to be sent to our minister containing that modification shall be agreed upon between him & the British Court as a part of the Treaty*—the ratification not to [be] exchanged without further instruction from this country unless accepted in this sense and with this qualification.

This was the course the Senate took, voting on June 24 to ratify all of Jay's treaty except the twelfth article. Officially, the treaty remained a "mystery." Unofficially, its provisions were published in the New York press three days after John Jay took office as governor on July 1, 1795. But new British captures of American ships made Washington reluctant to sign the agreement, and he sought Hamilton's opinion. The former Secretary promptly sent the President his "Remarks."

[New York, July 9–11, 1795]

The truly important side of this Treaty is that it closes and upon the whole as reasonably as could have been expected the controverted points between the two Countries—and thereby gives us the prospect of repossessing our Western Posts, an object of primary consequence in our affairs—of escaping finally from

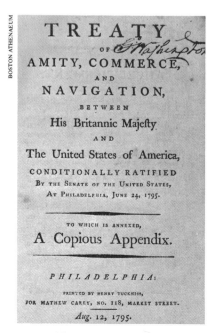

TREATY
OF *Washington*

AMITY, COMMERCE,
AND
NAVIGATION,
BETWEEN
His Britannic Majesty
AND
The United States of America,
CONDITIONALLY RATIFIED
By the Senate of the United States,
At Philadelphia, June 24, 1795.

TO WHICH IS ANNEXED,
A Copious Appendix.

PHILADELPHIA:
PRINTED BY HENRY TUCKNISS,
FOR MATHEW CAREY, NO. 118, MARKET STREET.
Aug. 12, 1795.

Washington's own signed copy of Jay's treaty with Great Britain

being implicated in the dreadful war which is ruining Europe—and of preserving ourselves in a state of peace for a considerable time to come.

Well considered, the greatest interest of this Country in its external relations is that of peace. The more or less of commercial advantages which we may acquire by particular treaties are of far less moment. With peace, the force of circumstances will enable us to make our way sufficiently fast in Trade. War at this time would give a serious wound to our growth and prosperity. Can we escape it for ten or twelve years more, we may then meet it without much inquieture and may advance and support with ener[g]y and effect any just pretensions to greater commercial advantages than we may enjoy.

It follows that the objects contained in the permanent articles are of real and great value to us.... The terms are no way inconsistent with national honor.

Despite Hamilton's arguments, Washington left for Mount Vernon without having signed the treaty. His hesitation only encouraged critics, who called for a meeting at City Hall in New York on July 18 to consider the best "mode of communicating to the President their disapprobation of the English treaty." Hamilton attended as well, and the New York *Journal* described the events of the weekend.

New-York, July 22 [1795].

At the moment the clock struck *twelve*, Mr. *Hamilton*, who was mounted upon a stoop in Broad-street, supported by *Mr. King*...&c. attempted to harrangue the people. He had proceeded no farther than an expression of his ignorance *who called the meeting*, before he was interrupted by the call, "Let us have a chairman;" on which *Col. William S. Smith* was nominated, appointed, and took his stand upon the balcony of the Federal Hall.

Mr. Peter R. Livingston then attempted to address the chair, but was interrupted by Mr. Hamilton; on which a question of order took place, whether Mr. H. or Mr. L. should speak first; this was...carried, by a large majority, in favor of Mr. L. Mr. Livingston then attempted to state the business of the meeting,...but the confusion was so great, that he could not be heard— and, finding that there was an intention, by the oppo-

This 1797 water color, the only existing contemporary view of New York's upper Broad Street, looks uptown to Federal Hall.

site party, to defeat the object of the meeting, and prevent the questions being taken on the treaty, he moved, *"That those who disapproved of the treaty, should go to the right, and those who approved of it, to the left;"* which motion was but partly carried into effect; a large body marched up to the church, a large body still remained on the ground, and none, upon the question being reversed, moved to the left....

Finding it impossible to effect a division, those who had drawn off now returned; but finding a great tumult, about 500 of them drew off again, proceeded to the battery, formed a circle, and there BURNT *the treaty*, opposite the government house.

During this interval, Mr. Hamilton introduced a resolution, said to be pened by *Mr.* King, and transmitted it to the Chairman, who attempted to read it, and, behold, a momentary silence took place—but when the citizens found that the resolution *declared it unnecessary to give an opinion on the treaty*, they roared, as with one voice *we'll hear no more of it; tear it up*, &c.

The question was then moved, and carried, for the appointment of a committee of 15, to draft RESOLUTIONS *"expressive of their disapprobation of the treaty."*...

Mr. Hamilton, before the appointment of the Committee, finding the question of his resolutions could not obtain in the *great body*, put the question *(himself)* to those around him, some of whom cried *aye*—after which he called to the *friends of order* to follow him, and they moved off the ground, but the number that followed was small.

New York's customhouse, c. 1796

Not only was Hamilton's circle of friends small that day, but the number of his enemies was increasing. When he tried to play peacemaker between Federalist Josiah Ogden Hoffman and Republican James Nicholson, he found himself the target of Nicholson's anger. Trying to clarify matters, Hamilton later prepared a formal description of his version of the incident.

[New York, July 25–26, 1795]

Mr. Hamilton declares & would repeat that when he interposed in the altercation between Mr. Nicholson & Mr. Hoffman what he said was addressed to both & was purely intended without offence to either to pre-

Jay burned in effigy by opponents of his treaty with Great Britain

vent the continuance of a controversy which might lead to disturbance & riot.

Mr. Nicholson replied very harshly to Mr. Hamilton that he was not the man to prevent his quarrelling called him an Abettor of Tories and used some other harsh expressions which are forgotten.

Mr. Hamilton replied that that was not a place for altercation & Mr. Nicholson & he would discuss it upon a more fit occasion.

Mr. Nicholson replied he & Mr. Hamilton would not pursue the affair for he [Hamilton] had declined an interview upon a former occasion.

Mr. Hamilton replied that no man could affirm that with truth & that he pledged himself to convince Mr. Nicholson of his mistake.

On July 20, Hamilton challenged Commodore Nicholson to a duel. For almost forty-eight hours, Hamilton and Nicholson exchanged notes. Then their seconds tried to work out some form of apology that would settle the affair. Agreement was finally reached, and the Commodore and the Colonel were able to avoid a duel with their reputations intact. This was of considerable value to the Federalists, since Hamilton had begun to publish his monumental defense of Jay's treaty, the essays of "Camillus." This series, titled "The Defence," was signed with the name of the legendary hero who had saved Rome from invasion by the Gauls in the fourth century. The first number, printed in the New York *Argus*, warned Americans of a threat of another kind.

[New York, July 22, 1795]

It is only to know the vanity and vindictiveness of human nature, to be convinced, that while this generation lasts, there will always exist among us, men irreconciliable to our present national constitution....It is a material inference from this, that such men will watch with Lynx's eyes for opportunities of discrediting the proceedings of the government, and will display a hostile and malignant zeal upon every occation, where they think there are any prepossessions of the community to favor their enterprizes. A treaty with Great Britain was too fruitful an occasion not to call forth all their activity.

It is only to consult the history of nations to perceive, that every country, at all times, is cursed by the existence of men, who, actuated by an irregular

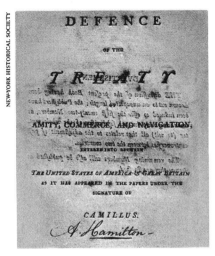

*Title page of Hamilton's personal
copy of his essays by "Camillus"*

ambition, scruple nothing which they imagine will contribute to their own advancement and importance. In monarchies, supple courtiers; in republics, fawning or turbulent demagogues, worshipping still the idol power wherever placed, whether in the hands of a prince, or of the people, and trafficking in the weaknesses, vices, frailties, or prejudices of the one or the other. It was to have been expected, that such men, counting more on the passions than on the reason of their fellow citizens, and anticipating that the treaty would have to struggle with prejudices, would be disposed to make an alliance with popular discontent, to nourish it, and to press it into the service of their particular views.

By the end of August, Washington had signed the treaty, but Hamilton still defended Administration policies in public as "Camillus" and offered advice to the Government in private. More than ever Washington needed the aid of his former Secretary of the Treasury. Edmund Randolph had resigned as Secretary of State after an intercepted dispatch from Fauchet, the former French minister, made it appear that he had solicited a bribe. Randolph's departure and the death of Attorney General William Bradford created two vacancies in the Cabinet. But no one seemed eager to join the Administration, and by the time Washington wrote to Hamilton on October 29 to ask, "What am I to do for a Secretary of State," four men had refused the post. A week later, Hamilton replied, reporting, first of all, that a fifth man, Rufus King, had now rejected the President's offer.

New York November 5th 1795
Circumstances of the moment conspire with the disgust which a virtuous and independent mind feels at placing itself *in but* to the foul and venomous shafts of calumny which are continually shot by an odious confederacy against Virtue—to give Mr. King a decided disinclination to the office.

I wish Sir I could present to you any useful ideas as a substitute. But the embarrassment is extreme as to Secretary of State. An Attorney General I believe may be easily fixed upon by a satisfactory choice....

But for a Secretary of State I know not what to say. [William Loughton] *Smith* [congressman from South Carolina] though not of full size is very respectable for talent & has pretty various information. I think he has more real talent than the last incumbent of the Office. But there are strong objections to his appointment. I fear he is of an uncomfortable temper. He is popular with no description of men from a certain *hardness* of character and he more than most other men is considered as tinctured with prejudices towards the British....

Mr. Innis [James Innes], I fear is too absolutely lazy for Secy of State. The objection would weigh less as to Atty General....

Judge [Nathaniel] Pendleton writes well is of respectable abilities and a Gentlemanlike smooth man. If I were sure of his political views I should be much disposed to advise his appointment under the circumstances. But I fear he has been somewhat tainted with the prejudices of Mr. Jefferson & Mr. Madison & I have afflicting suspicions concerning these men....

In fact a first rate character is not attainable. A second rate must be taken with good dispositions & barely decent qualifications. I wish I could throw more light. Tis a sad omen for the Government.

Apparently conceding that a "first rate character" could not be found, Washington transferred Timothy Pickering to the State Department. Two months later, Hamilton visited Philadelphia for the first time since his resignation from the Cabinet. The Government's case for the constitutionality of the "carriage tax" was being argued before the Supreme Court, and since this tax had been enacted at his own urging in June, 1794, Hamilton felt a special responsibility for its vindication. Opponents contended that it was a "direct" tax, which, under the Constitution, had to be levied in proportion to state population. Hamilton persuaded the Court to uphold the measure with this common-sense argument on the definition of "direct" and "indirect" taxes.

February 24, 179[6]

The following are presumed to be the only direct taxes.

Capitation or poll taxes.

Taxes on lands and buildings.

General assessments, whether on the whole property of individuals, or on their whole real or personal estates....

To apply a rule of apportionment according to numbers to taxes of the above description, has some *rationale* in it; but to extend an apportionment of that kind to other cases, would, in many instances, produce ... preposterous consequences, and would greatly embarrass the operations of the government....

The Constitution gives power to Congress to lay and collect the taxes, duties, imposts, and excises, requiring that all duties, imposts, and excises shall be uniform throughout the United States.

Here *duties*, *imposts*, and *excises* appear to be contradistinguished from *taxes*, and while the latter is left to apportionment, the former are enjoined to be uniform.

But, unfortunately, there is equally here a want of criterion to distinguish *duties*, *imposts* and *excises* from taxes.

If the meaning of the word *excise* is to be sought in the British statutes, it will be found to include the duty on carriages... and not liable to apportionment; consequently not a direct tax.

An argument results from this, though not perhaps a conclusive one: yet where so important a distinction in the Constitution is to be realized, it is fair to seek the meaning of terms in the statutory language of that country from which our jurisprudence is derived.

Timothy Pickering

James McHenry's appointment as Secretary of War and Charles Lee's nomination as Attorney General completed the roster of "second rate" men who now made up Washington's official family of advisers. Such men made it more difficult than ever to handle pressing issues, and during Hamilton's stay in Philadelphia the President often turned to him for advice and counsel—particularly concerning Republican opposition to Jay's treaty. Having finally received official notice that ratifications had been exchanged in London, the President had proclaimed the treaty in effect and had submitted it to the House of Representatives on March 1. The House was responsible for voting funds to implement the agreement, and even though congressional Republicans could not undo the treaty, they could still embarrass the Administration. Thus, when Edward Livingston of New York introduced resolutions demanding that House members be allowed to see Jay's official instructions and correspondence, Hamilton wrote to Washington suggesting a plan of action.

New York March 7th. 1796

If the motion succeeds, it ought not to be complied with. Besides that in a matter of such a nature the production of the papers cannot fail to start [a] new and unpleasant Game—it will be fatal to the Negotiating Power of the Government if it is to be a matter of

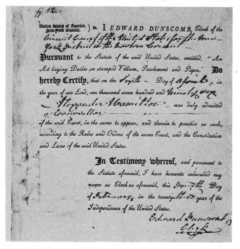

Hamilton's 1796 certificate to practice law before the United States Circuit Court

course for a call of either House of Congress to bring forth all the communication however confidential.

It seems to me that something like the following answer by the President will be adviseable.

"A right in the House of Representatives, to demand and have as a matter of course, and without specification of any object all communications respecting a negotiation with a foreign power cannot be admitted without danger of much inconvenience. A discretion in the Executive Department how far and where to comply in such cases is essential to the due conduct of foreign negotiations and is essential to preserve the limits between the Legislative and Executive Departments. The present call is altogether indefinite and without any declared purpose. The Executive has no cases on which to judge of the propriety of a compliance with it and cannot therefore without forming a very dangerous precedent comply."

Washington refused the House demand, but the Republicans attacked on another front. On April 15, the House adopted resolutions submitted by Congressman William Blount (and drafted by James Madison) declaring that Congress had a right to pass on portions of treaties involving matters that were the constitutional responsibility of the House, and further, that the President must make available any information that concerned House functions. In effect, these resolutions were intended to justify the House's refusal to vote funds for implementing Jay's treaty. When he heard of these developments, Hamilton wrote to Senator Rufus King.

New York April 15. 1796

To me our true plan appears to be the following....

I The President ought immediately after the House has taken the ground of refusal to send them a solemn Protest....

A copy of this protest to be sent to the Senate for their information. The Senate by resolutions to express strongly their approbation of his principles, to assure him of their firm support & to advise him to proceed in the execution of the Treaty....

Then the Merchants to meet in the Cities & second by their resolutions the measures of the President & Senate further addressing their fellow Citizens to cooperate with them. Petitions afterwards to be handed

Patrick Henry

throughout the U States.

The Senate to hold fast & consent to no adjournment till the expiration of the term of service of the present House unless provision [is] made.

The President to cause a confidential communication to be made to the British stating candidly what has happened; his regrets, his adherence nevertheless to the Treaty....

I prefer that measures should begin with a Protest of the President—as it will be in itself proper & there will be more chance of success if the Contest appears to be with him & the Senate auxiliaries than in the reverse.

But in all this business celerity decision & an imposing attitude are indispensable. The Glory of the President, the safety of the Constitution, the greatest interests, depend upon it. Nothing will be wanting here. I do not write to the President on the subject.

Congressional Republicans backed down and voted funds for Jay's treaty, not so much because of merchants' protests as because of Rufus King's threat to make appropriations for this treaty a rider to any and all treaty bills that came to the Senate. Federalists could now concentrate on choosing a candidate to succeed Washington in the fall elections. King had wooed Patrick Henry of Virginia, a former Antifederalist. Thomas Pinckney, America's minister to Britain, was also mentioned prominently. Either of these southerners, it was believed, would have a better chance than would Vice President John Adams. Early in May, Hamilton discussed Federalist strategy with King.

[New York] May 4 1796

I am intirely of opinion that P. H [Patrick Henry] declining Mr. P_____ [Pinckney] ought to be our man. It is even an idea of which I am fond in various lights. Indeed on latter reflection, I rather wish to be rid of P.H, that we may be at full liberty to take up Pinckney.

In the event of Pinck[n]ey's return to this Country, I am of opinion all circumstances considered, it is expedient you should replace him. I hope no great question will in a short period agitate our Councils & I am sure you will do much good on the scene in question. I have called on Jay, but happened not to find him disengaged. I shall quickly see him & shall with great pleasure do every thing requisite on my part.

Thomas Pinckney

343

Senator King admitted that he was "not a little tired" of his legislative burden, and Hamilton passed the information along to Washington. The President reacted promptly by naming King as Thomas Pinckney's successor. Meanwhile, another problem arose that required Hamilton's advice. Rumor had it that members of the French Directory were so displeased with Jay's treaty that they were going to send a special envoy to raise protests and perhaps even demand that the United States aid the French colonies in the West Indies. As yet, no such person had arrived, but Washington was worried about what his response should be, and he asked Hamilton to discuss the matter with Jay. Hamilton replied calmly that it was pointless to be apprehensive before America learned the intentions of the Directory; and he counseled the President about the possibility that France might go so far as to demand a renunciation of Jay's treaty.

New York May 20. 1796

The answer will naturally be that this sacrifice of the positive & recent engagements of the country is pregnant with consequences too humiliating and injurious to us to allow us to believe that the expectation can be persisted in by France since it is to require a thing impossible & to establish as the price of the continuance of Friendship with us the sacrifice of our honor by an act of perfidy which would destroy the value of our friendship to any Nation. That, besides, the Executive...is not competent to it—it being of the province of Congress by a declaration of War or otherwise in the proper cases to annul the operation of Treaties....

If the Guarantee of the West Indies should be claimed—The answer may be—

"That the decision of this question belongs to Congress who if it be desired will be convened to deliberate upon it." I presume & hope they will have adjourned. For to [gain] time is every thing.

Hamilton had been conscientiously reporting to Washington every rumor of French attacks on merchant vessels, and the President responded with understandable alarm. Troubled, too, by the conduct of his minister to Paris, James Monroe, who was an enthusiastic supporter of the Directory, Washington asked Hamilton and Governor Jay to discuss, among "other interesting matters," the possibility of sending a new special envoy to France. Hamilton reported the results of these conferences to the President.

New York July 5. 1796

We are both of opinion there is *no* power in the President to appoint an Envoy Extraordinary, without the concurrence of the Senate, & that the information in question is *not* a sufficient ground for extraordinarily convening the senate. If however the President from his *information collectively* be convinced that a dangerous state of things exists between us & France and that an envoy extraordinary to avert the danger is a necessary measure, I believe this would in the sense of the constitution warrant the calling of the Senate for the purpose....

Mr. Jay & Myself though somewhat out of your question talked of the expediency of removing Monroe, and though we perceive there are weighty reasons against it, we think those for it preponderate—if a proper man can be found. But here we feel both immense embarrassment, for he ought to be at the same time a friend to the Government & understood to be *not unfriendly* to the French Revolution. General [Charles Cotesworth] Pinckney is the only man we can think of who fully satisfies the idea, & unfortunately every past experiment forbids the hope that he would accept—though but for a short time. But if a character of tolerable fitness can be thought of, it would seem expedient to send him. At any rate it is to be feared, if...no *actual* & *full* explanation takes place, it will bring serious censure upon the Executive. It will be said that it did not display as much zeal to avoid misunderstanding with France as with G Britain....

As to your resignation, Sir, it is not to be regretted that the declaration of your intention should be suspended as long as possible & suffer me to add that you should *really hold the thing undecided to the last moment.* I do not think it is in the power of party to throw any slur upon the lateness of your decl[a]ration. And you have an obvious justification in the state of things. If a storm gathers, how can you retreat? This is a most serious question.

Washington wears a lace cravat in Adolph Wertmüller's 1795 portrait.

Washington replied that he should have issued a farewell address the day after Congress adjourned and urged Hamilton to finish drafting such a message as quickly as possible. Meanwhile, the President decided to send Charles Pinckney to Paris to replace James Monroe. On July 30, Hamilton completed the manuscript of the President's Farewell Address. He had tried, he told Washington, to make it *"importantly* and *lastingly* useful." With the exception of some of the more partisan passages, Washington found it to be just that. Opening with a declaration that Washington would decline reelection, Hamilton's draft then turned to "some sentiments" on the nation's future course.

[New York, July 30, 1796]

Interwoven as is the love of Liberty with every fibre of your hearts no recommendation is necessary to fortify your attachment to it. Next to this that unity of Government which constitutes you one people claims your vigilant care & guardianship—as a main pillar of your real independence of your peace safety freedom and happiness.

This being the point in your political fortress against which the batteries of internal and external enemies will be most constantly and actively however covertly and insidiously levelled, it is of the utmost importance that you should appreciate in its full force the immense value of your political Union to your national and individual happiness—that you should cherish towards it an affectionate and immoveable attachment and that you should watch for its preservation with jealous solicitude....

The great rule of conduct for us in regard to foreign Nations ought to be to have as little *political* connection with them as possible—so far as we have already formed engagements let them be fulfilled—with circumspection indeed but with perfect good faith. Here let us stop.

Europe has a set of primary interests which have none or a very remote relation to us. Hence she must be involved in frequent contests the causes of which will be essentially foreign to us....

Our detached and distant situation invites us to a different course & enables us to pursue it. If we remain a united people under an efficient Government the period is not distant when we may defy material injury from external annoyance—when we may take such an attitude as will cause the neutrality we shall at any time resolve to observe to be violated with caution...when we may choose peace or war as our interest guided by justice shall dictate.

Why should we forego the advantages of so felicitous a situation? Why quit our own ground to stand upon Foreign ground? Why by interweaving our destiny with any part of Europe should we intangle our prosperity and peace in the nets of European Ambition rivalship interest or Caprice?

Permanent alliance, intimate connection with any part of the foreign world is to be avoided.

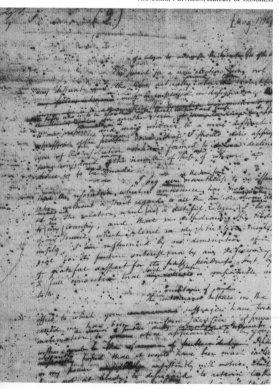

The first page of Hamilton's draft of Washington's Farewell Address

Even when the Farewell Address had been revised and published, Washington was not free of official burdens. Arriving in Philadelphia to serve out the last months of his term, he discovered in an issue of the *Aurora* a letter to Pickering from Pierre Adet, the new French minister, complaining that France's protests had not been answered by the American Government. Because it was not clear whether Adet had taken this step on order from the Directory, Washington—in what was now a familiar pattern—asked Hamilton and Jay to discuss Adet's status. Hamilton sent the President this report.

Pierre Adet

[New York] November 4. 1796

We settled our opinion on one point—(viz) That whether Mr. Adet acted with or without instruction from his Government in publishing his communication, he committed a disrespect towards our government which ought not to pass *unnoticed,* and would most properly be *noticed* to him as the Representative or Agent. That the manner of noticing it, in the first instance at least, ought to be *negative,* that is, by the *personal conduct* of the President towards the Minister. That the true rule on this point would be to receive the Minister...with a *dignified reserve,* holding an *exact medium* between an *offensive coldness* and *cordiality.* The *point* is [a] nice one to be hit, but no one will know better how to do it than the President.

Meanwhile, Washington decided to publish a reply to Adet's appeal, prepared by Secretary Pickering. The exchanges between Adet and the Secretary of State continued until November 15. Then, deliberately timing his announcement to coincide with the American elections, the French minister declared that his Government considered Jay's treaty a violation of the 1778 Franco-American treaties of alliance and commerce and equivalent to an alliance with Great Britain; and that therefore he had been ordered "to suspend...his ministerial functions." Three weeks later, the New York *Minerva* carried Hamilton's essay, "The Answer," which opened with this analysis of French policies.

[December 8, 1796]

The French republic have, at various times, during the present war, complained of certain principles, and decisions of the American government, as being violations of its neutrality, or infractions of the treaty made with France in the year 1778....They are now not only renewed with great exaggeration, but the French government have directed that it should be done *in the tone of*

James Watson

reproach, instead of the language of friendship. The apparent intention of this menacing tone, at this particular time, is to influence timid minds to vote agreeable to their wishes in the election of president and vice-president, and probably with this view, the memorial was published in the news-papers. This is certainly a practice that must not be permitted. If one foreign minister is permitted to publish what he pleases to the people, in the name of his government, every other foreign minister must be indulged with the same right. What then will be our situation on the election of a president and vice president, when the government is insulted, the persons who administer it, traduced, and the electors menaced by public addresses from these intriguing agents?

Adet's publications came too late to affect the choice of presidential electors in most states, but the New York congressional elections were not held until December. One New York newspaper remarked that Hamilton "patroles the whole city and strains every nerve in favor of the yankey candidate," Federalist James Watson. But when the polls opened on December 13, the incumbent congressman, Republican Edward Livingston, pulled ahead. Within a few days, Hamilton had learned enough about the races for the Electoral College and for the New York delegation to Congress to send this summary of the political picture to Rufus King in London.

Edward Livingston

New York Decr. 16. 1796

If we may trust our information, which there is every reason to trust, it is now decided that neither *Jefferson* nor *Burr* can be President. It must be either *Adams* or *Pinckney*, the *first most probably.* By the throwing away of votes in New England lest *Pinkney* should outrun *Adams,* it is not unlikely that Jefferson will be *Vice* President. The event will not a little mortify *Burr....*

After giving you these consolatory accounts, I am now to dash the Cup a little, by telling you that *Livingston* is in all probability reelected in the City....

But in the state at large we shall better our representation, and I hope for a majority in the next house of Representatives. As an omen of this, there are several *new members* in Congress from different states, who hitherto vote with our friends.

The favourable change in the conduct of Great Britain towards us strengthens the hand of the friends of Order & peace....

As Hamilton had predicted, John Adams won election as the second President of the United States. But Washington, even in the last weeks of his term, still faced major problems. Some advisers suggested that a special envoy be sent to Paris, just as John Jay had been sent to London in a similar crisis in 1794; but Washington hesitated to take this step lest it offend his newly appointed minister to Paris, Charles Cotesworth Pinckney. Once again, the President asked Hamilton's advice, and the former Secretary made this suggestion.

[New York, January 25–31, 1797]

I have reflected as maturely as time has permitted on the idea of an extraordinary mission to France, and notwithstanding the objections, I rather incline to it under some shape or other. As an imitation of what was done in the case of Great Britain, it will argue to the people equal solicitude. To France it will have a similar aspect (for Pinckney will be considered there as a mere substitute in ordinary course to Mr. Monroe) and will in some degree soothe her pride. The influence on party, if a man in whom the opposition has confidence is sent, will be considerable in the event of non success. And it will be to France a bridge over which she may more easily retreat.

The best form of the thing in my view is a commission including three persons who may be called "*Commissioners* Plenipotentiary & extraordinary." Two of the three should be Mr. Madison and Mr. Pinckney. A third may be taken from the Northern states and I know none better than Mr. [George] *Cabot*—who or any *two* of whom may be empowered to act. . . .

Or (which however I think less eligible) Mr. Madison & Mr. Pinkney only may be joint Commissioners—without a third person.

Mr. Cabot . . . will I think certainly go. If not the other two may act without him. . . .

Unless Mr. *Madison* will go there is scarcely another character that will afford advantage.

ADAMS NATIONAL HISTORIC SITE

This portrait of John Adams was painted by William Winstanley in 1798, during Adams's Presidency.

Despite Hamilton's urging, Washington did not appoint a commission. Writing to Rufus King, Hamilton saw little reason for optimism in the conduct of Congress or in the new Administration of John Adams.

[New York] Feby. 15. 1797

The present session of Congress is likely to be very unproductive. That body is in the situation which we foresaw certain *anti* executive maxims would bring them to.

Mr. Adams is President, Mr. Jefferson Vice President. Our Jacobins say they are well pleased and that the *Lion* & the *Lamb* are to lie down together. Mr. Adam's *personal* friends talk a little in the same way. Mr. *Jefferson* is not half so ill a man as we have been accustommed to think him. There is to be a united and a vigorous administration. Sceptics like me quietly look forward to the event—willing to hope but not prepared to believe. If Mr. Adams has *Vanity* to plan a plot has been laid to take hold of it. We trust his real good sense and integrity will be a sufficient shield.

On reflection, Hamilton realized that Adams could appoint the commission and might be in a better position to do so than Washington had been. Toward the end of February, Hamilton began his campaign to influence the new Executive with this letter to Adams's old friend Theodore Sedgwick.

[New York] Feby. 26. 1797

It is a fact, that the resentment of the French Government is very much levelled at the actual President. A change of the person (however undespicable in other respects) may give a change to the passion, and may also furnish a bridge to retreat over. This is a great advantage for a new President & the most ought to be made of it. For it is much our interest to preserve peace, if we can with honor, and if we cannot it will be very important to prove that no endeavour to do it has been omitted.

Were I Mr. Adams, then I believe I should begin my Presidency by naming an extraordinary Commission to the French Republic. And I think it would consist of three persons, Mr. Madison Mr. Pinkney & Mr. Cabot.

As a result of dispatches from Paris, opinion in favor of a special mission to France began growing during March. The Directory, having accepted James Monroe's letter of recall, had refused to receive Charles Pinckney as his successor until French grievances were remedied. Hamilton knew the time was propitious to reintroduce his plan. His task was easier, since John Adams had retained all the members of Washington's Cabinet, and these were men who were used to receiving and following the advice of the former Secretary of the Treasury. In mid-March, Hamilton wrote to Secretary of State Pickering.

A page from the letter in which Hamilton supplied the answers to the questions John Adams asked of his War Secretary in April, 1797

[New York] March 22. 1797

It is now ascertained that Mr. Pinckney has been refused and with circumstances of indignity. What is to be done? The share I have had in the public administration added to my interest as a Citizen make me extremely anxious that at this delicate Crisis a course of conduct exactly proper may be adopted. I offer to your consideration without ceremony what appears to me such a course.

First. I would appoint a day of humiliation and prayer.... it will be politically useful to impress our nation that there is a serious state of things — to strengthen religious ideas in a contest which in its progress may require that our people may consider themselves as the defenders of their Country against Atheism conquest & anarchy. It is far from evident to me that the progress of the war may not call on us to defend our fire sides & our altars. And any plan which does not look forward to this as possible will in my opinion be a superficial one.

Second. I would call Congress together at as *short a day* as a majority of both houses can assemble.

3 When assembled I would appoint a Commission extraordinary to consist of Mr. Jefferson, or Mr. Madison, together with Mr Cabot & Mr. Pinckney....

4 The Congress should be urged to take defensive measures.

Pickering replied that Adams had already decided to call Congress into session. From Secretary Wolcott, Hamilton learned that the President had also decided to send a mission to France, although he did not agree with Hamilton's choice of members. Hamilton's first letters to Adams's hand-me-down Cabinet were unsolicited, but the secretaries did not hesitate to seek his opinions, nor were they reluctant to share information with him. Hamilton's most useful channel of influence within the Administration was James McHenry, the Secretary of War. In late April, while occupied in Albany with "court avocations" and his father-in-law's illness, Hamilton received an urgent letter from his friend "Mac," who enclosed a series of questions that Adams had submitted to the Cabinet for written opinions. McHenry asked for Hamilton's "answer at length" and begged him to tell no one of this request. In his reply, Hamilton considered each of Adams's queries on foreign policy, beginning with the question of whether France's rejection of Pinckney was a bar to future negotiations.

[Albany] April 29. 1797

The former relations of the U States to France — the

James McHenry

agency of that power in promoting our revolution—are reasons in the nature of things for not lightly running into a quarrel with—even for bearing and forbearing to a considerable extent. There is perhaps in such a case peculiar dignity in moderation.

France in declining to receive Mr Pinckney has not gone to the *ne plus ultra.* She has declined to receive a minister till grievances, of which she complains, are redressed. She has not absolutely ordered away a minister as the preliminary to war....It is not even clear that she means to say she will not receive an *extraordinary* minister. This leaves some vacant ground between her act and *rupture.* The U States may occupy it by a further attempt at negotiation. This further attempt seems to be that which must carry us to the point beyond which we cannot go....

But to preserve character abroad—and esteem for the Government at home, it is essential that the idea of further negotiation be accompanied by measures that shall demonstrate a spirit of resistance in case of failure—that shall yield present protection—and promise future security.

With this *adjunct,* it is believed that the Government in pursuing the plan of further negotiation will raise rather than depress the character of the Nation abroad & will preserve the dignity of the American mind & the esteem of the American people.

McHenry found Hamilton's suggestions so useful that he simply recopied the letter, added a few paragraphs, and presented the document to the President as his own work. In May, before a joint session of Congress, Adams outlined his policy toward France. His decisions—to stand firm and to send a commission to Paris—enraged the Republicans and pleased Hamilton. But the "continuance of peace" in Hamilton's private affairs was threatened anew in the first week of July, when James Monroe's return from Paris coincided with the publication of a series of pamphlets entitled "The History of the United States for 1796." The pamphlets charged that Hamilton and other Federalists who had been calling for Monroe's removal from the Paris ministry were seeking revenge for the part Monroe had played in investigating the Reynolds affair in December, 1792. Also printed were the documents concerning that inquiry, along with hints that Hamilton's "volunteer acknowledgement of seduction" concealed grave misconduct in office. As soon as Hamilton read the pamphlets, he wrote indignantly to Monroe and to the other men who had taken part in the investigation, Frederick Muhlenberg and Abraham Venable.

New York July 5. 1797

The peculiar nature of this transaction renders it impossible that you should not recollect it in all its parts and that your own declarations to me at the time contradicts absolutely the construction which the Editor of the Pamphlet puts upon the affair.

I think myself intitled to ask from your Candour and Justice a declaration equivalent to that which was made me at the time in the presence of Mr. Wolcott by yourself and the two other Gentlemen accompanied by a contradiction of the representations in the comments cited above. And I shall rely upon your delicacy that the manner of doing it will be such as one Gentleman has a right to expect from another—especially as you must be sensible that the present appearance of the papers is contrary to the course which was understood between us to be proper and includes a dishonorable infidelity somewhere....

I send you the copy of a Memorandum of the substance of your declaration made by me the morning after our interview....

Memorandum . . . of Messrs. Monroe Mughlenburgh & Venable concerning the affair of J Reynolds.

That they regreted the trouble and uneasiness which they had occasioned to me in consequence of the representations made to them. That they were perfectly satisfied with the explanation I had given and that there was nothing in the transaction which ought to affect my character as a public Officer or lessen the public confidence in my integrity.

A page from Hamilton's memorandum to Monroe, Muhlenberg, and Venable

James Monroe received this letter just as he was about to leave Philadelphia for New York. In Manhattan, his misunderstanding with Hamilton grew more serious. The pamphlets revealed that Monroe had continued to correspond with Jacob Clingman, James Reynolds's partner in crime, after his meetings with Hamilton in December, 1792. This information convinced Hamilton that there was a wide-ranging plot against him. On July 11, he and his wife's brother-in-law John Church went to Monroe's lodgings for a confrontation with the Virginian and his friend David Gelston. Gelston, who left a record of the morning's events, recalled that Hamilton was "very much agitated" when he came to the meeting. Monroe tried to soothe him by explaining that he had received his letter late at night before leaving Philadelphia and had not had time to prepare a joint statement on the subject with Venable and Muhlenberg. Monroe gave assurances that such a statement would be prepared as soon as he returned to Philadelphia, but Hamilton was not satisfied.

John Church

[New York] Tuesday Morning July 11th. 1797
Colo. M then observed if he Colo. H. wished him to give a relation of the facts...as they appeared to him, he would do it then. Colo. H. said he should like to hear it, Colo. M. then proceeded upon a history of the business... and said that the packet of papers before alluded to he yet believed remained sealed with his friend in Virginia and after getting through Colo. H. said this as your representation is totally false...upon which the Gentlemen both instantly rose Colo. M. rising first and saying do you say I represented falsely, you are a Scoundrel. Colo. H said I will meet you like a Gentleman Colo. M said I am ready get your pistols, both said we shall not or it will not be settled any other way. Mr C[hurch] & myself rising at the same moment put our selves between them Mr. C. repeating Gentlemen Gentlemen be moderate... we all sat down & the two Gentn, Colo. M & Colo. H. soon got moderate, I observed however very clearly to my mind that Colo. H. appeared extremely agitated & Colo. M. appeared soon to get quite cool and repeated his intire ignorance of the publication & his surprize to find it published, observing to Colo. H. if he would not be so warm & intemperate he would explain everything he knew of the business & how it appeared to him.

Hamilton was persuaded to let matters rest until Monroe could talk to Muhlenberg and Venable. Although his wife was expecting their sixth child in a few weeks, Hamilton left New York on July 12 to take part in these talks. In Philadelphia, he argued with Monroe and Muhlenberg over the terms of the statement they should issue, and he was determined not to leave until his name was cleared. When his departure was delayed by Monroe's reluctance to produce a satisfactory account of his transactions with Jacob Clingman, Hamilton sent him this bitter complaint.

[Philadelphia, July 22, 1797]
There appears a design at all events to drive me to the necessity of a formal defence—while you know that the extreme delicacy of its nature might be very disagreeable to me. It is my opinion that as you have been the cause...

Engraved portrait of James Monroe

of the business appearing in a shape which gives it an adventitious importance,... it was incumbent upon you as a man of honor and sensibility to have come forward in a manner that would have shielded me completely from the unpleasant effects brought upon me by your agency. This you have not done.

On the contrary by the affected reference of the matter to a defence which I am to make, and by which you profess your opinion is to be decided—you imply that your suspicions are still alive. And as nothing appears to have shaken your original conviction but the wretched tale of Clingman,... it follows that you are pleased to attach a degree of weight to that communication which cannot be accounted for on any fair principle. The result in my mind is that you have been and are actuated by motives towards me malignant and dishonorable; nor can I doubt that this will be the universal opinion when the publication of the whole affair which I am about to make shall be seen.

Shortly after having written this letter, Hamilton rejoined his wife in New York in time for the birth of their fifth son, William. His correspondence with Monroe continued for another two weeks, and at one point it seemed that the affair might end in a duel. Instead, the incident closed with a move by Hamilton that was more puzzling than any of the bizarre events that had occurred earlier. On August 25, a pamphlet appeared in New York with the title *Observations on Certain Documents...in which the Charge of Speculation against Alexander Hamilton...is Fully Refuted. Written by Himself.* The tract was more interesting than its name indicated, for Hamilton included not only the documents involved in the investigation of 1792, but also his correspondence with Maria and James Reynolds and the details of his career as lover and victim of blackmail. Anticipating criticism, Hamilton offered this explanation for his decision to expose his follies.

[August 31, 1797]

I owe perhaps to my friends an apology for condescending to give a public explanation. A just pride with reluctance stoops to a formal vindication against so despicable a contrivance and is inclined rather to oppose to it the uniform evidence of an upright character. This would be my conduct on the present occasion, did not the tale seem to derive a sanction from the names of three men of some weight and consequence in the society:

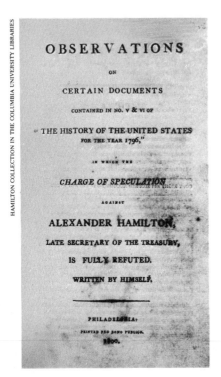

Title page of an 1800 edition of Hamilton's Observations, *his defense against charges of speculation*

a circumstance, which I trust will excuse me for paying attention to a slander that without this prop, would defeat itself by intrinsic circumstances of absurdity and malice.

The charge against me is a connection with one James Reynolds for purposes of improper pecuniary speculation. My real crime is an amorous connection with his wife, for a considerable time with his privity and connivance, if not originally brought on by a combination between the husband and wife with the design to extort money from me.

This confession is not made without a blush. I cannot be the apologist of any vice because the ardour of passion may have made it mine. I can never cease to condemn myself for the pang, which it may inflict in a bosom eminently intitled to all my gratitude, fidelity and love. But that bosom will approve, that even at so great an expence, I should effectually wipe away a more serious stain from a name, which it cherishes with no less elevation than tenderness. The public too will I trust excuse the confession. The necessity of it to my defence against a more heinous charge could alone have extorted from me so painful an indecorum.

In the three years of his retirement from the Treasury, Hamilton's life had come full circle. He had left office pinning his hopes for America's peace on a diplomatic mission to England. At the close of 1797, he waited for word of the joint commission to Paris that could save America from "rupture" with the French Republic. He had begun his venture in private life with heavy obligations to his wife and children. There was now another son to be educated, and Elizabeth Hamilton had a stronger claim than ever on her husband's heart and conscience. Hamilton's experiment with withdrawal from public duty had hardly been successful. He felt too strong a commitment to the measures he had begun as Secretary of the Treasury to abandon them. He had challenged James Nicholson to a duel in a dispute over Jay's treaty and shamed his family with the exposure of his affair with Maria Reynolds to uphold his reputation for honesty as a public official. And now, as an unofficial adviser to the Cabinet, he was occupied with the progress of the three-man mission to France. Hamilton would not be a completely private citizen until that mission had succeeded.

Chapter 13

Seeds of Conflict

Hamilton's vows to devote himself to his family and his profession were more seriously threatened by the joint commission to France than they had been by Jay's mission to England. Jay had brought back a controversial treaty for his friend to defend; the reports of the insults that the French Government heaped on the members of the joint commission— Elbridge Gerry, Charles Pinckney, and John Marshall—helped precipitate America into a quasi war with her Revolutionary ally. France's Foreign Minister, Talleyrand, forced the commissioners to bargain through his agents, whom they dubbed "W," "X," "Y," and "Z" in their dispatches. The price of negotiation, they learned, was to be a "loan" to France and a "gift" to Talleyrand himself. When the commissioners' reports of the XYZ affair reached Philadelphia, the United States embarked on a strange undeclared war, which saw no land battles and only a few minor naval engagements.

For Hamilton, the Quasi War offered an opportunity to introduce "respectability" into America's military establishment, as he had done with the nation's finances. Unfortunately, it also gave him a chance for closer contact with President John Adams, who had reacted to Hamilton's part in the 1796 elections by calling him "as great an hypochrite as any in the U.S." It was only a matter of time before the two men would find new reasons for mutual distrust. Hamilton had limited but sincere respect for Adams. He had worked for Adams's election as Vice President in 1789 and 1792 and appreciated the New Englander's support of his program for discharging the public debt via the Sinking Fund Commission. But generally their early relations had not been close. Adams was a proud and suspicious man who resented Hamilton's efforts in 1789 to see that votes in the Electoral College were balanced so that Washington would not accidentally lose the Presidency. To Adams, this was a personal insult that had barred him from an "equal" chance at the office of Chief Executive.

Luckily, Adams was ignorant of Hamilton's work as secret adviser to his

Cabinet in 1798. One reason for this was Adams's habit of leaving Philadelphia as soon as Congress adjourned and remaining at his home in Quincy, Massachusetts, until the legislature reconvened. Had Adams spent more time in the capital, he might have learned sooner of Hamilton's meddling in the Administration. Indeed, if Adams had not been an absentee President, the secretaries might have had less reason to consult Hamilton when prompt decisions were needed. As it happened, the advice Hamilton gave the Cabinet in 1797 and 1798 coincided with the President's own views. But in the progress of the Quasi War their ideas diverged, and Adams learned, as had Thomas Jefferson, that the more he knew of Hamilton, the less he found to admire. When he finally discovered Hamilton's role in the Administration, his anger revealed the depth of his hostility.

At first, however, the President and the former Secretary were united in their determination to assert America's rights and dignity. Even before the Government learned of the extortion attempt by W, X, Y, and Z, James McHenry had asked Hamilton for his suggestions on Administration policy in case the joint mission should fail. The course that Hamilton outlined was remarkably similar to Adams's own conclusions.

[New York, January 27–February 11] 1798

The measures to be taken by the Executive will therefore be—

To communicate to Congress with *manly* but *calm* and *sedate* firmness & without strut, the ill success of the attempt to negotiate & the circumstances attending it—

To deplore the failure of the measure—

To inculcate that the crisis is a very serious one & looking forward to possible events in Europe may involve the safety liberty & prosperity of this Country—

That the situation points out two objects 1 measures of immediate defence to our Commerce and 2 of ulterior security in the event of open Rupture....

The idea to be thrown in that the hope of an accommodation without proceeding to open Rupture ought not to be abandonned or precluded while measures of self preservation ought not to be omitted or delayed & ought to be prosecuted with a vigour commensurate with the present urgency & eventual greatness of the danger....

In addition to these measures Let the President recommend a day to be observed as a day of fasting humiliation & prayer. On religious ground this is very proper—On political, it is very expedient. The Government will be very unwise, if it does not make the most of the religious prepossessions of our people—opposing

358

the honest enthusiasm of Religious Opinion to the phrenzy of Political fanaticism.

February passed with no word from the commissioners. Hamilton rode to Albany to argue the case of Louis Le Guen, a French merchant whose legal problems kept Hamilton profitably employed for several years in a series of trials that became among the most famous in the early history of American business law. Shortly after his return to New York City, Hamilton learned of the humiliating treatment of the American commission by W, X, Y, and Z. Too indignant to keep silent, he protested to Secretary of State Pickering.

American suspicions of French motives were rife when this plan of a supposed French invasion of England and Ireland was published in Philadelphia in April, 1798.

New York March 17. 1798

I look upon the Question before the Public as nothing less than whether we shall maintain our Independence and I am prepared to do it in every event and at every hazard. I am therefore of opinion that our Executive should come forth on this basis.

I wish to see a *temperate*, but *grave solemn* and *firm* communication from the President to the two houses on the result of the advices from our Commissioners. This communication to review summarily the course of our affairs with France from the beginning to the present moment . . . to consider her refusal to receive our Ministers as a virtual denial of our Independence and as evidence that if circumstances favour the plan we shall be called to defend that Independence our political institutions & our liberty against her enterprizes—to conclude that leaving still the door to accommodation open & not proceeding to final rupture. Our duty our honor & safety require that we shall take vigorous comprehensive measures of defence adequate to the immediate protection of our Commerce to the security of our Ports and to our eventual defence in case of Invas[ion] with a view to these great objects calling forth and organising all the resources of the Country.

I_n *perfect confidence,"* Pickering responded by giving Hamilton secret details of the XYZ affair, and outlined the Administration's plans to recall the commissioners. As Congress considered the implications of the diplomatic crisis, Hamilton adopted a new pen name, "Titus Manlius," and began treating his readers to a lively exposé of French politics. His basic goal, however, was to persuade Americans and their

Government to arm for their own defense—and to arm "respectably." In his sixth essay, he confronted what was perhaps the greatest barrier to military preparedness: the American people's traditional hostility to a standing army.

A page from Washington's letter assessing the crisis with France and offering Hamilton a position as major general in the event of war

[New York, April 19, 1798]

The resolution to raise an army, it is to be feared, is that one of the measures suggested, which will meet with greatest obstacle; and yet it is the one which ought most to unite opinion. Being merely a precaution for internal security, it can in no sense tend to provoke war, and looking to eventual security in a case, which if it should happen would threaten our very existence as a nation, it is the most important.

The history of our revolution-war is a serious admonition to it. The American cause had nearly been lost for want of creating in the first instance a solid force commensurate in duration with the war....

Suppose an invasion, & that we are left to depend on Militia alone. Can it be doubted that a rapid and formidable progress would in the first instance be made by the invader? Who can answer what dismay this might inspire—how far it might go to create general panic—to rally under the banners of the enemy the false and the timid?...To have a good army on foot will be best of all precautions to prevent as well as to repel invasion.

Hamilton kept himself available for whatever form the "public call" might take in this crisis, although he declined Governor Jay's suggestion that he accept an appointment to an unexpired term in the United States Senate. But Hamilton was not so vain or unrealistic as to think that he would be the first patriot summoned by that "public call." To his mind there was only one man, George Washington, who could lend enough prestige to the new military establishment to make national defense a reality. Accordingly, Hamilton urged the former President to leave his peaceful retirement at Mount Vernon.

New York May 19. 1798

In such a state of public affairs it is impossible not to look up to you; and to wish that your influence could in some proper mode be brought into direct action. Among the ideas which have passed through my mind for this purpose—I have asked myself whether it might not be expedient for you to make a circuit through Virginia and North Carolina under some pretence of health &c. This would call forth addresses public dinners &c. which would give you an opportunity of expressing sentiments in Answers Toasts &c. which would throw the weight of your character into the scale of the Government and revive an enthusiasm for your person that may be turned into the right channel....

You ought also to be aware, My Dear Sir, that in the event of an open rupture with France, the public voice will again call you to command the armies of your Country; and though all who are attached to you will from attachment, as well as public considerations, deplore an occasion which should once more tear you from that repose to which you have so good a right—yet it is the opinion of all those with whom I converse that you will be compelled to make the sacrifice. All your past labour may demand to give it efficacy this further, this very great sacrifice.

Washington replied that he would have no choice but to return to public life if he were called, but would do so with "as much reluctance ... as I should do to the tombs of my Ancestors." Although the General ruled out a southern tour, Hamilton was encouraged by his response and sent him the following reply.

A view of Mount Vernon in 1798

New York June 2d 1798

It is a great satisfaction to me to ascertain what I had anticipated in hope, that you are not determined in an *adequate emergency* against affording once more your Military services.... You intimate a desire to be informed what would be my part in such an event as to entering into military service. I have no scruple about opening myself to you on this point. If I am invited *to a station in which the service I may render may be proportioned to the sacrifice I am to make*, I shall be willing to go into army. If you command, the place in which I should hope to be most useful is that of Inspector General with a command in the line. This I would accept.... I have no knowlege of any arrangement contemplated but I take it for granted the services of all the former officers worth having may be commanded & that your choice would regulate the Executive. With decision & care in selection an excellent army may be formed.

By the end of June, Congress had made considerable progress in working out measures for the creation of a larger Navy, an "Additional Army" that would serve during the international crisis, and a "Provisional Army" that would only be called up in an actual state of war. Hamilton, meanwhile, had been spending more and more time sending advice to his friends in the Cabinet. Finding that he could no longer resist giving advice in person, he set off for Philadelphia, arriving in the first week of July. There he learned that Adams had named Washington Commander in Chief of the armed forces, and that the Senate had confirmed the nomination—all without Washington's knowledge. In accepting his appointment, Washington refused to serve in the field unless absolutely necessary and demanded the right to choose his principal staff officers. He submitted a list of these men to Adams, with Hamilton's name first, as Inspector General with the rank of major general. Washington confessed to Hamilton that he expected his former aide to be his "Coadjutor, and assistant," but if the commissions were issued in the order given by the new Commander, Hamilton would have seniority over two other major generals, Henry Knox and Charles Pinckney, who had outranked him at the end of the Revolution. The President postponed sending the commissions lest Knox or Pinckney should take offense. Timothy Pickering loyally reported on this delicate matter, and Hamilton made his position clear in a letter to the Secretary of State.

Hamilton's commission as Inspector General of the Army, signed by President John Adams, July, 1798

[New York] July 17 [1798]

I had contemplated the possibility that *Knox* might come into service & was content to be second to him, if *thought indispensable. Pinckney,* if placed over me, puts me a grade lower. I dont believe it to be necessary. I am far from certain that he will not be content to serve under me—but I am willing that the affair should be so managed as that the relative ranks may remain open to future settlement, to ascertain the effect of the arrangement which has been contemplated. I am not however ready to say that I shall be satisfied with the appointment of Inspector General with the rank & command of Major General on the principle that every officer of higher rank in the late army who may be appointed is to be above me. I am frank to own that this will not accord with my opinion of my own pretensions & I have every reason to believe that it will fall far short of public opinion. Few have made so many sacrifices as myself— to few would a change of situation for a military appointment be so injurious as to myself—if with this sacrifice, I am to be degraded below my just claim in public opinion —ought I to acquiesce?

Even when the Senate approved the list of officers that Washington had prepared, Adams hesitated to take a firm stand on the relative rank of the three generals. The President left for his home in Quincy, Massachusetts, without having dispatched the signed commissions to the major generals. At this point in the growing dispute, Adams was in favor of issuing all the commissions on the same day, with no explicit statement on seniority. The relative rank of the three major generals at the end of the Revolution, he assumed, would determine their standing in the command of the Quasi War. By the end of July, Hamilton had become increasingly annoyed at the delay and a bit more emphatic on what "justice" should be done him—as he showed in a letter to Washington.

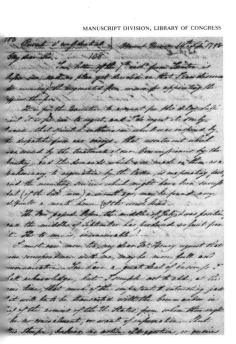

A copy of Washington's letter to James McHenry commenting on John Adams's initial reluctance to appoint Hamilton second-in-command

Philadelphia July 29[–August 1] 1798
With regard to the delicate subject of the relative rank of the Major Generals, it is very natural for me to be a partial judge, and it is not very easy for me to speak upon it. If I know myself however, this at least I may say, that were I convinced of injustice being done to oth[ers] in my favour, I should not hesitate even to volun[teer] a correction of it, as far as my consent could avail. But in a case like this, am I not to take the opinion of others as my guide? If I am, the conclusion is that the Gentlemen concerned ought to acquiesce. It is a fact, of which there is a flood of evidence that a great majority of leading fœderal men were of opinion, that in the event of your declining command of the army, it ought to devolve upon me, and that in case of your acceptance, which every body ardently desired, the place of second in command ought to be mine. It is not for me to examine the justness of this opinion. . . .

After saying this much, I [must] add that regard to the public interest is ever predominant with me—that if the Gentlemen concerned are dissatisfied & the service likely to suffer by the preference given to me—I stand ready to submit our relative pretensions to an impartial decision and to wave the preference. It shall never be said, with any color of truth, that my ambition or interest has stood in the way of the public good. . . .

[Next, Hamilton turned to a "matter of far greater moment" than the rank of the general officers.]

It is that my friend, McHenry, is wholly insufficient for his place, with the additional misfortune of not having himself the least suspicion of the fact! This generally

363

General Henry Knox

will not surprise you, when you take into view the large scale upon which he is now to act. But you perhaps may not be aware of the whole extent of the insufficiency. It is so great as to leave no probability that the business of the War Department can make any tolerable progress in his hands. . . .

My real friendship for McHenry concurring with my zeal for the service predisposed me to aid him in all that he could properly throw upon me. And I thought that he would have been glad in the organisation of the army and in the conduct of the recruiting service, to make me useful to him. With this view I came to this City & I previously opened the way, as far as I could with the least decency. But the idea has been thus far very partially embraced and . . . I shall return to New York without much fruit of my journey. I mention this purely to apprise you of the course of things and the probable results.

Hamilton now concentrated his attention on aiding James McHenry, suggesting that the Secretary of War summon the major generals to begin military planning. Henry Knox, however, refused to accept his appointment unless he were given clear rank over Hamilton and Pinckney. Adams, reluctant to offend Knox for fear of injuring the Government's cause in Massachusetts, finally decided to issue the commissions and to make Knox the senior major general. Learning from McHenry of the President's decision, Hamilton wrote to the Secretary of War.

> New York Sepr. 8th. 1798
> I postponed a reply 'till to day because I wished first to reflect maturely. My mind is unalterably made up. I shall certainly not hold the commission on the plan proposed, and only wait an official communication to say so.
>
> I return you the inclosures in your letter. You may depend on my fidelity to your friendly confidence. I shall regret whatever of inconvenience may attend you. You doubtless will take care that you retain in your own power all the evidences of this transaction.

But just as Hamilton was about to abandon his "military character," Washington demanded that Adams appoint the general officers in the order that he had indicated when he accepted command of America's provisional and additional forces. Adams acquiesced and sent the signed commissions to the Secretary of War. Summoning all his courage, McHenry issued the commissions and called the new Inspector General to a conference in Philadelphia. Hamilton replied to his timid friend.

> N York Oct 19. 1798
>
> It was essential for you to take a decisive course & to leave the blame of further delay at some other door. There can be no doubt of the propriety of combining the aid of General Officers. But *Pinckney* being now arrived, it seems to me very proper & necessary that he also should be called upon. You will learn with pleasure that he sent me a message...purporting his intire satisfaction with the military arrangement & readiness to serve under my command. Communicate this to our friend *Pickering* & *Wolcott,* as I am not well enough to write them by this post.

The matter of "priority" settled, Washington asked Hamilton to "give, without delay, your *full* aid to the Secy of War." Henry Knox having declined his appointment, Hamilton, Pinckney, and Washington were left to bring some order to the War Department and to handle the military arrangements. At Washington's request, Hamilton prepared the staff officers' recommendations on McHenry's requests for information and advice. The reports, which were sent to the Secretary of War over Washington's signature on December 13, revealed Hamilton's own views on the long-range goals of the new armies. His reply to McHenry's questions concerning the wisdom of withdrawing troops from the southern and western frontiers to guard the seaboard, reflected Hamilton's interest in military affairs in the wilderness.

> [Philadelphia, December 13, 1798]
>
> It is not adviseable to withdraw any of the troops from the quarters of the Country, which you mention, towards the Atlantic frontier. But the disposition in those quarters probably requires careful revision. It is not impossible that it will be found to admit of alterations favourable both to œconomy and to the military objects to be attained. The local knowledge of [Brigadier] General [James] Wilkinson [commander of the Western Army] would be so useful in an investigation of this sort, that it is deemed very important to direct him forthwith to repair to Philadelphia. If this be impracticable by land, he mav it is presumed come by way of New Orleans. It is observed that in his late communications with the

Spanish Governor he has taken pains to obviate jealousy of the views of the UStates. This was prudent, and he ought to be encouraged to continue the policy. It will also be useful to employ a judicious Engineer to survey our posts on the [Great] Lakes in order that it may be ascertained in the various relations of trade and defence, what beneficial changes, if any, can be made.

Although Hamilton, Washington, and Pinckney had left McHenry with clear guidelines, the Secretary did little to implement their plans. Hamilton, for instance, had been assigned the duty of supervising recruitment of the new troops, but had been issued no official directions. Without these orders, Hamilton received no pay and, as he reminded McHenry, he was reluctant to take more time from his legal practice without some assurance of compensation.

Private   New York Decr. 16. 1798

To be frank with you, it is utterly out of my power to apply my time to the public service, without the compensations, scanty enough, which the law annexes to the office. If I were to receive them from the day of the appoint[ment] I should be at least a thousand pounds the worse for my acceptance. From the time it was first known that I had reengaged in military life, the uncertainty of my being able to render services for which I might be retained drove away more than half my professional practice, which I may moderately estimate at four thousand pounds a year. My pecuniary sacrifices already to the public ought to produce the reverse of a disposition every where to compel me to greater than the law imposes. This remark, I am well aware, is not necessary for you personally. . . .

It is always disagreeable to speak of compensations for one's self but a man past 40 with a wife and six Children, and a very *small* property beforehand, is compelled to wave the scruples which his nicety would otherwise dictate.

McHenry's abbreviated version of Washington's recommendations was not submitted to Congress until December 31. Hamilton, unsalaried though he was, took more and more burdens from the Secretary of War in January, drafting legislation for McHenry to present to the House and giving advice on the most minute points. Since Washington refused to take active command until needed in the field, Hamilton and Pinckney were to share responsibility for the additional and provisional forces. McHenry turned to the Inspector General for his "ideas," and Hamilton outlined this division of authority.

VOLUNTEER COMPANIES, who have affociated, and intend offering their Services to the PRESIDENT of the UNITED STATES in the PROVISIONAL ARMY.

A broadside of November 1, 1798, ordering volunteer companies of militia to report for duty

New York January 24th 1799

If I rightly understood the Commander in Chief, his wish was that all the Military points and military force everywhere should be put under the direction of the two Major Generals, who alone should be the Organs of the department of War. The objects of this plan are to disburthen the head of that department of infinite details which must unavoidably clog his general arrangements, and to establish a vigilant military superintendence over all the military points. There is no difficulty in this plan except as to the Western Army. It will be a very natural disposition to give to the Inspector General the command of all the Troops and Posts North of Maryland and to General Pinckney the command of all the Troops and Posts South of the district assigned to the Inspector General. How will this plan as to the Western Army answer? Let all the troops upon the Lakes, including those on the Miami which communicat[es] with Lake Erie, be united under the command of one Officer.... Let all the Troops in Tennessee be united under the command of one Officer.... Let them consider themselves as under the orders of the General who commands the Western Army—and let the whole be placed under the superintendence of the Inspector General....

At the end of January, Hamilton was able to assume his duties and "emoluments" as Inspector General, but his pleasure in his new work was overshadowed by new "attacks" from the "declared enemies" of government in the South. The Kentucky and Virginia legislatures issued angry resolutions against the 1798 Alien and Sedition Acts, and there were even rumors that Virginia was planning armed resistance. Hamilton wrote anxiously to Massachusetts Congressman Theodore Sedgwick.

New York Feby 2. 1799

What, My Dear Sir, are you going to do with Virginia? This is a very serious business, which will call for all the wisdom and firmness of the Government. The following are the ideas which occur to me on the occasion.

The first thing in all great operations of such a Government as ours is to secure the opinion of the people. To

*William Vans Murray, in a portrait
painted in London by Mather Brown*

this end, the proceedings of Virginia and Kentucke with the two laws complained of should be referred to a special Committee. That Committee should make a report exhibiting with great luminousness and particularity the reasons which support the constitutionality and expediency of those laws—the tendency of the doctrines advanced by Virginia and Kentucke to destroy the Constitution...and, with calm dignity united with pathos, the full evidence which they afford of a regular conspiracy to overturn the government. And the Report should likewise dwell upon the inevitable effect and probably the intention of these proceedings to encourage a hostile foreign power to decline accommodation and proceed in hostility. The Government must [not] merely [de]fend itself [b]ut must attack and arraign its enemies. But in all this, there should be great care to distinguish the people of Virginia from the legislature and even the greater part of those who may have concurred in the legislature from the chiefs; manifesting indeed a strong confidence in the good sense and patriotism of the people, that they will not be the dupes of an insidious plan to disunite the people of America to break down their constitution & expose them to the enterprises of a foreign power.

With the command of America's forces now divided between himself and Pinckney, Hamilton began working out a plan for securing America's western frontiers. But in mid-February he received word from Sedgwick that John Adams, having consulted neither Congress nor his own Cabinet, had announced that William Vans Murray, the American minister at The Hague, was to represent the nation at Paris. It was the President's intention to ignore French insults to America's pride and to make yet another attempt at peaceful negotiations. Republicans were delighted, but the Federalists balked. As a compromise, Adams was forced to include Murray as part of a new three-man commission. Furthermore, Murray was not to be joined by his colleagues until the American Government had firm reason for believing that the Directory would negotiate. Within a month, Hamilton's hopes for strong American defense policies were threatened again when the citizens of three Pennsylvania counties, led by one John Fries, took up arms to protest a land and house tax enacted to finance military preparedness. Adams proclaimed a state of rebellion, yet even as Hamilton was sending men into the field to suppress Fries' Rebellion, he was writing cautiously to McHenry.

Private   New York March 18. 1799

Beware, my Dear Sir, of magnifying a riot into an insurrection, by employing in the first instance an inadequate force. Tis better far to err on the other side. Whenever the Government appears in arms it ought to appear like a *Hercules,* and inspire respect by the display of strength. The consideration of expence is of no moment compared with the advantages of energy. Tis true this is always a relative question — but tis always important to make no mistake. I only offer a *principle* and a *caution.*

Militia and Regular Army forces prepared to move against the insurgents, but mismanagement plagued the troops more seriously than did Fries and his followers. James McHenry's unwillingness to reform the Army supply system hamstrung Hamilton's efforts to enlist troops, and only after a personal visit to the War Department in Philadelphia could Hamilton send Washington this mildly encouraging report.

Private   New York May 3d. 1799

At length the recruiting for the additional regiments has begun in *Connecticut New York New Jersey Pensylvania* and *Delaware.* The enclosed return of cloathing will sufficiently explain to you that it has commenced at least as soon as the preparations by the Department of War would permit. It might now also proceed in Maryland and Massachusettes, and the next post will I trust enable me to add Virginia — but that I do not think it expedient to outgo our supply of Cloathing. It will have the worst possible effect — if the recruits are to wait a length of time for their cloathing....

The Secretary of War imputes the deficiency in the article of Cloathing to a failure of a contract which he had made and to the difficulty of suddenly finding a substitute by purchases in the market. It is however obvious that the means which have been since pursued have not been the best calculated for dispatch.

Shadow portraits of George and Martha Washington, thought to have been done by Washington's stepgranddaughter, Eleanor Custis

Mount Vernon and its Associations
BY BENSON J. LOSSING, 1883

As Hamilton had predicted, the insurrection was quickly stifled as soon as the Government made a strong show of force. Fries was captured easily, convicted of treason, and sentenced to death, although he was later pardoned. Hamilton's mood improved considerably. The Army, he hoped, would be "at its complement" by autumn. In August, however, worried about the efficient supply of food and clothing during the approaching winter months, Hamilton renewed his campaign to force McHenry to delegate responsibility in the interests of the service.

> New York Aug 19. 1799
>
> It is one thing for business to drag on—another for it to go well. The business of supply in all its branches (except as to provisions) proceeds heavily and without order or punctuality—in a manner equally ill adapted to œconomy on a large scale as to efficiency and the contentment of the army. It is painful to observe how disjointed and peace-meal a business it is. Among other evils is this that the head of the War Department and the Chief of the several divisions of the army exhaust their time in details, which, beyond a general superintendence are foreign to them. And plans for giving perfection to our military system are unavoidably neglected.
>
> Let me repeat, my Dear friend, my earnest advice, that you proceed to organise without delay the several branches of the Department of supply, that is to fix the plan and appoint the agents.... The saving from better management will infinitely overpay the expence of salaries.

Meanwhile, Hamilton was growing increasingly apprehensive about the prospect of peace negotiations. Recent dispatches from William Vans Murray indicated that the Directory might be willing to negotiate, and any sign of peace would shorten the time in which the Adams Administration would allot energy or funds for completing military "arrangements." Hamilton's frayed temper was clear in this letter to James McHenry.

> New York Sepr. 21. 1799
>
> Symptoms bordering on mutiny for the want of pay have been reported to me as having appeared in the twelveth and thirteenth Regiments. And discontents less turbulent have been communicated from several other quarters. An explosion any where would injure and discredit the service, and wherever the blame might really be would be shared by all.
>
> No one can be more deeply impressed than I am with the necessity of a strict adherence to general rules and to established forms. But there will occur circumstances in which these ought to be dispensed with. And it is equally important, to judge rightly when exceptions ought to be admitted as when the general rule ought to be maintained.

A view of Trenton in 1789, when a triumphal arch was erected in honor of Washington, who was on his way to be inaugurated in New York

The creation of a new army, in which every officer from the highest to the lowest is of new appointment, & in respect to which in and out of the administration there is a deficiency of some essential organs, presents a case which with the utmost diligence and care will require and justify relaxations....

...Muster and Pay-Rolls are to be in certain precise forms prescribed by the Treasury. These forms were received by me only four days since, and consequently could not hitherto be in the possession of the commandants of Regiments, It will not be said that I ought to have called for them; because certainly it lies with the department to communicate its own regulations uncalled for. Are the soldiery to suffer a privation of pay for several months, because these forms never prescribed, have not been fulfilled?

A few days later, learning that General Charles Pinckney was in Rhode Island, Hamilton urged the General to come to his aid. Pinckney agreed to join Hamilton, McHenry, and Major General James Wilkinson, commander of defenses in the West, for a meeting at Trenton, where the Cabinet had taken refuge from another of Philadelphia's yellow fever epidemics. At the same time that these men were converging on the small New Jersey town, John Adams was on his way south from Quincy to discuss the peace commission with Secretary Pickering, while Chief Justice Oliver Ellsworth and Governor William R. Davie, the two envoys who were to join William Vans Murray in Europe, were journeying to Trenton to learn how a recent "revolution" in the French Directory would affect their appointments. Hamilton later described the results of the coincidental meeting, in mid-October, 1799, of this remarkable assortment of American statesmen—an encounter that ended Hamilton's hopes for the nation's military "respectability."

[September, 1800]

It happened that I arrived at Trenton a short time before the President—Chief Justice Elsworth a short time after him. This was considered as evidence of a combination between the heads of Departments, the Chief-Justice and myself, to endeavour to influence or counteract him [the President] in the affair of the Mission.

The truth, nevertheless, most certainly is, that I went to Trenton with General Wilkinson, pursuant to a preconcert with him of some weeks standing...that when I left New-York upon this journey, I had no expectation, what-

Peacefield was John Adams's home in Quincy, Massachusetts.

ever, that the President would come to Trenton, and that I did not stay at this place a day longer than was indispensable to the object I have stated. . . .

As to Chief Justice Elsworth, the design of his journey was understood to be to meet his colleague, Governor Davy, at the seat of the Government, where they would be at the fountain head of information, and would obtain any lights or explanations which they might suppose useful. . . .

Yet these simple occurrences were to the jealous mind of Mr. Adams, "confirmations strong," of some mischievous plot against his independence. . . .

[Hamilton's mere presence at Trenton convinced Adams of the existence of a "plot." When the Inspector General tried to dissuade him from sending Ellsworth and Davie to France, the President became implacable. Hamilton later recalled what had taken place.]

When the news of the Revolution in the Directory arrived, Mr. Adams was at his seat in Massachusetts. His Ministers addressed to him a joint letter, communicating the intelligence, and submitting to his consideration, whether that event ought not to suspend the projected mission. In a letter which he afterwards wrote from the same place, he directed the preparation of a draft of instructions for the Envoys, and intimated that their departure would be suspended *for some time.*

Shortly after he came to Trenton, where he adjusted with his Ministers the tenor of the instructions to be given; but he observed a profound silence on the question, whether it was expedient that the Mission should proceed. The morning after the instructions were settled, he signified to the Secretary of State that the Envoys were immediately to depart.

He is reported to have assigned as reason of his silence, that he knew the opinions of his Ministers from their letter; that he had irrevocably adopted an opposite one; and that he deemed it most delicate not to embarrass them by a useless discussion.

Hamilton returned to New York shaken by Adams's abrupt move. The likelihood of the mission's success destroyed his hopes for military reform and restored the reputation of the Jeffersonians, who had been badly hurt by anti-French opinion at the beginning of the Quasi War. Furthermore, peace would put an end to Hamilton's new Army career, returning him inevitably to the hazardous world of partisan politics, where the President was now his avowed enemy. But Hamilton was determined to make some contribution to military reform before leaving his Army post. Realizing there was no longer a chance to create a large, "respectable" army, he concentrated instead on peacetime measures that would give America military security without an unpopular standing army. A central point in his plan was the creation of a "Military Academy," as he reported to James McHenry.

> New-York Novr. 23d. 1799
>
> Since it is agreed, that we are not to keep on foot numerous forces instructed and disciplined, military science in its various branches ought to be cultivated, with peculiar care, in proper Nurseries; so that there may always exist a sufficient body of it ready to be imparted and diffused, and a competent number of persons qualified to act as instructors to the additional troops, which events may successively require to be raised. This will be to substitute the elements of an army to the thing itself, and it will greatly tend to enable the Government to dispense with a large body of standing forces, from the facility which it will give of forming Officers and Soldiers promptly upon emergencies.
>
> No sound mind can doubt the essentiality of Military Science in time of war, any more than the moral certainty that the most pacific policy, on the part of a Government, will not preserve it from being engaged in War, more or less frequently. To avoid great evils, it must either have a respectable force prepared for service, or the means of preparing such a force with expedition. The latter, most agreable to the genius of our Government and Nation is the object of a Military Academy.
>
> I propose that this Academy shall consist of five Schools: One to be called "The Fundamental School"—another "The School of Engineers & Artillerists" another "The School of Cavalry"—another "The School of Infantry" and a fifth "The School of the Navy."...
>
> These Schools to be provided with proper Apparatus and instruments for philosophical and Chemical experiments, for Astronomical and Nautical observation for surveying and for such other processes as are requisite to the illustration of the several topics of instruction.

The Cadets of the Army and young persons who are destined for military and Naval service ought to study two years in the Fundamental School—and if destined for the Corps of Engineers and Artillerists, or for the Navy two years more in the appropriate School. If for the Cavalry or Infantry one year more in the appropriate School. . . .

In addition to these, Detachments of Officers and non commissioned Officers of the Army ought to attend the Academy in rotation for the purposes of Instruction and Exercise, according to the nature of the corps to which they respectively belong.

To salvage what he could from the wreckage of the Army, Hamilton traveled to Philadelphia in mid-December to confer with McHenry. His stay was marred by the news of Washington's death at Mount Vernon. Deeply grieved, Hamilton wrote to Charles Pinckney.

Philadelphia Decr. [22] 1799

The death of our beloved commander in Chief was known to you before it was to me. I can be at no loss to anticipate what have been your feelings. I need not tell you what are mine. Perhaps no friend of his has more cause to lament, on personal account, than myself. The public misfortune is one which all the friends of our Government will view in the same light. I will not dwell on the subject. My Imagination is gloomy my heart sad.

Writing letters of condolence was no easier for the author of the "Publius" and "Camillus" essays than for other men. It was four weeks after Washington's death before Hamilton could send this message to Martha Washington.

New York Jany. 12. 1800

I did not think it proper, Madam, to intrude amidst the first effusions of your grief. But I can no longer restrain my sensibility from conveying to you an imperfect expression of my affectionate sympathy in the sorrows you experience. No one, better than myself, knows the greatness of your loss, or how much your excellent heart is formed to feel it in all its extent. Satisfied that you cannot receive consolation, I will attempt to offer none. Resignation to the will of Heaven, which the practice of your life ensures, can alone alleviate the sufferings of so heartrending an affliction.

There can be few, who equally with me participate in the loss you deplore.... I cannot say in how many ways the continuance of that confidence and friendship was necessary to me in future relations.

With Washington's death, Hamilton lost his most consistent and influential sponsor in public life. John Adams, more hostile than ever, was left to plague the Inspector General. In the first week of the new year, 1800, Hamilton commented to Rufus King.

Gen. GEORGE WASHINGTON

This memorial portrait of Washington accompanied a funeral oration published the year after his death.

New York January 5 1800

In our Councils there is no fixed plan. Some are for preserving and invigorating the Navy and destroying the army. Some, among the friends of Government, for diminishing both on pecuniary considerations.

My plan is to complete the Navy to the contemplated extent... And finally to preserve the Organs of the existing force; reducing the men to a very moderate number. For this plan there are various Reasons that appear to me solid. I much doubt however that it will finally prevail....

I must hasten to a Conclusion. It was unnecessary for me to have told you that for the loss of our illustrious friend [Washington] every heart is in mourning.

Adieu God bless you

P S   Who is to be the Commander in Chief? Not the next in Command. The appointment will probably be deferred.

As Hamilton predicted, no successor was named for Washington. A new baby daughter, Elizabeth, born in October, gave Hamilton an added motive for looking after his family's welfare, and he now resumed his legal practice. In mid-January, he rode to Albany to argue the case of Louis Le Guen. From there he wrote this fond letter to his wife.

[Albany] Sunday Jany 26 [1800]

I was quite disappointed and pained, My Dear Eliza, when I found, that the Post of Saturday had brought me no letter from you; especially as I was very anxious to hear of the health of my *little* Betsey. But I was consoled in the Evening by your affectionate letter of which *Mr. Leguen* was the bearer. It is absolutely necessary to me when absent to hear frequently of you and my dear Children. While all other passions decline in me, those of love and friendship gain new strength. It will be more and more my endeavour to abstract myself from all pursuits which interfere with those of Affection. Tis here only I can find true pleasure. In this I know your good and kind heart responses to mine.

I hope in about ten days to commence my return-journey. Need I tell that I shall not delay a moment longer than is unavoidable?

But again Hamilton could not forget his public duty. Back in New York in February, his thoughts turned to the presidential election. Congressional Federalists had endorsed Adams as their candidate earlier that winter, and Hamilton wrote to Theodore Sedgwick about the turn of events.

New York, Feb. 27, 1800.
When will Congress probably adjourn? Will any thing be settled as to a certain *Election*? Will my presence be requisite as to this or any other purpose, and when? I observe more and more that by the jealousy and envy of some, the miserlyness of others and the concurring influence of *all foreign powers,* America, if she attains to greatness, must *creep* to it. Well be it so. Slow and sure is no bad maxim. Snails are a wise generation.

P S—Unless for indispensable reasons I had rather not come.

Hamilton's political speculations were momentarily interrupted in March when he received orders to disband all "additional" troops. The Quasi War was dying out. There was now little likelihood that American forces would be called into battle, and a peace settlement was not far off. Meanwhile, New York voters went to the polls in April to choose the state legislators who would select presidential electors in the fall. The Republicans had been demanding that state law be changed to permit direct voting for the Electoral College. The Federalists had ignored their demands. But when the Republicans triumphed at the polls under the skillful leadership of Aaron Burr, the continuance of Federalist rule in America suddenly seemed uncertain. Writing to Governor Jay, Hamilton reconsidered the idea of direct voting.

New York May 7. 1800
The moral certainty therefore is that there will be an Antifœderal Majority in the Ensuing Legislature, and this very high probability is that this will bring *Jefferson*

into the Chief Magistracy; unless it be prevented by the measure which I shall now submit to your consideration, namely the immediate calling together of the existing Legislature.

I am aware that there are weighty objections to the measure; but the reasons for it appear to me to outweigh the objections. And in times like these in which we live, it will not do to be overscrupulous. It is easy to sacrifice substantial interests of society by a strict adherence to ordinary rules.

In observing this, I shall not be supposed to mean that any thing ought to be done which integrity will forbid — but merely that the scruples of delicacy and propriety, as relative to a common course of things, ought to yield to the extraordinary nature of the crisis. They ought not to hinder the taking of a *legal* and *constitutional* step, to prevent an *Atheist* in Religion and a *Fanatic* in politics from getting possession of the helm of the State....

The calling of the Legislature will have for object the choosing of Electors by the people in Districts. This... will insure a Majority of votes in the U States for a Fœderal Candidate.

The measure will not fail to be approved by all the Fœderal Party; while it will no doubt be condemned by the opposite. As to its intrinsic nature it is justified by unequivocal reasons of *public safety.*

The reasonable part of the world will I believe approve it. They will see it as a proceeding out of the common course but warranted by the particular nature of the crisis and the great cause of social order.

Theodore Sedgwick

J ay ignored this proposal as "a measure for party purposes wh[ich]. I think it w[oul]d. not become me to adopt." New York's Republican legislature would be allowed to choose the electors. Hamilton, however, had already turned to a new strategy when he suggested to Theodore Sedgwick that Federalists of all states agree to give equal support to Adams and Charles Pinckney. Sedgwick reported that at least one Federalist, Samuel Dexter, hesitated to give such a pledge, since it seemed like an attempt to abandon the President and would "crumble the federal party to atoms." Hamilton would have none of this and sent Sedgwick his opinion of Dexter's arguments.

New York May 10. 1800

He is I am persuaded much mistaken as to the opinion

entertained of Mr Adams by the Fœderal party. Were I to determine from my own observation I should say, *most* of the *most influential men* of that party consider him as a very *unfit* and *incapable* character.

For my individual part my mind is made up. I will never more be responsible for him by my direct support — even though the consequence should be the election of *Jefferson*. If we must have an *enemy* at the head of the Government, let it be one whom we can oppose & for whom we are not responsible, who will not involve our party in the disgrace of his foolish and bad measures. Under *Adams* as under *Jefferson* the government will sink. The party in the hands of whose chief it shall sink will sink with it and the advantage will all be on the side of his adversaries.

Tis a notable expedient for keeping the Fœderal party together to have at the head of it a man who hates and is distrusted by those men of it who in time past have been its most efficient supporters.

If the cause is to be sacrificed to a weak and perverse man, I withdraw from the party & act upon my own ground — never certainly against my principles but in pursuance of them in my own way. I am mistaken if others will not do the same.

The only way to prevent a fatal scism in the Fœderal party is to support G Pinckney in good earnest.

If I can be perfectly satisfied that Adams & Pinckney will be upheld in the East with intire good faith, on the ground of conformity I will wherever my influence may extend pursue the same plan. If not I will pursue Mr. Pinkny as my single object.

CULVER PICTURES, INC.

Charles Cotesworth Pinckney

The congressional caucus grudgingly agreed to give "equal" support to Adams and Pinckney. Learning that Adams had dismissed Timothy Pickering from the Cabinet and that McHenry had resigned, Hamilton sent this urgent request to the Secretary of State a few days later.

[New York, May 14, 1800]

I perceive that you as well as Mc.Henry are quitting the Administration. I am not informed how all this has been, though I conjecture. Allow me to suggest, that you ought to take with you copies and extracts of all such documents as will enable you to *explain* both *Jefferson* & *Adams.* You are aware of a very curious journal of the latter when he was in Europe, a tissue of weakness and vanity.

The time is coming when men of real integrity & energy must unite against all Empirics.

At the beginning of June, Hamilton received a letter from James McHenry describing the Secretary of War's clash with Adams. The President had called Hamilton "a Bastard" and declared he would rather be Jefferson's Vice President "or even Minister resident at the Hague, than indebted to such a being as Hamilton for the Presidency." Hamilton returned the document with this comment.

> June 6. 1800 New York
>
> I thank you My *Dear Mac* for the perusal of the Inclosed and wish you had not thought it necessary to forbid my taking a copy. Such a paper to be shewn confidentially would be very important. Charles Carroll of Carrolton ought as soon as possible to be apprized of all the circumstances.
>
> The man is more mad than I ever thought him and I shall soon be led to say as wicked as he is mad.
>
> Pray favour me with as many circumstances as may appear to you . . . to shew the probability of Coalitions with Mr. Jefferson &c which are spoken of.

In his last month as Inspector General, Hamilton made a tour of New England Army posts to bid farewell to the troops. But he may not have gone north solely out of concern for the undermanned additional army and provisional recruits—loyal soldiers who had never fought a skirmish. Along the way, at meetings with Federalists in New Hampshire, Connecticut, Rhode Island, and Massachusetts, Hamilton found that there was another army in New England: an army of men who were as dissatisfied with Adams as he was. Hamilton returned from his inspection tour with reason to believe that his strategy for electing Charles Pinckney had a good chance for success. The Quasi War had given the nation no fireworks on battlefields, but its aftermath promised an entertaining battle royal between the Federalist President and his Inspector General. For, by the end of that fruitless exercise in military preparedness, Hamilton had learned to dislike John Adams as thoroughly as the Massachusetts statesman had always detested him.

Chapter 14

Last Encounters

The last four years of Hamilton's life were overshadowed by the consequences of his decision to oppose Adams's reelection in 1800. The electoral system involved any would-be campaign manager in delicate calculations and complicated bargains that could easily misfire. The flaws of the Electoral College, where electors could not designate which of their two ballots was for President and which for Vice President, had become a major problem with the development of two parties. Each group now had to guess in advance how many votes could safely be "thrown away" from its vice presidential candidate to insure that it would elect its own men in the right order. Had there been effective party discipline, this would have been easy, but the election of 1796 had shown that there were no guarantees that Federalists or Republicans would vote as their leaders wished. That year Adams's supporters had thrown away too many votes, and the Federalist nominee for Vice President had lost to Thomas Jefferson.

In 1800, political observers agreed that the race would be very close. Hamilton had to convince Federalists in all sections to give "equal" support to Adams and Charles Cotesworth Pinckney. If New Englanders threw away a few votes in Adams's favor and southerners threw away a few more to insure Pinckney's success, Jefferson would win. Beyond this, equal support would result in a tie in the Electoral College, and the final choice would lie with the House of Representatives. In that quarter, Hamilton might be able to persuade congressmen to choose Pinckney over Adams as the next President.

With this plan in mind, Hamilton returned from his tour of New England at the end of June, 1800. On leaving the office of Inspector General, he had made the usual resolutions to devote himself to his family. There were also plans for an impressive country residence on thirty acres of land in upper Manhattan, which he had purchased in 1799. But both the completion of the Grange (named after the ancestral home in Scotland) and attention to his family would have to come after public duty. Back in New York, Hamilton set about convincing Federalists that only an "equal chance" for Charles Pinckney and John Adams would save the party, and that ultimately Adams must be defeated. Hamilton began mobilizing his campaign against the President with letters like this one to Oliver Wolcott.

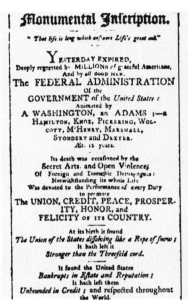

Monumental Inscription.

" *That life is long which answers Life's great end.*"

YESTERDAY EXPIRED,
Deeply regretted by MILLIONS of graceful Americans,
And by all GOOD MEN,
The FEDERAL ADMINISTRATION
Of the
GOVERNMENT of the *United States :*
Animated by
A WASHINGTON, an ADAMS ;—a
HAMILTON, KNOX, PICKERING, WOL-
COTT, M'HENRY, MARSHALL,
STODDERT and DEXTER.
Æt. 12 years.

Its death was occasioned by the
Secret Arts. and Open Violence
Of Foreign and Domestic Demagogues :
Notwithstanding its whole Life
was devoted to the Performance of every Duty
to promote
The UNION, CREDIT, PEACE, PROSPER-
ITY, HONOR, and
FELICITY of its COUNTRY.

At its birth it found
The Union of the States dissolving like a Rope of snow :
It hath left it
Stronger than the Threefold cord.

It found the United States
Bankrupts in Estate and Reputation :
It hath left them
Unbounded in Credit ; and respected throughout
the World.

In March, 1801, after Jefferson's election to the Presidency, the death of the Federalist party was announced in the Boston Centinel.

N Y July 1. 1800

It is essential to inform the most discreet...of the facts which denote unfitness in Mr. Adams. I have promised confidential friends a correct statement. To be able to give it, I must derive aid from you. Any thing you may write shall if you please be returned to you. But you must be exact & much in detail. The history of the mission to France from the first steps...down to the last proceedings is very important.

I have serious thoughts of writing to the *President* to tell him That I have heared of his having repeatedly mentioned the existence of a British Faction in this Country & alluded to me as one of that faction—requesting that he will inform me of the truth of this information & if true what have been the grounds of the suggestion.

His friends are industrious in propagating the idea to defeat the efforts to unite for Pinckney. The inquiry I propose may furnish an antidote and vindicate character. What think you of the Idea?

For my part I can set Malice at defiance.

Although Wolcott still served in the Cabinet, he was as determined as Hamilton to see that the President did not win a second term. Wolcott replied to Hamilton's letter by hinting that Adams had sent Ellsworth and Davie to France solely to gain political advantage. He encouraged Hamilton to write to Adams concerning the rumors of a "British Faction," and Hamilton sent this message to the President at Quincy.

New York August 1. 1800

It has been repeatedly mentioned to me that you have on different occasions, asserted the existence of a *British Faction* in this Country, embracing a number of leading or influential characters of the *Fœderal Party* (as usually denominated) and that you have sometimes named me, at other times plainly alluded to me, as one of this description of persons: And I have likewise been assured that of late some of your warm adherents, for electioneering purposes, have employed a corresponding language.

I must, Sir, take it for granted, that you cannot have

381

made such assertions or insinuations without being willing to avow them, and to assign the reasons to a party who may conceive himself injured by them. I therefore trust that you will not deem it improper that I apply directly to yourself, to ascertain from you, in reference to your own declarations, whether the information, I have received, has been correct or not, and if correct what are the grounds upon which you have founded the suggestion.

By this time, Hamilton had heard accusations that he opposed Adams because of "personal pique" growing out of his failure to be named Washington's successor as Commander in Chief. He began to plan a way to publicize his real motives and wrote to Wolcott.

John Adams, from a 1799 broadside

New York Aug 3. 1800

I have serious thoughts of giving to the public my opinion respecting Mr. Adams with my reasons in a letter to a friend with my signature. This seems to me the most authentic way of conveying the information & best suited to the plain dealing of my character. There are however reasons against it and a very strong one is that some of the principal causes of my disapprobation proceed from yourself & other members of the Administration who would be understood to be the sources of my information whatever cover I might give the thing.

What say you to this measure? I would predicate it on the fact that I am abused by the friends of Mr. Adams who ascribe my opposition to pique & disappointment & would give it the shape of a *defence of myself.*

During the rest of the summer, Hamilton opened "mutual communication of information & opinions" with Federalist leaders in other states and started work on a "letter to a friend" that would expose Adams. Circulation of the draft version was delayed when Hamilton received reactions to the project from New England. George Cabot, for instance, urged restraint, since in the end the party might have to support Adams. Meanwhile, Hamilton had also written to the President, giving Adams a second chance to clarify his remarks about a "British Faction." When Adams ignored this letter from the "Creole bastard," as he had the first, Hamilton delayed no longer. His *Letter... Concerning the Public Conduct of John Adams...* appeared in pamphlet form in early October. Intended for private circulation, the *Letter* traced his differences with Adams's theories and policies since the Revolution, opening with this explanation.

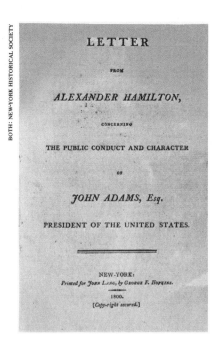

Title pages of Hamilton's pamphlet attacking John Adams (top) and of one published in his defense

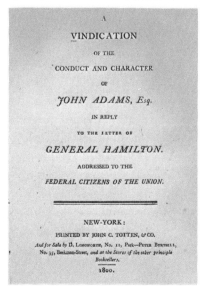

[October 17–21, 1800]

Some of the warm personal friends of Mr. Adams are taking unwearied pains to disparage the motives of those Federalists, who advocate the equal support of Gen. Pinckney, at the approaching election of President and Vice-President....

In addition to a full share of the obloquy vented against this description of persons collectively, peculiar accusations have been devised, to swell the catalogue of my demerits. Among these, the resentment of disappointed ambition, forms a prominent feature. It is pretended, that had the President, upon the demise of General Washington, appointed me Commander in Chief, he would have been, in my estimation, all that is wise, and good and great.

It is necessary, for the public cause, to repel these slanders; by stating the real views of the persons who are calumniated, and the reasons of their conduct.

In executing this task, with particular reference to myself, I ought to premise, that the ground upon which I stand, is different from that of most of those who are confounded with me as in pursuit of the same plan. While our object is common, our motives are variously dissimilar. A part, well affected to Mr. Adams, have no other wish than to take a double chance against Mr. Jefferson. Another part, feeling a diminution of confidence in him, still hope that the general tenor of his conduct will be essentially right. Few go as far in their objections as I do. Not denying to Mr. Adams patriotism and integrity, and even talents of a certain kind, I should be deficient in candor, were I to conceal the conviction, that he does not possess the talents adapted to the *Administration* of Government, and that there are great and intrinsic defects in his character, which unfit him for the office of Chief Magistrate.

It is difficult to understand how Hamilton believed this pamphlet could be kept secret. A confederate of Aaron Burr's, the Republican vice presidential candidate, obtained a copy and extracts were published in the Philadelphia *Aurora* on October 22.

Although Hamilton's friends dissuaded him from further publications, he had already given the Republicans (or Democratic-Republicans, as party members were by then being called) their finest piece of propaganda for the 1800 campaign. Electors met in the states on December 4, and it soon became clear that the vote in the Electoral College would be a tie—not, as Hamilton had planned, between the Federalist nominees, but between the Democratic-Republicans Thomas Jefferson and Aaron Burr. The final outcome would have to be decided in the House of Representatives, and Hamilton wrote to Oliver Wolcott urging that Federalists throw their support to Jefferson as the lesser of two evils.

New York Decr. 16. 1800

It is now, my Dear Sir, ascertained that Jefferson or Burr will be President and it seems probable that they will come with equal votes to the House of Representatives. It is also circulated here that in this event the Fœderalists in Congress or some of them talk of preferring Burr. I trust New England at least will not so far lose its head as to fall into this snare. There is no doubt but that upon every virtuous and prudent calculation Jefferson is to be preferred. He is by far not so dangerous a man and he has pretensions to character. . . .

But early measures must be taken to fix on this point the opinions of the Fœderalists. Among them, from different motives—Burr will find partisans. If the thing be neglected he may possibly go far.

Having helped to destroy his own party's chances for electing a President, Hamilton now fought to see that Jefferson, not Burr, won the office of Chief Executive. Although his campaign to discredit Burr was the continuation of a long-standing political conflict that would eventually destroy them both, even Hamilton admitted that his personal relationship with Burr was pleasant. The two men had often been joint counsel for the same clients in New York and were cordial to each other outside the courtroom. Had their political views been closer, they might have found enough mutual interests and traits of personality to become friends. Burr came from a distinguished and well-established American family (he was the grandson of Jonathan Edwards), but he, like Hamilton, had grown up without his parents and faced the world with more talents than financial resources. Both were handsome, dapper men who enjoyed the practice of politics and the law. But Hamilton had chosen the road of "respectability" and "propriety" for his public career. In the Revolution, he had been Washington's aide and had won the Commander's support for his later ventures. His marriage to Elizabeth Schuyler placed him in one of New York's leading families. Burr, on the other hand, had aligned himself with Horatio Gates in the military feuds of the war, and his marriage to Theodosia Prevost, a widow ten years his senior with five children, did nothing to advance his ambitions. In public life, Burr chose "democracy," organizing the political clubs of New York and exploiting popular issues with a skill Hamilton both envied and despised. In the election of 1800, Hamilton's campaign against Burr began in earnest. He wrote to his friend Gouverneur Morris, now a United States Senator from New York, who could be counted on to use his influence with Federalists in the lower house of Congress.

New York Decr. 24, 1800

Jefferson or *Burr?*—the former without all doubt. The latter in my judgment has no principle public or private— could be bound by no agreement—will listen to no monitor but his ambition; & for this purpose will use the *worst* part of the community as a ladder to climb to permant power & an instrument to crush the better part. He is bankrupt beyond redemption except by the resources that grow out of war and disorder or by a sale to a foreign power or by great peculation. War with Great Britain would be the immediate instrument. He is sanguine enough to hope every thing—daring enough to attempt every thing—wicked enough to scruple nothing. From the elevation of such a man heaven preserve the Country!

Let our situation be improved to obtain from Jefferson assurances on certain points—the maintenance of the present system especially on the cardinal points of public Credit, a *Navy, Neutrality.*

Make any discreet use you think fit of this letter.

Miniature, by Trumbull, of Oliver Wolcott, Hamilton's successor as Treasury Secretary, and later elected Governor of Connecticut

The votes of the Electoral College would not be officially tallied until February, and Hamilton used the next weeks to persuade wavering Federalists of the perils that would follow Burr's election. Because congressmen were to vote by states, Delaware's single Representative, James Bayard, would cast a vote equal to that of the larger delegations from New York and Virginia. Bayard accordingly became an important object of Hamilton's attention and a frequent recipient of his letters.

New-York Jany. 16th. 180[1]

I was glad to find my dear sir, by your letter, that you had not yet determined to go with the current of the Fœderal Party in the support of Mr *Burr* & that you were resolved to hold yourself disengaged till the moment of final decision. Your resolution to separate yourself, in this instance, from the Fœderal Party if your conviction shall be strong of the unfitness of Mr Burr, is certainly laudable. So much does it coincide with my ideas, that if the Party shall by supporting Mr Burr as President adopt him for their official Chief—I shall be obliged to consider myself as an *isolated* man. It will be impossible for me to reconcile with my notions of *honor* or policy, the continuing to be of a Party which according to my apprehension will have degraded itself & the country.

On Tuesday, February 17, House Federalists gave Jefferson the Presidency on their thirty-fifth ballot. The deadlock was broken when Federalist members of three delegations cast blank ballots; Bayard of Delaware was one of these. Hamilton's letters had not persuaded him to back Jefferson, but at the last minute he had withdrawn support from Burr. Hamilton made one more stand for Federalist principles in the spring of 1801 when he campaigned against George Clinton, who had emerged from retirement to seek another term as governor. Clinton won, and Hamilton discarded politics for the time to tend to business and plan the finishing touches for the Grange. In May, he sent Elizabeth this note.

Fish Kill Sunday Evening [May 10, 1801]

Wife Children and *hobby* are the only things upon which I have permitted my thoughts to run. As often as I write, you may expect to hear something about the *latter*.

Don't lose any opportunity which may offer of ploughing up the new garden spot and let the waggon make a tour of the ground lately purchased to collect the dung upon it to be scattered over that spot.

When it is too cold to go on with grubbing, our men may be employed in cutting and clearing away the underbrush in the Grove and the other woods; only let the *center* of the principal wood in the line of the different rocks remain rough and wild.

The Country people all agree that to fat fowls, it is essential to keep them well supplied with gravel. One, of whom I inquired, informed me, that sea shore gravel, not too large, is particularly good. They also say the coops must be cleaned out every two or three days. After the Fowls have had a sufficient opportunity of drinking, the remaining water must be removed.

Jefferson, by Rembrandt Peale

The life of a prosperous attorney and country gentleman seemed to satisfy Hamilton. That summer New York Republicans celebrated Independence Day by gathering at Manhattan's Brick Church to hear a violently anti-Federalist speech by Captain George Eacker, but Hamilton made no comment on the oration. Collecting legal fees and "Setts of Italian Marble" for his new home seemed more worthwhile. Much of Hamilton's contentment as a private citizen came from his pleasure at seeing the progress of his brilliant eldest son, Philip. When the boy graduated from Columbia College in 1800 and began studying for the law, Hamilton had drawn up these strict but affectionate guidelines for the young student.

[New York, 1800]

This 1781 view of upper Manhattan and the Hudson River looks north toward Fort Washington and the site of Hamilton's home, the Grange.

Rules for *Mr Philip Hamilton*

From the first of April to the first of October he is to rise not later than Six Oclock. The rest of the year not later than Seven. If Earlier he will deserve commendation. Ten will be his hour of going to bed throughout the year.

From the time he is dressed in the morning till Nine o clock (the time for breakfast Excepted) he is to read law.

At nine he goes to the office & continues there till dinner time. He will be occupied partly in the writing and partly in reading law.

After Dinner he reads law at home till five O clock. From this hour till seven he disposes of his time as he pleases. From Seven to ten he reads and studies what ever he pleases.

From twelve on Saturday he is at liberty to amuse himself.

On Sunday he will attend the morning Church. The rest of the day may be applied to innocent recreations.

He must not Depart from any of these rules without my permission.

But on the evening of November 20, 1801, Philip visited a New York theater, where he started a quarrel with George Eacker, the Republicans' Fourth of July orator. On November 23, Eacker and young Hamilton crossed the Hudson to New Jersey, where gentlemen could still legally defend their honor by dueling. Philip fell, mortally wounded, and was brought back to Manhattan, where his parents watched his sufferings for almost twenty hours. At the funeral, Alexander Hamilton "was with difficulty supported to the grave of his hopes." He could not bring himself to answer any letters of condolence. Instead he buried himself in a furious attack on Thomas Jefferson's recent message to Congress. The *New-York*

Evening Post (which Hamilton had helped found earlier that year) carried the first of eighteen installments of Hamilton's *Examination* ten days after Jefferson had presented his program at Washington.

Life of Alexander Hamilton BY ALLAN MCLANE HAMILTON, 1910

Hamilton's eldest son, Philip, as he looked at the age of twenty

[December 17, 1801]

Whoever considers the temper of the day, must be satisfied that this message is likely to add much to the popularity of our chief magistrate. It conforms, as far as would be tolerated at this early stage of our progress in political perfection, to the bewitching tenets of that illuminated doctrine, which promises man, ere long, an emancipation from the burdens and restraints of government; giving a foretaste of that pure felicity which the apostles of this doctrine have predicted.... And should the viands, which they offer, prove baneful poisons instead of wholesome aliments, the justification is both plain and easy — *Good patriots must, at all events, please the People.* But those whose patriotism is of the OLD SCHOOL, who differ so widely from the disciples of the new creed, that they would rather risk incurring the displeasure of the people, by speaking unpalatable truths, than betray their interest by fostering their prejudices; will never be deterred by an impure tide of popular opinion, from honestly pointing out the mistakes or the faults of weak or wicked men, who may have been selected as guardians of the public weal.

The Message of the President, by whatever motives it may have been dictated, is a performance which ought to alarm all who are anxious for the safety of our Government, for the respectability and welfare of our nation. It makes, or aims at making, a most prodigal sacrifice of constitutional energy, of sound principle, and of public interest, to the popularity of one man.

Hamilton's *Examination* distracted him from his grief that winter. By February, 1802, he was again making public appearances, speaking against Jefferson's plan to repeal the Judiciary Act, which had been passed by the "lame duck" Federalist Congress a year earlier. By repealing the act, Jefferson could simply do away with the new judicial posts that Adams had filled with Federalists before he left office. Hamilton was enraged at this threat to the independence of the judiciary, but his pleas that Federalists oppose the repeal measure in a temperate and dignified manner only irritated others in his party. In February, he wrote sadly to Gouverneur Morris, who was battling the repeal bill in the Senate.

[New York, February 27, 1802]

Mine is an odd destiny. Perhaps no man in the UStates has sacrificed or done more for the present Constitution than myself—and contrary to all my anticipations of its fate, as you know from the very begginning I am still labouring to prop the frail and worthless fabric. Yet I have the murmurs of its friends no less than the curses of its foes for my reward. What can I do better than withdraw from the Scene? Every day proves to me more and more that this American world was not made for me....

You, friend Morris, are by *birth* a native of this Country but by *genius* an exotic. You mistake if you fancy that you are more a favourite than myself or that you are in any sort upon a theatre s[uited] to you.

Jefferson's repeal bill was passed, but the battle had restored Hamilton's spirits and he was at last able to reply to his friends' notes of sympathy at Philip's death. At the end of March, he wrote to Dr. Benjamin Rush, a Philadelphia physician who had entertained Philip in his home.

New York March 29. 1802

I felt all the weight of the obligation which I owed to you and to your amiable family, for the tender concern they manifested in an event, beyond comparison, the most afflicting of my life. But I was obliged to wait for a moment of greater calm, to express my sense of the kindness.

My loss is indeed great. The highest as well as the eldest hope of my family has been taken from me. You estimated him rightly. He was truly a fine youth. But why should I repine? It was the will of heaven; and he is now out of the reach of the seductions and calamities of a world, full of folly, full of vice, full of danger—of least value in proportion as it is best known. I firmly trust also that he has safely reached the haven of eternal repose and felicity.

You will easily imagine that every memorial of the goodness of his heart must be precious to me. You allude to one recorded in a letter to your son. If no special reasons forbid it, I should be very glad to have a copy of that letter.

Mrs. Hamilton, who has drank deeply of the cup of

Benjamin Rush

sorrow, joins me in affectionate thanks to Mrs. Rush and yourself. Our wishes for your happiness will be unceasing.

Through all the personal difficulties of the past months, Hamilton had not lost his interest in reorganizing the Federalist party. He saw an opportunity to achieve that goal when he learned to his satisfaction that Virginia's Democratic-Republicans were growing increasingly distrustful of Vice President Aaron Burr. Federalists in Congress planned a caucus to "concert an uniform plan" for taking advantage of the situation. At James Bayard's request, Hamilton sent his advice, suggesting that Federalists borrow Democratic-Republican methods to achieve their own ends.

New-York April [16–18] 1802

Men are rather reasoning than reasonable animals for the most part governed by the impulse of passion. This is a truth well understood by our adversaries who have practised upon it with no small benefit to their cause.

It is no less true that the Foederalists seem not to have attended to the fact sufficiently; and that they erred in relying so much on the rectitude & utility of their measures, as to have neglected the cultivation of popular favour by fair & justifiable expedients.... Yet unless we can contrive to take hold of & carry along with us some strong feelings of the mind we shall in vain calculate upon any substantial or durable results. Whatever plan we may adopt, to be successful must be founded on the truth of this proposition. And perhaps it is not very easy for us to give it full effect; especially not without some deviations from what on other occasions we have maintained to be right. But in determining upon the propriety of the deviations, we must consider whether it be possible for us to succeed without in some degree employing the weapons which have been employed against us, & whether the actual state & future prospect of things be not such as to justify the reciprocal use of them. I need not tell you that I do not mean to countenance the imitation of things intrinsically unworthy, but only of such as may be denominated irregular, such as in a sound & stable order of things ought not to exist. Neither are you to infer that any revolutionary result is contemplated. In my opinion the present Constitution is the standard to which we are to cling. Under its banners... must we combat our political foes, rejecting all changes but through the channel itself provides for amendments....I now offer you the outline of the plan....Let an Association be formed to be denominated, "The Christian Constitutional Society." It's objects to be, 1st The support of the Christian Religion. 2nd The support of the Constitution of the United States....

[This society, Hamilton explained, would have a national "directing council," a "sub-directing council" in each state, and local societies under the "sub-directing" boards. He then outlined "Its Means."]

1st   The diffusion of information. For this purpose not only the Newspapers but pamphlets must be la[r]gely employed & to do this a fund must be created. 5 dollars annually for 8 years, to be contributed by each member who can really afford it....It is essential to be able to disseminate *gratis* useful publications. Whenever it can be done, & there is a press, clubs should be formed to meet once a week, read the newspapers & prepare essays, paragraphs &ct

2nd   The use of all lawful means in *concert* to promote the election of *fit men*. A lively correspondence must be kept up between the different Societies.

3rd   The promoting of institutions of a charitable & useful nature in the management of Fœderalists. The populous cities ought particularly to be attended to. Perhaps it will be well to institute in such places 1st Societies for the relief of Emigrants—2nd. Academies each with one professor instructing the different Classes of Mechanics in the principles of Mechanics & Elements of Chemistry.

James A. Bayard of Delaware

Bayard replied regretfully that such "Clubs" would only "revive a thousand jealousies & suspicions," and concluded that Federalists must let the Democratic-Republicans defeat themselves. But although Hamilton's proposals for Federalist reorganization had failed, his personal fortunes seemed to be on the rise once again. The continuing war in Europe, with its raids on neutral shipping, was providing Hamilton with a lucrative practice in insurance law. In June, Elizabeth gave birth to a baby boy, who was named Philip, after his dead brother, and six months later, the Hamiltons moved into their new country home in upper Manhattan. It was as one gentleman farmer to another that Hamilton wrote to Charles Pinckney at the end of December.

The Grange

Grange (NY) Decr. 29. 1802

A garden, you know, is a very usual refuge of a disappointed politician. Accordingly, I have purchased a few acres about 9 Miles from Town, have built a house and am cultivating a Garden. The melons in your country are very fine. Will you have the goodness to send me some seed both of the Water & Muss Melons?

My daughter adds another request, which is for three or four of your peroquets [parakeets]. She is very fond of birds. If there be any thing in this quarter the sending of which can give you pleasure, you have only to name them. As Farmers a new source of sympathy has arisen between us; and I am pleased with every thing in which our likings and taste can be approximated.

Amidst the triumphant reign of Democracy, do you retain sufficient interest in public affairs to feel any curiosity about what is going on? In my opinion the follies and vices of the Administration have as yet made no material impression to their disadvantage. On the contrary, I think the malady is rather progressive than upon the decline in our Northern Quarter. The last *lullaby* message [Jefferson's message to Congress], instead of inspiring contempt, attracts praise. Mankind are forever destined to be the dupes of bold & cunning imposture.

With no national or statewide elections to tempt him from his "garden," Hamilton's first winter at the Grange was a quiet one. There was more sorrow for the family in March, 1803, when Elizabeth Hamilton's mother died in Albany. While his wife traveled to the funeral, Hamilton stayed in New York and sent her this affectionate report on their household.

Sunday Evening March 20 [1803] Grange

I am here my beloved Betsy with my two little boys *John* & *William* who will be my bed fellows to night. The day I have passed was as agreeable as it could be in your absence; but you need not be told how much difference your presence would have made. Things are now going on here pretty and pretty briskly. I am making some innovations which I am sure you will approve.

The remainder of the Children were well yesterday.

Eliza pouts and plays, and displays more and more her ample stock of Caprice.

I am anxious to hear of your arrival at Albany & shall be glad to be informed that Your Father and all of you are composed. I pray you to exert yourself & I repeat my exhortation that you will bear in mind it is your business to comfort and not to distress.

Although he made a few appearances on behalf of Federalist candidates in 1803, Hamilton was compelled to concentrate mainly on his private interests. Building the Grange had cost more than expected, and other investments had gone wrong. Richard Peters spoke truer, perhaps, than he knew when he advised Hamilton to make the farm his "Plaything—but see that you have other Business, that you may afford to pay for the Rattle." Despite ill health, Hamilton rode to Albany to earn fees to pay for his "plaything" and wrote to his wife to suggest new embellishments for his expensive toy.

Claverack [New York] Oct 14. 1803

There are some things necessary to be done which I omitted mentioning to you. I wish the Carpenters to make and insert two Chimnies for ventilating the Ice-House, each about two feet square & four feet long half above and half below the ground—to have a cap on the top sloping downwards so that the rain may not easily enter—the aperture for letting in and out the air to be about a foot and a half square in the side immediately below the cap....

Let a separate compost bed be formed near the present one; to consist of 3 barrels full of the *clay* which I bought 6 barrels of *black mould* 2 waggon loads of the best clay on the Hill opposite the *Quakers place*... and one waggon load of pure cow-dung. Let these be well and repeatedly mixed and pounded together to be made use of hereafter for the Vines.

I hope the apple trees will have been planted so as to profit by this moderate and wet weather. If not done— Let *Tough* be reminded that a temporary fence is to be put up...so as to prevent the cattle injuring the young trees....

Remember that the piazzas are also to be caulked & that additional accommodations for the pidgeons are to be Made.

You see I do not forget the Grange. No that I do not;

nor any one that inhabits it. Accept yourself my tenderest affection. Give my Love to your Children.

Hamilton enjoyed the luxury of private life throughout 1803. But in 1804, state voters were to decide on a President, a governor, and congressmen, and when Hamilton traveled again to Albany in February of that year his business was both legal and political. His legal affairs concerned the case of Harry Crosswell, a Federalist printer indicted for libel a year before. Crosswell had asked Hamilton for help in the summer of 1803, but other obligations kept Hamilton from appearing until the following winter, when a complicated series of appeals and counter-appeals brought Crosswell's case to the New York Court of Errors. In his appearance before the court in February, 1804, Hamilton presented some of the most important arguments on the law of libel and the freedom of the press heard in an American courtroom in the early nineteenth century. His plea for Crosswell centered on the contention that the truth of a publication must be accepted as a defense against a charge of libel, and that juries must be allowed to decide on the truth or falsehood of such statements. As one judge remarked, Hamilton's "whole soul, was inlisted in the cause," and he closed his case for Crosswell with this description of the role of a free press in America.

[Albany, February, 1804]
We have been careful that when one party comes in, it shall not be able to break down and bear away the others. If this be not so, in vain have we made Constitutions, for, if it be not so, then we must go into anarchy, and from thence to despotism and to a master. Against this I know there is an almost insurmountable obstacle in the spirit of the people. They would not submit to be thus enslaved. Every tongue, every arm would be uplifted against it; they would resist, and assist, and resist, till they hurled from their seats, those who dared make the attempt. To watch the progress of such endeavours is the office of a free press. To give us early alarm and put us on our guard against the encroachments of power. This, then, is a right of the utmost importance, one for which, instead of yielding it up, we ought rather to spill our blood. . . . Never can tyranny be introduced into this country by arms; these can never get rid of a popular spirit of enquiry; the only way to crush it down is by a servile tribunal. It is only by the abuse of the forms of justice that we can be enslaved. An army never can do it. For ages it can never

be attempted. The spirit of the country with arms in their hands, and disciplined as a militia, would render it impossible. Every pretence that liberty can be thus invaded, is idle declamation. It is not to be endangered by a few thousand of miserable, pitiful military. It is not thus that the liberty of this country is to be destroyed. It is to be subverted only by a pretence of adhering to all the forms of law, and yet by breaking down the substance of our liberties. By devoting a wretched, but honest man as the victim of a nominal trial.

Hamilton's eloquence did not win Harry Crosswell immediate exoneration: the court divided on the question of granting the printer a new trial. But Hamilton's powers of persuasion were not confined to the courtroom that month. Aaron Burr's personal and political differences with Jefferson had driven him back to local politics. George Clinton had declined another term, and the Democratic-Republicans endorsed Chancellor John Lansing, Jr., as his successor, while a splinter group in the party backed Burr. Many New York Federalists favored joining Burr, and Albany party men were to caucus on this point on February 16. Six days before that meeting, Hamilton spoke in support of Lansing.

[Albany, February 10, 1804]

If he [Burr] be truly, as the fœderalists have believed, a man of irregular and insatiable ambition, if his plan has been to rise to power on the ladder of Jacobinic principles, it is natural to conclude that he will endeavour to fix himself in power by the same instrument, that he will not lean on a fallen [and] falling party, generally speaking of a character not to favour usurpation and the ascendancy of a despotic chief. Every day shews more and more the much to be regretted tendency of governments intirely popular to dissolution and disorder. Is it rational to expect, that a man who had the sagacity to foresee this tendency, and whose temper would permit him to bottom his aggrandisement on popular prejudices and vices would desert this system at a time, when more than ever the state of things invites him to adhere to it?

...If Lansing is Governor his personal character affords some security against pernicious extremes, and at the same time renders it morally certain, that the democratic party already much divided and weakened will moulder and break asunder more and more....

Hamilton's copy of Don Quixote, *from his library at the Grange*

May it not lead to a recasting of parties by which the fœderalists will gain a great accession of force from former opponents. At any rate, is it not wiser in them to promote a course of things by which scism [among the] democrats will be fostered and increased [than one likely, upon a] fair calculation to give them a chief better able than any they have yet had to unite and direct them.

When Lansing refused the nomination, the Clintonians chose Chief Justice Morgan Lewis as their candidate. Meanwhile Hamilton, who was the self-appointed chief of the anti-Burr movement, was receiving his full share of personal abuse. In the last week of February, he heard Judge Ebenezer Purdy's accusations that "*Monarchy*" was the Federalists' objective, and that he, Hamilton, had circulated a letter proposing an English prince on an American throne. When confronted, Purdy asserted that George Clinton had seen such a letter in 1787. Hamilton wrote to the Governor, demanding an explanation.

Albany Febr. 27. 1804

It is now a long time since a very odious slander has been in circulation to the prejudice of my character. It has come to my ears in more than one way, but always 'till lately without the disclosure of any source to which I could resort for explanation or detection. Within a few days, Mr. Kane of this City related to me a story as coming from Judge Purdy, in substance very similar to the calumny to which I have alluded....your name is implicated in the transaction, with what warrant it would be improper for me to prejudge. But the very mention of your name adds importance to the affair and increases the motives to investigation.

The charge...is of a nature too derogatory to permit me to pass it lightly over. It is essential that its origin and progress should be traced as fully as may be practicable, in order to the thorough exposure of its falshood and malignity.

The assertions of Judge Purdy authorise me to appeal to you for a frank and candid explanation of so much of the matter as relates to yourself. This explanation I request as speedily as may be.

An anti-Lewis broadside of 1804

Clinton replied graciously to Hamilton's questions. While he had seen such a letter, the copy he read had no signature or address, and he declared that he had never believed or said that Hamilton was connected with it. The Governor promised to search for this mysterious letter and send it to Hamilton. He concluded, "I am pleased to find that however much we may differ on other political Subjects we agree in Sentiment as to this." Soon afterward, Hamilton returned to Manhattan to work for the candidacy of Morgan Lewis, thus allying himself with Clinton, his old antagonist. There are no written records of his campaign against Burr, nor any newspaper accounts of speeches he may have made that spring. In the closing days of the gubernatorial race, Hamilton sent this prophetic advice to a friend who had suffered personal reverses.

New York April 13th. 1804

'Tis by patience and perseverance that we can expect to vanquish difficulties, and better our unpleasant condition.

Arraign not the dispensations of Providence—they must be founded in wisdom and goodness; and when they do not suit us, it must be because there is some fault in ourselves, which deserves chastisement, or because there is a kind intent to correct in us some vice or failing, of which, perhaps we may not be conscious; or because the general plan requires that we should suffer partial ill.

In this situation it is our duty to cultivate resignation, and even humility, bearing in mind, in the language of the Poet, that it was *Pride which lost the blest abodes.*

Morgan Lewis, by Charles Curran

Hamilton had no presentiment that his own pride would soon threaten his family. On the contrary, with Burr's defeat, Hamilton probably foresaw for himself nothing but a comfortable life as a Federalist citizen. But, as discreetly as Hamilton had conducted his battle against Burr, the Vice President eventually learned of it. In June, Burr saw printed in a newspaper a letter from Dr. Charles Cooper describing remarks Hamilton had made after a dinner at Albany in February. On June 18, Burr demanded from Hamilton "a prompt and unqualified acknowledgement or denial of the use of any expressions which could warrant the assertions of Dr. Cooper." Hamilton replied two days later, taking refuge in the vagueness of Cooper's language as an excuse for neither admitting nor denying the truth of his charges.

New York June 20, 1804

I have maturely reflected on the subject of your letter ... and the more I have reflected the more I have become convinced, that I could not, without manifest impropriety, make the avowal or disavowal which you seem to think necessary.

The clause pointed out ... is in these terms, "I could

397

detail to you a *still more despicable opinion,* which General Hamilton has expressed of Mr. Burr." To endeavour to discover the meaning of this declaration, I was obliged to seek in the antecedent part of the letter for the opinion to which it referred.... I found it in these words "General Hamilton and Judge Kent have declared, *in substance,* that they looked upon Mr. Burr to be a *dangerous man,* and one *who ought not to be trusted with the reins of Government."* The language of Doctor Cooper plainly implies, that he considered this opinion of you, which he attributes to me, as a *despicable* one; but he affirms that I have expressed some other *still more despicable;* without however mentioning to whom, when, or where.... the phrase...admits of infinite shades....

Repeating, that I cannot reconcile it with propriety to make the acknowlegement, or denial, you desire, I will add, that I deem it inadmissible, on principle, to consent to be interrogated as to the justness of the *inferences,* which may be drawn by *others,* from whatever I may have said of a political opponent in the course of a fifteen years competition....

I stand ready to avow or disavow promptly and explicitly any precise or definite opinion, which I may be charged with having declared of any Gentleman. More than this cannot fitly be expected from me; and especially it cannot reasonably be expected, that I shall enter into an explanation upon a basis so vague as that which you have adopted. I trust, on more reflection, you will see the matter in the same light with me. If not, I can only regret the circumstance, and must abide the consequences.

Aaron Burr, as he looked in 1805

With some justice, Burr replied that this note contained "nothing of that sincerity and delicacy which you profess to Value." Hamilton's letter, Burr declared, only "furnished me with new reasons for requiring a definite reply." Burr's friend William Van Ness delivered this message to Hamilton and recorded his reactions.

[New York, June 22, 1804]

General Hamilton perused it, & said it was such a letter as he had hoped not to have received, that it contained several offensive expressions & seemed to close the door to all further reply, that he had hoped the answer he had returned to Col Burr's first letter would have given a different direction to the controversy, that he thought Mr Burr would have perceived that there was a difficulty in his making a more specific reply, & would have desired him to state what had fallen from him that might have given rise to the inference of Doctor Cooper. He would have done this frankly, & he believed it would not have been found to exceed the limits justifiable among political opponents. If Mr Burr should upon the suggestion of these ideas be disposed to give a different complexion to the discussion, he was willing to consider the last letter not delivered; but if that communication was not withdrawn he could make no reply and Mr Burr must pursue such course as he should deem most proper.

This second evasion did not settle the matter. In the next days, Van Ness tried to work out the problem with Hamilton and Hamilton's friend Nathaniel Pendleton, but Burr was now convinced that Hamilton's remarks in Albany were part of a long-standing plot to blacken his character. On June 25, he demanded a "General disavowal of any intention on the part of Genl Hamilton in his various conversations to convey impressions derogatory to the honor of Mr Burr." Hamilton drafted this reply for Pendleton to present to Van Ness.

> [New York] 26 june 1804
>
> The expectations now disclosed as on the part of Colo. Burr, appear to him [Hamilton] to have greatly changed and extended the original ground of inquiry, and instead of presenting a particular and definite case for explanation, seem to aim at nothing less than an inquisition into his most confidential as well as other conversations through the whole period of his acquaintance with Col Burr. While he was prepared to meet the particular case fully and fairly he thinks it inadmissible that he should be expected to answer at large as to any thing that he may possibly have said in relation to the character of Colo. Burr, at any time or upon any occasion.... He does not however mean to authorise any conclusion as to the real nature of his Conduct in relation to Col. Burr, by his declining so loose and vague a basis of explanation; and he disavows an unwillingness to come to a satisfactory, provided it be an honorable accommodation. His objection is to the very indefinite ground which Col. Burr has assumed, in which he is sorry to be able to discover nothing short of predetermined hostility.

399

This letter sealed Hamilton's fate. The next morning, Van Ness delivered Burr's challenge to a duel that would "vindicate that honor at such hazard as the nature of the case demands." Hamilton received the challenge the evening of July 27 and began preparing for his meeting with the Vice President. Pendleton and Van Ness worked out the details of time and place while the principals put their affairs in order. In the next two weeks, Hamilton finished as much outstanding legal work as possible and prepared a series of documents to be left with Pendleton. While most of these concerned Hamilton's business affairs, one was a summary of his beliefs on dueling in general and his quarrel with Burr in particular.

[New York, June 28–July 11, 1804]

1. My religious and moral principles are strongly opposed to the practice of Duelling and it would ever give me pain to be obliged to shed the blood of a fellow in a private combat forbidden by the laws.

2   My wife and Children are extremely dear to me, and my life is of the utmost importance to them, in various views.

3. I feel a sense of obligation towards my creditors; who in case of accident to me . . . may be in some degree sufferers. . . .

4   I am conscious of no *ill-will* to Col Burr, distinct from political opposition. . . .

Lastly, I shall hazard much, and can possibly gain nothing by the issue of the interview.

But it was, as I conceive, impossible for me to avoid it. There are *intrinsick* difficulties in the thing, and *artificial* embarrassments, from the manner of proceeding on the part of Col. Burr.

Intrinsick—because it is not to be denied, that my animadversions on the political principles character and views of Col Burr have been extremely severe, and on different occasions I, in common with many others, have made very unfavourable criticisms on particular instances of the private conduct of this Gentleman.

. . . The disavowal required of me by Col Burr, in a general and indefinite form, was out of my power. . . . Yet I wished, as far as might be practicable, to leave a door open to accommodation. . . .

I am not sure, whether under all the circumstances I did not go further in the attempt to accommodate, than a puntilious delicacy will justify. If so, I hope the motives I have stated will excuse me. . . .

To those, who with abhorring the practice of Duelling

A view of Weehawken, New Jersey

may think that I ought on no account to have added to the number of bad examples, I answer that my *relative* situation, as well in public as private appeals, inforcing all the considerations which constitute what men of the world denominate honor, impressed on me (as I thought) a peculiar necessity not to decline the call. The ability to be in future useful, whether in resisting mischief or effecting good, in those crises of our public affairs, which seem likely to happen, would probably be inseparable from a conformity with public prejudice in this particular.

Scrupulously efficient as ever, Hamilton prepared for his duel by arranging for his estate, naming executors, and drawing up his will. Elizabeth was to be his sole beneficiary if anything were left after the payment of his debts. The most difficult part of Hamilton's preparations was providing for his children's "dear Mother." He left two letters for Elizabeth with Pendleton; the first was written a week before he was to meet Burr in New Jersey.

[New York] July 4. 1804

This letter, my very dear Eliza, will not be delivered to you, unless I shall first have terminated my earthly career; to begin, as I humbly hope from redeeming grace and divine mercy, a happy immortality.

If it had been possible for me to have avoided the interview, my love for you and my precious children would have been alone a decisive motive. But it was not possible, without sacrifices which would have rendered me unworthy of your esteem. I need not tell you of the pangs I feel, from the idea of quitting you and exposing you to the anguish which I know you would feel. Nor could I dwell on the topic lest it should unman me.

The consolations of Religion, my beloved, can alone support you; and these you have a right to enjoy. Fly to the bosom of your God and be comforted. With my last idea, I shall cherish the sweet hope of meeting you in a better world.

Adieu best of wives and best of Women. Embrace all my darling Children for me. Ever yours

AH

Eastman Johnson made this portrait of Mrs. Alexander Hamilton in 1846. She died in 1854 at the age of ninety-seven, having outlived her husband by fifty years.

Just before he went to bed on the evening before his duel, Hamilton again wrote to his wife.

[New York, July 10, 1804]

Tuesday Evening 10 O Cl[ock]

The Scruples [of a Christian have deter]mined me to expose my own [life to any] extent rather than subject my[self to the] guilt of taking the life of [another.] This must increase my hazards & redoubles my pangs for you. But you had rather I should die innocent than live guilty. Heaven can [preserve] me [and I humbly] hope will, but in the contrary event, I charge you to remember that you are a Christian. God's will be done! The will of a merciful God must be good.

Once more Adieu My Darling darling Wife

AH

Hamilton had decided to "expose" himself by reserving his first shot in the duel—and perhaps even his second—so that Burr would have "a double opportunity to...pause and to reflect." At 5 A.M., July 11, Hamilton crossed the river to Weehawken, New Jersey. By seven o'clock, all parties were present, and the seconds, Van Ness and Pendleton, worked out the details of the duel. Van Ness left this record of the morning's events.

[July 11, 1804]

While his second was explaining these rules [for the duel] Genl Hamilton raised & levelled his pistol, as if to try his position, and lowering it said, I beg pardon for delaying you but the direction of the light, sometimes renders glasses necessary. He then drew from his pocket a pair of spectacles & having put them on, observed that he was ready to proceed....

The parties being...asked if they were prepared, being answered in the affirmative he [Pendleton] gave the word *present* as had been agreed on, and both of the parties took aim & fired in succession....The pistols were discharged within a few seconds of each other and the fire of Col: Burr took effect; Genl Hamilton almost instantly fell, Col: Burr then advanced toward Genl H__n with a manner and gesture that appeared to Genl Hamilton's friend to be expressive of regret, but without Speaking turned about & withdrew—Being urged from the field by his friend...with a view to prevent his being recognised by the Surgeon and Bargemen who were then approaching. No farther communication took place between the principals and the Barge that carried Col: Burr immediately returned to the City.

This portrait of Hamilton was drawn from memory by Gordon Fairman the year after Hamilton's death.

The account of Dr. David Hosack, the physician whom Burr and Hamilton had chosen to attend the duel, takes up the story after Hamilton fell. The doctor's account appeared in a newspaper two months later.

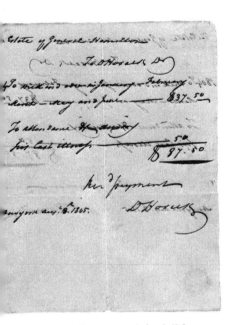

Dr. Hosack presented this bill for $87.50 to Hamilton's estate for "attendance during his last illness."

[New York] August 17th, 1804.

I found him half sitting on the ground, supported in the arms of Mr. Pendleton. His countenance of death I shall never forget—He had at that instant just strength to say, "This is a mortal wound, Doctor;" when he sunk away, and became to all appearances lifeless. I immediately stripped up his clothes, and soon, alas! ascertained that the direction of the ball must have been through some vital part. [On performing an autopsy, Hosack found "the ball struck the second or third false rib, fractured it about in the middle; it then passed through the liver and diaphragm, and...lodged in the first or second lumbar vertebra...."] His pulses were not to be felt; his respiration was entirely suspended; and upon laying my hand on his heart, and perceiving no motion there, I considered him as irrecoverably gone. I however observed to Mr. Pendleton, that the only chance for his reviving was immediately to get him upon the water. We therefore lifted him up, and carried him out of the wood, to the margin of the bank, where the bargemen aided us in conveying him into the boat, which immediately put off. During all this time I could not discover the least symptom of returning life....

[In the boat, Dr. Hosack rubbed Hamilton's face and body with "spirits of hartshorne." Fifty yards from shore, Hammilton regained consciousness. Dr. Hosack's account here is at variance with Van Ness's earlier report that both pistols "were discharged within a few seconds of each other."]

He breathed; his eyes, hardly opened, wandered, without fixing upon any objects; to our great joy he at length spoke: "My vision is indistinct," were his first words. His pulse became more perceptible; his respiration more regular; his sight returned.... Soon after recovering his sight, he happened to cast his eye upon the case of pistols, and observing the one that he had had in his hand lying on the outside, he said, "Take care of that pistol; it is undischarged, and still cocked; it may go off and do harm;

—Pendleton knows, (attempting to turn his head towards him) that I did not intend to fire at him." "Yes," said Mr. Pendleton..."I have already made Dr. Hosack acquainted with your determination as to that." He then closed his eyes, and remained calm, without any disposition to speak....He asked me once or twice, how I found his pulse; and he informed me that his lower extremities had lost all feeling; manifesting to me that he entertained no hopes that he should long survive....Perceiving that we approached the shore, he said, "Let Mrs. Hamilton be immediately sent for—let the event be gradually broken to her; but give her hopes." Looking up we saw his friend Mr. [William] Bayard standing on the wharf in great agitation....when I called to him to have a cot prepared, and he at the same moment saw his poor friend lying in the bottom of the boat, he threw up his eyes and burst into a flood of tears and lamentation. Hamilton alone appeared tranquil and composed. We then conveyed him as tenderly as possible up to the house....

Upon our reaching the house he became more languid....I gave him a little weak wine and water. When he recovered his feelings, he complained of pain in his back; we immediately undressed him, laid him in bed, and darkened the room. I then gave him a large anodyne, which I frequently repeated. During the first day he took upwards of an ounce of laudanum [tincture of opium]....Yet were his sufferings, during the whole of the day, almost intolerable.

The Reverend Benjamin Moore

As soon as Hamilton was brought to Bayard's house, a message was sent to Benjamin Moore, Episcopal bishop of New York. Moore went immediately, but delayed giving Hamilton Communion until the General had had "time for serious reflection." A few hours later, Moore wrote, he received another summons.

[New York] Thursday evening, July 12 [1804]. At one o'clock I was again called on to visit him. Upon my entering the room and approaching his bed, with the utmost calmness and composure he said, "My dear Sir, you perceive my unfortunate situation, and no doubt have been made acquainted with the circumstances which led to it. It is my desire to receive the Communion at your hands. I hope you will not conceive there is any impropriety in my request." He added, "It has for some time past been the wish of my heart, and it was my intention to take an early opportunity of uniting myself to the church, by the reception of that holy ordinance." I observed to him, that...however desirous I might be to afford consolation to a fellow mortal in distress; still, it was my duty as a minister of the gospel, to hold up the law of God...and that...I must unequivocally condemn the practice which had brought him to his present unhappy condition. He acknowledged the propriety of these sentiments, and declared that he viewed the late transaction with sorrow and contrition. I then asked him, "Should it please God, to restore you to health, Sir, will you never be again engaged in a similar transaction? and will you employ all your influence in society to discountenance this barbarous custom?" His answer was, "That, Sir, is my deliberate intention."...

[Bishop Moore discussed the meaning of the Communion with Hamilton. At last he questioned the dying man.]

"Do you sincerely repent of your sins past? Have you a lively faith in God's mercy through Christ, with a thankful remembrance of the death of Christ? And are you disposed to live in love and charity with all men?" He lifted up his hands and said, "With the utmost sincerity of heart I can answer those questions in the affirmative —I have no ill will against Col. Burr. I met him with a fixed resolution to do him no harm—I forgive all that happened." I then observed...that I had no reason to doubt his sincerity, and would proceed immediately to gratify his wishes. The Communion was then administered, which he received with great devotion, and his heart afterwards appeared to be perfectly at rest.

On Saturday, July 14, 1804, Hamilton was buried in Trinity churchyard, at the head of Wall Street in lower Manhattan.

Although Dr. Hosack had "not the shadow of a hope" of Hamilton's recovery, he summoned other medical experts for consultations. These doctors confirmed his gloomy diagnosis, and Hamilton's sufferings continued—as Dr. Hosack later recalled.

[New York] August 17th, 1804.
During the night, he had some imperfect sleep; but the succeeding morning his symptoms were aggravated, attended however with a diminution of pain. His mind retained all its usual strength and composure. The great

405

The Hamilton memorial engraving above was published circa 1804.

source of his anxiety seemed to be in his sympathy with his half distracted wife and children. He spoke to me frequently of them—"My beloved wife and children," were always his expressions. But his fortitude triumphed over his situation, dreadful as it was; once, indeed, at the sight of his children brought to the bed-side together, seven in number, his utterance forsook him; he opened his eyes, gave them one look, and closed them again, till they were taken away. As a proof of his extraordinary composure of mind, let me add, that he alone could calm the frantic grief of their mother. *"Remember, my Eliza, you are a Christian,"* were the expressions with which he frequently, with a firm voice, but in a pathetic and impressive manner, addressed her. His words, and the tone in which they were uttered, will never be effaced from my memory.

Bishop Moore returned to Hamilton's bedside the morning of Thursday, July 12, and remained there until 2 P.M., when Hamilton "expired without a struggle, and almost without a groan." Thus the most spirited and vocal warrior of the Federalist cause left his wife and children, his unpaid debts, and his unfulfilled dreams. He left, as well, a great mystery for American historians. His premature death helped make Hamilton a comparatively vague personality among the Founding Fathers. Unlike Jefferson, Madison, and Adams, he had no years of quiet retirement in which to write his memoirs or answer questions about his early career. In his forty-nine years, Hamilton had been too pressed by public duty and family obligations to spare time for reminiscence.

Hamilton's death was perhaps the most puzzling incident in his short life. Biographers return again and again to two questions: Why had he not given Aaron Burr some form of apology and avoided a challenge? And why, once that challenge had been issued, did Hamilton not decline the duel on the grounds of his religious and moral convictions?

Some have speculated that Hamilton was motivated by some sort of "death wish," a subconscious desire for self-destruction. Certainly Hamilton's letters in the last three years of his life reflected a feeling that he was out of place in Jeffersonian America. Politically, both Hamilton and Burr had run the course of their careers by the time they met for their "interview" in Weehawken. In 1802, Hamilton's friends had ignored his suggestions for remodeling the Federalist party, and the party would never fully recover from the bitter division of 1800. Burr in his turn had alienated the southern wing of his party, and his life after the duel was a series of fantastic schemes and pathetic failures. His plans to establish a colony in the West, possibly even to form a new nation, brought him to trial for treason in 1807.

But any attempt to conduct posthumous psychoanalysis on either man is fruitless and quite unnecessary. There is an answer to the riddle of Hamilton's death in the clear patterns of his life. Hamilton could not offer Burr a satisfactory explanation or apology because there was none. In the course of the years, Hamilton had insulted Burr's family, impugned his financial solvency, and accused him of almost everything from accepting bribes to showing cowardice in the Army. If any man deserved "satisfaction" from him, Hamilton knew that it was Aaron Burr. By Hamilton's own standards of "honor," he had given Burr reason for a challenge. Those same standards forced Hamilton to accept Burr's invitation to the meeting at Weehawken. Hamilton would not have criticized any man for refusing to participate in a duel if that man was opposed in principle, as he himself was, to this form of ritual bloodshed; but Hamilton felt a special need to prove his own right to a "reputation," to "honor." A self-made man, Hamilton molded his life after the image of those who had been born to wealth and power in the aristocratic, Colonial tradition. Determined to prove that America, though a new republic, could be "respectable" in the most strict definition of the word, Hamilton demanded as much of himself. If this meant embracing old, outmoded standards of honor, he would do so. And he followed this terrible, relentless logic to its tragic conclusion when he crossed the Hudson to Weehawken.

Other men and other patriots felt concern for national respectability without losing their sense of proportion in this way. But Hamilton had a special reason for guarding the reputation he had earned. As long as there was one man who, like John Adams, could dismiss him as "a bastard brat of a Scotch pedlar," Hamilton's struggle to give his name legitimacy and stature was pointless. If he were to be "useful" to the nation, Hamilton believed that he must preserve that reputation by any means.

At Hamilton's funeral, Gouverneur Morris begged Americans "to remember this solemn testimonial, that he was not ambitious. . . . He was ambitious only of glory." Morris had known Hamilton well and understood his friend's desperate need for recognition. He demanded of his audience at Trinity Church, *I charge you to protect his fame* — it is all he has left — all that these poor orphan children will inherit from their father." And this was all that Hamilton had hoped to leave. It was not power or wealth, but "fame" and "glory" that had driven Hamilton throughout his short life. Thirty years as an American, a career as a soldier and a statesman, a loving family, and warm friends had never erased the fears and frustrations in the heart of Nicholas Cruger's clerk, who longed for a "war" to rescue him from his drudgery. Few men contributed more than Alexander Hamilton to the establishment of the new American nation, which held out the promise of a new life, with new standards of a man's worth. The tragedy of Hamilton's life was that he was so often at odds with the new nation he had helped to create.

Selected Bibliography

Bemis, Samuel Flagg. *Jay's Treaty: A Study in Commerce and Diplomacy.* New York: Macmillan, 1923.

Bowers, Claude G. *Jefferson and Hamilton: The Struggle for Democracy in America.* Boston: Houghton Mifflin, 1925.

Cooke, Jacob E., ed. *The Federalist.* Middletown, Conn.: Wesleyan University Press, 1961.

De Conde, Alexander. *Entangling Alliance: Politics and Diplomacy under George Washington.* Durham: Duke University Press, 1958.

————.*The Quasi-War: The Politics and Diplomacy of the Undeclared War with France, 1797–1801.* New York: Charles Scribner's Sons, 1966.

DePauw, Linda G. *The Eleventh Pillar: New York State and the Federal Constitution.* Ithaca: Cornell University Press, 1966.

Hacker, Louis M. *Alexander Hamilton in the American Tradition.* New York: McGraw-Hill, 1957.

Hamilton, Alexander. *The Law Practice of Alexander Hamilton: Documents and Commentary.* Edited by Julius Goebel, Jr., *et al.* 2 vols. to date. New York: Columbia University Press, 1964 – .

————. *The Papers of Alexander Hamilton.* Edited by Harold C. Syrett *et al.* 19 vols. to date. New York: Columbia University Press, 1961 – .

————. *The Works of Alexander Hamilton.* Edited by John C. Hamilton. 7 vols. New York: J. F. Trow, 1850–51.

————. *The Works of Alexander Hamilton.* Edited by Henry Cabot Lodge. 9 vols. New York: G. P. Putnam's Sons, 1885–86.

Hamilton, Allan McLane. *The Intimate Life of Alexander Hamilton.* New York: Charles Scribner's Sons, 1910.

Hamilton, John C. *A History of the Republic of the United States of America, as Traced in the Writings of Alexander Hamilton and of his Contemporaries.* 7 vols. New York: Appleton, 1857–64.

Lodge, Henry Cabot. *Alexander Hamilton.* Boston: Houghton Mifflin, 1882.

Lycan, Gilbert L. *Alexander Hamilton and American Foreign Policy: A Design for Greatness.* Norman, Okla.: University of Oklahoma Press, 1970.

Miller, John C. *Alexander Hamilton: A Portrait in Paradox.* New York: Harper & Row, 1959.

————. *The Federalist Era, 1789–1801.* New York: Harper & Row, 1960.

Mitchell, Broadus. *Alexander Hamilton.* 2 vols. New York: Macmillan, 1957–62.

Rossiter, Clinton L. *Alexander Hamilton and the Constitution.* New York: Harcourt, Brace & World, 1964.

————. *1787: The Grand Convention.* New York: Macmillan, 1966.

Schachner, Nathan. *Alexander Hamilton.* New York: Yoseloff, 1957.

Stourzh, Gerald. *Alexander Hamilton and the Idea of Republican Government.* Stanford: Stanford University Press, 1970.

Syrett, Harold C., and Cooke, Jean G., eds. *Interview in Weehawken: The Burr-Hamilton Duel, as Told in the Original Documents.* Middletown, Conn.: Wesleyan University Press, 1960.

White, Leonard D. *The Federalists: A Study in Administrative History.* New York: Macmillan, 1948.

Acknowledgments

Unless otherwise specifically credited below, all documents reproduced in this volume are from the Alexander Hamilton Papers, Library of Congress, Washington, D.C., the greatest collection of Hamilton documents in existence, and other collections at the Library of Congress. In addition the Editors would like to thank the following institutions for permission to reprint documents in their possession:

American Philosophical Society, Philadelphia, Penna., page 379(center)
Bank of New York, New York, N.Y., pages 265(bottom)–266(top)
Charleston Library Society, Charleston, S. C., page 392(top)
Columbia University, New York, N.Y., pages 310(center), 337(bottom)–338(top), 370(top), 376(bottom)–377, 393(bottom)–394(top)
Connecticut Historical Society, Hartford, pages 319–320(top), 384
Henry E. Huntington Library, San Marino, Calif., pages 373–74(top)
Historical Society of Pennsylvania, Philadelphia, pages 266(center), 323(bottom)–324(top)
Lehigh University, Bethlehem, Penna., page 353
Library Collection of Philadelphia, pages 389(bottom)–390(top)
Maryland Hall Records, Annapolis, page 324 (center)
Massachusetts Historical Society, Boston, pages 351(top), 359(center), 362, 367(bottom)–368, 378(bottom)–379(top), 381(bottom)–382(top)
National Archives, Washington, D.C., page 247(top)
New-York Historical Society, New York, N.Y., page 146, 327(bottom), 333, 335(center), 336(bottom)–337, 342(bottom)–343(top), 348(bottom)–349(top), 349(bottom)–350(top), 375(center), 400–401(top)
New York Public Library, New York, N.Y., pages 344(bottom)–345, 390–91
New York State Historical Association, Weehawken, pages 397(bottom)–398(top), 398(bottom)–399(top), 399(bottom), 402(bottom)
Pennsylvania Archives, Harrisburg, page 320(center)
Public Records Office, London, pages 285(bottom)–286(top)
Public Records Office — Foreign Office, London, page 316(top)
Rhode Island Historical Society, Providence, page 248(top)
United States Naval Academy, Annapolis, Md., pages 358–59(top)
University of Virginia, Charlottesville, pages 374(bottom)–375
Yale University Library, New Haven, Conn., page 334(bottom)

The Editors also make grateful acknowledgment for the use of documents from the following works:

Hamilton, James A. *Reminiscences of James A. Hamilton; or, Men and Events, at Home & Abroad, During Three Quarters of a Century.* New York, 1869. Page 329(bottom)
Hamilton, John Church. *Life of Alexander Hamilton, a History of the Republic of the United States of America.* Boston, 1879. Page 267(bottom)

The Editors wish to express their appreciation of the many institutions and individuals who made available their pictorial material for use in this volume. In particular the Editors are grateful to:

Mrs. Joseph Carson, Philadelphia, Penna.
Chase Manhattan Bank Money Museum, New York, N.Y.
Columbiana Collection, Columbia University Libraries, New York, N.Y. — Alice Bonnell
Danish Maritime Museum, Kronborg Castle, Helsingor, Denmark
Hamilton Collection, Columbia University Libraries, New York, N.Y. — Kenneth Lohf
Independence National Historical Park Collection, Philadelphia, Penna.
Eva Lawaetz, St. Croix, Virgin Islands
Mr. and Mrs. Walter Lewisohn, Yorktown Heights, N.Y.
Library of Congress, Washington, D.C. — John D. Knowlton
National Archives, Washington, D.C.
New-York Historical Society, New York, N.Y.
New York Public Library, New York, N.Y.
The Royal Library, Copenhagen, Denmark
University of Copenhagen Library, Copenhagen, Denmark
Yale University Art Gallery, New Haven, Conn.

Index

be treated of in a

by uniting

proceeding ~~measures~~ as may

for that purpose, m

Jn

The President & Directors

of the Bank of the United Sta